Materialism

Moral and Social Consequences

BY THE SAME AUTHOR

Ageing: Challenges and Opportunities (1991)

Alcohol and Drug Abuse: A Psychosocial and Spiritual Approach to Prevention (2007)

Alzheimer's Disease: An Eclipse before Sunset (2016)

Creative Dimensions of Suffering (2009)

'Depression: Biological, Psychosocial, and Spiritual Dimensions and Treatment' (2015)

Doukhobors and the Bahá'í Faith: Tolstoy and His Appreciation of the Bahá'í Faith (1989)

Environment and Psychopathology, ed. with H. E. Lehmann (1993)

In Search of Nirvana: A New Perspective on Alcohol and Drug Dependency (1985, 1989)

'Intergenerational Responses to Persecution' (1998)

'Psychological and Spiritual Dimensions of Persecution and Suffering' (1994)

Steadfastness in the Covenant: Responding to Tests and Tribulations (2014)

Substance Abuse: A Bahá'í Perspective (2000)

WHO Course on Psychiatric Hospital Organization and Management (1983)

Materialism

Moral and Social Consequences

Second edition

Abdu'l-Missagh Ghadirian, M. D.

GEORGE RONALD
OXFORD

George Ronald, Publisher
Oxford
www.grbooks.com

A catalogue record for this book is available from the British Library

ISBN 978-0-85398-607-2

Cover Design: Steiner Graphics

CONTENTS

INTRODUCTION TO THE SECOND EDITION

Materialism and materialistic philosophy contend that whatever we experience in the world can be explained in physical terms and that matter is the centre of all aspects of life. Materialism as a concept has been defined in different ways in the literature. It 'can refer either to the simple preoccupation with the material world, as opposed to intellectual or spiritual concepts, or to the theory that physical matter is all there is'.[1] It may also refer to a prevalent doctrine suggesting that material success is the highest value, that it gives meaning to life and that existence is primarily explainable in material terms: 'This theory is far more than a simple focus on material possessions. It states that everything in the universe is matter, without any true spiritual or intellectual existence . . .This doctrine appears to be prevalent in western society today.'[2]

The opponents of the above concept of materialism believe that scientific discoveries in the fields of quantum physics and biological sciences suggest that the universe and its material aspects are connected through a network of energy, and that therefore the concept of matter as comprising everything in the universe needs to be revised. Moreover, '[w]e live in a world surrounded by and composed of matter. It is natural, therefore, that we may become distracted from spiritual or intellectual pursuits by material possessions, but this is frequently where problems occur. We can become obsessed by a desire to obtain them, or simply frustrated by the need to maintain them.'[3]

In a Yiddish story as told by Charles Moore, a rich man 'is persuaded to pay a visit to a rebbe':

> The rebbe leads him to the window. 'Look out there,' the rebbe says, and the rich man looks out at the street. 'What do you see?' 'I see people,' he answers.
>
> Then the rebbe leads him to the mirror. 'What do you see now?' The rich man answers, 'Now I see myself.'
>
> 'So,' the rebbe says. 'In the window there is glass and in the mirror there is glass. But the glass of the mirror is covered with silver, and no sooner is the silver added than you cease to see others but see only yourself.' [4]

Moore then comments: 'Today's consumers look in the mirror and crave meaning . . . When we confine our ambition to trying to satisfy our disparate desires, the result is that we become increasingly self-absorbed and increasingly unable to care for others.'[5]

In some people the accumulation of material possessions may reflect their efforts to fill an inner void or existential vacuum. Human beings are unique both inwardly and outwardly. In our outward relationship with society and cultural forces we are influenced by a variety of ideologies, beliefs and psychosocial factors which can impact our way of life and the choices we make. Society, culture, religion and socio-economic developments define or influence our personal values and social expectations. But within our inner selves and deeper reality we crave for greater understanding of the purpose of our life and the meaning of the challenges we face along our journey.

Science uncovers the mysteries of the unknown in the physical world and helps us to become creative in developing technology for a better and prosperous life. It shines a light on the landscape of our worldly existence and material civilization. It does not, however, shape our intrinsic values, nor does it provide us with a spiritual perspective on the purpose of life. This belongs to a different domain which transcends the material world and its limitations.

Material philosophy maintains that matter has priority over mind and spirit. Based on such a philosophical concept, the human mind, consciousness and spirit are by-products of matter and those who believe the contrary are deemed 'idealists'. Therefore, anyone who believes in the dualism of soul and body or in a transcendent God is automatically categorized as an 'idealist'[6] – a word nowadays related to 'unrealistic', 'impractical', 'unscientific'. Reductive materialism ascribes the entire domain of physical interactions, including human behaviour, to the mechanical laws of science and fails to recognize that human thought and reason are not purely mechanical processes.

In recent years there has been much debate about 'post-materialistic science' promoted by a group of authors and researchers. This emerging scientific point of view contends that materialistically-oriented scientists are biased in their interpretation of consciousness and that such a prejudice is not acceptable. More specifically, in the words of Dave Pruett: 'Consciousness is not the magical by-product of a mechanical cosmos. It is an inherent attribute of the stuff of the universe'.[7] Pruett, a former NASA researcher and Emeritus Professor of Mathematics at James Madison University, states that the proponents of post-materialistic science propose a radical paradigm which suggests that '[m]ind represents an aspect of reality as primordial as the physical world. Mind is fundamental in the universe; i.e., it cannot be derived from matter and reduced to anything more basic.'[8]

In theoretical terms there are different types of materialism: dialectical, historical, philosophical, cultural, scientific, nonreductive, and others. Materialism from a moral point of view is defined as 'a desire for wealth and material possessions with little interest in ethical or spiritual matters'.[9] In this context, materialistic people have a strong belief that owning or acquiring possessions constitutes the key to human happiness and well-being[10] and thus they have a constant concern for material wealth and an intense or excessive interest in worldly possessions.[11]

A philosophical analysis of historic or dialectic materialism is not the purpose of this book. Rather, it aims to examine the moral and psychosocial implications of a materialistic view of life in the context of attachment to worldly things and extrinsic values. With this objective, in order to provide a context for an explanation of materialism we need to understand it within a conceptual framework of life itself. One of the many definitions of life is a sequence of events or experiences in consciousness which occur during one's lifetime.[12] The human mind, through cognitive processes, makes it possible for a person to become conscious of these experiences. Thus the content and quality of life depend on what our attention has been directed to over time.[13]

Based on this concept of life, materialism is defined as a form of behavioural attitude characterized by 'excessive attention to goals that involve material objects: wanting to own them, consume them, or flaunt possession of them'.[14] In the words of the Universal House of Justice (2017):

> The forces of materialism promote a . . . line of thinking: that happiness comes from constant acquisition, that the more one has the better, that worry for the environment is for another day. These seductive messages fuel an increasingly entrenched sense of personal entitlement, which uses the language of justice and rights to disguise self-interest. Indifference to the hardship experienced by others becomes commonplace while entertainment and distracting amusements are voraciously consumed.'[15]

Devoting a certain degree of attention to material goals in order to live is normal, but when such attention consumes most of an individual's life, it overshadows other opportunities for development. Human beings are able either to transcend self-gratification whenever they find it necessary, or to heavily indulge in immediate satisfaction, depending on their personal goals and motivation. We have not only extrinsic needs to fulfil, but also intrinsic needs to attend to.

Materialism in this context is a state of mind, a trait and a lifestyle some people consciously choose – but many more possess it, unaware of its consuming effect on their daily life. Although materialism is more common among rich and prosperous nations, it recognizes no boundaries; it can affect poor and rich, educated and illiterate, young and old, religious or secular. In such a society, the gratification of physical and emotional desires takes centre stage in life and the body, not the soul, is in command. The light of a deeper understanding of the mysteries of life and the life beyond is obscured. In the more developed forms of materialistic society, materialism becomes like a cult with its own doctrines and practices. Belk, who in 1985 explored the psychosocial aspect of materialism, views it as a collection of personality characteristics which include three traits: envy, non-generosity and possessiveness.[16]

Proponents of materialism and nihilism maintain that 'nothing has any value, that no standards are binding, that no purpose exists, that there is nothing worth living or dying for, that everything is futile'.[17] 'Abdu'l-Baha once commented: '... the materialists of today are proud of their natural instincts and bondage. They state that nothing is entitled to belief and acceptance except that which is sensible or tangible. By their own statements they are captives of nature, unconscious of the spiritual world, uninformed of the divine Kingdom and unaware of heavenly bestowals...'[18]

Materialistic doctrine then, in its strict sense, values the physical frame alone, denying the notion of a spiritual dimension to human reality. But if we take materialism in a broader sense, with all its variations and implications, we find people with heavy material attachment who also believe in religion. Materialism can therefore be seen as a universal behavioural pattern characterized by excessive material attachment as a source of pride and pleasure, but bereft of altruism and moderation.

5

Materialistic notions can influence cultural attitudes and life style in society. As the Dalai Lama is reported to have stated: 'We have a largely materialistic lifestyle characterized by materialistic culture. However, this only provides us with temporary, sensory satisfaction, whereas long-term satisfaction is based not on the senses but on the mind.'[19]

CHAPTER 1

PERSPECTIVES ON MATERIALISM

Humanity is battered by forces of oppression, whether gener-
ated from the depths of religious prejudice or the pinnacles of
rampant materialism.
The Universal House of Justice[1]

Materialism has been studied and written about for centuries. Literature, philosophy, economics, politics, psychology and religion
all provide their different perspectives, but it is perhaps only with
the rising tide of materialism in the 20th century that the subject
has commanded academic attention. Since this book treats the
moral and social implications of materialism, this chapter gives a
brief overview of some of the more important ideas on the subject
from philosophy and psychology, including recent research.

Karl Marx and Friedrich Engels used the term 'social materialism' to refer to a theoretical perspective which holds that

> the satisfaction of everyday economic needs is the primary
> reality in every epoch of history. . . materialism takes the posi-
> tion that society and reality originate from a set of simple
> economic acts which human beings carry out in order to
> provide the material necessities of food, shelter, and clothing.
> Materialism takes as its starting point that before anything
> else, human beings must produce their everyday economic
> needs through their physical labor and practical productive

activity. This single economic act, Marx believed, gives rise to a system of social relations which include political, legal and religious structures of society.[2]

Materialism is a trait which characterizes much of North America and Europe, according to Swinyard et al (2001), and it is likely to spread worldwide through globalization. The authors indicate that its socio-cultural or individual aspects can be explored through research studies. On the individual level materialism can be defined as a phenomenon whereby people seek happiness by accumulating wealth and possessions.[3] It is a form of orientation with a focus on deriving joy through worldly possessions and social status. Consequently, the possession of material things may gain such significance that it becomes a major source of satisfaction and pleasure in life.

Richins and Dawson (1992) in their broader scheme of materialism consider it to be a value which guides the conduct and choices of the individual in a variety of situations. They propose the following three dimensions:[4]

- 'Acquisition Centrality': This involves individuals who place their possessions and acquisitions at the centre of their lives. For these people, material consumption becomes a goal in life.

- 'Acquisition as the Pursuit of Happiness': Satisfaction and happiness are derived from the acquisition and possession of goods essential for well-being.

- 'Possession as Defining Success': The success of individuals is measured by the quantity and quality of their accumulated possessions. Possessions are seen as indications of status in society.

Numerous studies have revealed a negative correlation between materialism and life satisfaction and happiness.[5] One of the reasons why materially-oriented people remain constantly dissatisfied in their lives is that their material goals constantly outpace them. Moreover, these individuals have greater ambitions and aspire to possess more and more. The gap between what they actually have and what they want constantly widens, and their dissatisfaction grows.[6]

Studies also recognize that religion plays an important role in defining true happiness and intrinsic values. But religious people can also be influenced by their own ego and socio-cultural ambitions to promote their self-interest. Allport and Ross (1967) present their concept of 'intrinsic' and 'extrinsic' religiosity as follows : '. . . the extrinsically-motivated person uses his religion, whereas the intrinsically-motivated lives his religion.'[7] In this statement the authors underline the view that intrinsically religious individuals are truly committed to their faith, as compared to those who are more self-serving – the extrinsically religious.

Although intrinsic religiosity in general is perceived to be one-dimensional, extrinsic religiosity consists of two or more components: the use of religion for personal benefit and to gain social rewards, writes Swinyard.[8] According to Kashdan and Breen (2007), 'strong materialistic values reflect a predominant orientation toward the purchase, consumption, and possession of wealth and physical goods. As a value, the importance of material goods directs a person's life choices and influences appraisals of self and others.'[9]

Most people with a materialistic mindset overvalue permissiveness and lean towards an excess of freedom. As a result, many of these individuals may find themselves in conflict with rules and regulations and in their relationships.[10]

Some of the great philosophers have held a broad view of materialism. Aristotle noted that people perceive the result of worldly possessions, health and fame to be happiness, and that happiness is valued for itself as the only intrinsic goal in life. But Epicurus, 2,300 years ago, believed that in order to enjoy a happy life one must develop self-discipline. His concept of materialism was based on the idea that one should be able to defer gratification. Further, he noted that although all pain is evil, this doesn't imply that pain should always be avoided.[11]

In the 18th century the utilitarian philosophers had a notion of human nature which was based on the principle of maximizing happiness. They believed that human actions were to be understood in terms of bringing happiness or failing to do so. F. W. Matson, a leading proponent of the utilitarian view, conceived happiness to be a mathematical expression of human behaviour – 'a sort of arithmetic of pleasure'. Later versions of this concept developed into the notion of a human being as a 'pleasure machine'. This materialistic notion led to the impression that human behaviour is based on instinctual drives to 'maximize pleasure and minimize pain'.[12]

Following the utilitarians, many today hold the view that the acquisition of wealth, fame, ownership of goods and long life are the royal road to happiness and well-being. This, together with a denial of a deeper meaning in life beyond matter, and of the spiritual nature of humankind, has become the hallmark of the pervasive culture of materialism. However, as one researcher in the field has noted, 'the virtual monopoly of materialism as the dominant ideology has come at the price of a civilization that has robbed it of much of the truth it once contained. In current use, it amounts to little more than a thoughtless hedonism, a call to do one's thing regardless of consequences, a belief that whatever feels good at the moment must be worth doing.'[13]

Another research study, by Kasser and Ryan (1993), demonstrates that excessive concern with financial success as well as material objectives is associated with lower levels of inner satisfaction and self-confidence. And Dean et al (2007) in their study of materialism have confirmed that materialistic attitudes in a married couple are associated with greater perceptions of financial problems, which are negatively correlated with degrees of marital satisfaction. Their analysis also revealed that such attitudes have a strong impact on couples' perception of financial difficulties as compared to their actual income.

It has also been suggested that in a death-denying culture a concern over mortality may contribute to material consumption and greed. Kasser and Sheldon in a study carried out in 2000 asked university students either to think about their own death or to listen to music. The participants were then asked questions about their expected financial status during the 15 years to come. The results showed an increase in financial expectations after reflecting upon death (as compared to listening to music). The participants inflated their expectations, including their overall worth and the amount of money they expected to spend on luxury items such as expensive clothing or entertainment. This finding may suggest that fear of mortality plays a role in the financial aspirations and superfluous consumption which have permeated American society.[14]

What is intriguing is that the participants of the study, instead of gaining a spiritual perspective on life and material possessions,[15] wanted to compensate for the possibility of death by over-indulging in material possessions as a defence against the reality of mortality. This perception, however, may not be shared by some other cultures. It may also reflect low self-esteem and unhappiness. People who are unhappy with their lives may try to compensate by acquiring material possessions in order to feel better.

Capitalism and materialism

Capitalism, also known as the free market economy, is the dominant economic system in the world today. Although existing in some form since the Middle Ages, it began to flourish in the 16th century. As of the beginning of the 18th century the focus of capitalist development shifted from commerce to industry, first in England, and then spreading to other parts of Europe and beyond. Capitalism is distinguished from previous economic systems by its use of the excess of production over consumption to enlarge productive capacity rather than using it for 'unproductive' purposes such as the building of pyramids or cathedrals. The ethic, promoted by the Protestant Reformation, of hard work and frugality – which also justified economic inequality, seeing wealth as a virtue – contributed to the spread of the system.[16]

The capitalistic theory of economics perceives individuals as being innately self-interested people who use their intellect to maximize their own benefits. The notions of self-interest, competition and profit maximization constitute the essential ingredients of a capitalist system. Although capitalism has proven to be successful in creating wealth and economic prosperity, it is less likely to maintain moral principles such as trust, empathy, compassion and generosity.[17]

In materialistic ideology, material attachment defines human worth and matter is the centrepiece of belief. Consumerism or consumer culture is an ideology which encourages an ever-increasing acquisition of goods and services. It is based on the view that consumption is needed as a machine to drive economic growth in modern society, the goal of a capitalistic society. In a materialistic society the acquisition and possession of objects constitutes an essential value, 'akin to a religion'.[18]

People whose economic ideology is mainly self-interest frequently encounter a serious dilemma in their daily life. They have to choose between protecting their own self-interest or supporting the collective requirements of society. Since the beginning of the 20th century social scientists have noted a dynamic connection between the economic environment and intrinsic values. Among those who have explored this connection is Ronald Inglehart, whose research has contributed significantly by introducing the modernization theory and the influence of economic environment on social values.[19] In light of Inglehart's research, Chavez Rojas (2014) hypothesizes that 'noble, higher-order values such as generosity will receive more approval and support as economic pressures decline with increased economic development. However, there is the possibility that individuals' attitudinal patterns . . . are also being influenced by the specific type of economic ideology adopted in each country around the world.'[20] His view on capitalism is that under its influence there is an erosion of moral values at the individual and societal level.[21]

The Bahá'í teachings emphasize that human nature and its development play an important role in our perception of the material world as it is related to spiritual reality: 'The human experience is essentially spiritual in nature: it is rooted in the inner reality – or what some call the "soul" – that we all share in common. The culture of consumerism, however, has tended to reduce human beings to competitive, insatiable consumers of goods and to objects of manipulation by the market.'[22]

In many developed countries, where glamour and the seductive influence of publicity and marketing have captivated the attention of the public, individuals often can't make a distinction between what they want as compared to what they need. In such an environment, the consumption of goods becomes a habit or an obsession with little attention to a rational need for such goods. Objectivity and moderation are the keys to change from a consumer culture to one based on healthy and rational choices with respect to consumption. To accomplish this we need to reflect on how society might make the transition to such an attitude. Ultimately, we need to see this 'transition to sustainable consumption and production as part of a global enterprise which enables all individuals to fulfill their dual purpose, namely to develop their inherent potentialities and contribute to the betterment of the wider community'.[23]

Pathways to a materialistic attitude

Kasser et al (2004) suggest two important 'pathways' through which people develop a materialistic attitude – or, as they put it, 'materialistic value orientation (MVO)'.

The first pathway includes experiences which impede or

undermine the satisfaction of psychological needs (love, security, affection). A materialistic value orientation in society may be related to a basic insecurity resulting from personal doubt and the fear of one's inability to cope with stress in an unpredictable world. Turning to material things and seeking safety in the shelter of wealth can become a way of compensation.[24] In such circumstances the possession of material goods provides not only a sense of satisfaction but also of control. Moreover, wealth and social status enable one to gain the approval of others and satisfy the need for safety and survival.[25]

However, dependency on material possessions or over-attachment to them itself carries a risk of another potential insecurity: the loss of wealth or income which would frustrate one's sense of security and control. Indeed, as Bahá'u'lláh writes, fear is hidden in wealth.[26] Since material wealth cannot always sustain security, the subsequent disappointment creates new anxieties which perpetuate a vicious circle.

Comparing one's financial status with that of others is another form of competition. It can reinforce the notion that being wealthy also means being powerful and thus gaining others' admiration. In a society where human values are measured by the size of income and assets, self-image becomes an important instrument of superiority. Despite these efforts, however, the underlying insecurity may persist because the extrinsic changes don't necessarily bring new insight and new intrinsic values. This tendency to compare and to compensate has been a feature of the spread of materialism into formerly communist and socialist countries and some of the developing nations.[27]

In order to maintain a sense of security, two factors are necessary: 1) an inner strength of self-esteem and contentment; and 2) an ability to rely on divine power at a time when no solution is in sight. Money gives a false sense of security and power. But in the absence of true self-esteem, the fear of loss of wealth can haunt individuals who possess a superficial sense of security. At the core of self-esteem lies a 'feeling of contentment' as a result of conviction and faith in a higher source of power and wisdom. In addition, there comes a capacity to love and to be loved and to be well-connected to family, friends and community. Self-esteem is also significantly enhanced through work, productivity and financial income, which are important in our daily life. But although earning money, and wealth, are essential for financial independence and a family life, reliance on these alone is not sufficient for maintaining stability of self-esteem and security.

The Kasser study also shows a link between economic deprivation and materialistic behaviour. Children whose families have suffered from socio-economic deprivation or disadvantages showed greater materialistic orientation.[28] This is partly because such children will try hard to prosper financially so that they don't fall into the plight of their parents.

The second pathway in the development of materialism relates to direct exposure to it, and the influence of materialistic values through socialization, internalization and materialistic models. As the researchers point out, people are exposed from birth to both implicit and explicit messages through advertising which endorses the importance of money and material possessions. This kind of media publicity, reinforced by peers and parents, will be internalized as values for a materialistic lifestyle in the family. Consequently, people are likely to accept these messages and incorporate them into their behavioural values. Messages from popular culture and commercial television shows such as 'The Price is Right' or 'Who Wants to Be a Millionaire?' are just a few examples of the promotion of the culture of consumption and materialism. Individuals who experience a greater level of insecurity are generally more susceptible to the influence of these commercial messages conveying the idea that the acquisition of products will benefit their well-being.[29]

Perspectives from psychology

The thinking and behavioural approaches of psychologists with regard to wealth, well-being and materialism are many and diverse. Some humanistic and existential psychologists such as Abraham Maslow, Erich Fromm and Carl Rogers have expressed critical views on the materialistic approach and lifestyle. In recent years enlightened researchers in the field such as Mihalyi Csikszentmihalyi, Richard Ryan, Tim Kasser and others have carried out extensive research in exploring the dynamics and consequences of materialistic pursuits. These psychologists have emphasized the role of authenticity in interpersonal relationships and the importance of personal growth and making a contribution to family and community life. They acknowledge the necessity of material comfort and well-being in fulfilling people's basic psychological and physical needs, but they also believe that 'a strong focus on materialistic pursuits not only distracts people from experiences conducive to psychological growth and health, but signals a fundamental alienation from what is truly meaningful'.[30] As Erich Fromm stated in 1941 in his book *Escape from Freedom*: 'In the medieval system capital was the servant of man, but in the modern system it became his master.'[31]

Moreover, materialistic values encourage activities which involve rewards. This system of motivating individuals may shift their attitude to becoming more reward-oriented. The long-term consequences of reward orientation are that people become less authentic and meaning-oriented. Consequently, they are unlikely to experience the deeper internal satisfaction and insight which occur when they are motivated by their own intrinsic values. In other words, their interest in the rewards of money, praise or position distracts them from a richer experience of reliance on their own initiative to take on life challenges with creative thinking. This does not mean that responding to reward as an incentive needs to be abandoned entirely, but rather that one should not become dependent on it for performance.[32]

Freud acknowledged that defining the purpose of life is a difficult task and that 'only religion can answer the question of the purpose of life'[33] – an astonishing statement by a man who also referred to religion as an 'illusion'.[34] In his book *Civilization and its Discontents* Freud proposed a materialistic understanding of the purpose of life in relation to the pleasure principle, stating that 'present-day man does not feel happy in his Godlike character',[35] and asserting that 'what decides the purpose of life is simply the programme of the pleasure principle. This principle dominates the operation of the mental apparatus from the start.'[36] He then postulated that there is no possibility that this pleasure principle can be carried through because 'all the regulations of the universe run counter to it. One feels inclined to say that the intention that man should be "happy" is not included in the plan of "Creation". What we call happiness in the strictest sense comes from the satisfaction of needs which have been dammed up to a high degree . . .'[37] By 'satisfaction of needs' he was most likely referring to biological needs such as eating, drinking, sleeping, sex, and so on, as well as psychological needs such as security and love.

This viewpoint reduces the meaning of happiness to a form of pleasure satisfaction, derived from Freud's pleasure principle and the quenching of instinctual needs. But human happiness is not always the result of satisfaction of needs, nor is happiness always the same as pleasure. Freud's contention that 'the regulations of the universe' counteract the fulfilment of the pleasure principle is a further indication that he equated human pleasure with animal pleasure: that is, sensory and instinctual gratification, and that this pleasure is restricted by the rules of ethics and social norms. His view of human happiness is that, on the one hand, it relates to the absence of pain and 'unpleasure', and on the other, it has to do with the experience of feelings of pleasure. According to him, in a narrow sense happiness relates only to pleasure.[38]

Freud believed that human beings are threatened with suffering from three sources or directions. One is from their own body, which not being eternal is doomed to decay and decomposition.

The body cannot even be free from pain and anxiety, which serve as warning signals. The second source of suffering is from the external world, which can attack people with merciless forces of destruction. The third and most important source, according to Freud, is suffering which comes from human relationships. He considered the latter to be probably the most painful kind of suffering, but admitted that it is no less inevitable than the two others.[39]

Under the pressure of these sufferings, Freud contended, people are accustomed to being moderate in their expectations of happiness and the fulfilment of the pleasure principle. Freud's ideology of the satisfaction of instincts, especially that of sexuality, is of paramount importance; in fact, his whole concept of happiness and suffering is connected to instinct satisfaction, with happiness often seen as a by-product:

> Just as a satisfaction of instinct spells happiness for us, so severe suffering is caused us if the external world lets us starve, if it refuses to sate our needs. One may therefore hope to be freed from a part of one's sufferings by influencing the instinctual impulses. This type of defence against suffering is no longer brought to bear on the sensory apparatus; it seeks to master the internal sources of our needs. The extreme form of this is brought about by killing off the instincts, as is prescribed by the worldly wisdom of the East and practised by Yoga.[40]

Clearly, Freud's reductionistic analysis of happiness and suffering misses a broader vision of life and the universe beyond the pleasure principle.

Freud viewed aggressiveness as a powerful element of human 'instinctual endowments'. He referred to it as a 'primary mutual hostility of human beings' which perpetually threatens society with disintegration and is the greatest impediment to civilization. Civilization must therefore mobilize all efforts to restrict human 'aggression instincts'.[41] He also believed that 'inclination

to aggression is an original, self-subsisting instinctual disposi-
tion'.[42] Having such a strong reductionistic and instinct-based
conviction about aggression, one may wonder if Freud did not go
too far in, for example, his theory of sexuality and neurosis, pre-
senting the individual as a prisoner of his/her biology and instinct
rather than a being who can change and grow through other forces
such as education. He also underestimated the role of the cultural
environment and the education of family and society in potenti-
ating or mitigating aggressive behaviour. If human aggression is
innate and engraved in human instincts, how will civilization be
able to survive this perpetual threat of disintegration? Humans
are neither machines nor subservient to their instinctual drives.
Their minds and souls can be trained and their aggressivity transformed into a positive force for peace and prosperity. Obviously
Freud underestimates the power of human conscience and the
role of religious teachings, when these are devoid of superstition
and fanaticism.

CHAPTER 2

EXPLOITING DESIRE: THE RISE OF CONSUMERISM

Earth provides enough to satisfy every man's need,
but not every man's greed.
Mahatma Gandhi[1]

From ancient times to the Industrial Revolution, people traditionally acquired goods according to their needs. However, with
the advancement of technology, the expansion of advertising and
easy access to goods through shopping malls, department stores
and more recently online, the psychological knowledge of the
human mind and motivation has been exploited to transform the
sense of 'need' into 'want'. This has led to a strong desire for consumption, especially in urban populations. The transformation
began with social and political activism for greater freedom in
society; this gradually changed into a movement aiming to create
more diverse products for marketing and to stimulate consumers' desire. This process has been well researched and publicized,
notably in 2002 in the BBC documentary *The Century of Self*
which explored the use of psychology as a tool to promote individualism in post-World War America.[2] The film reveals how the
Freudian concept of desire was used to manipulate people's minds
so that they bought more. The key to selling more goods was to
connect human emotions to specific products and bring about
a shift from contentment and fulfilment of needs to a desire
to obtain more and more goods. Consequently, consumption

came to be identified with American democracy and a materialistic way of thinking became the order of the day. Tapping the
deepest human desires, the culture of consumption – a 'happiness
machine' – became very popular in the 1920s until October 1929
when the US market crashed.

Richard Robbins in his book *Global Problems and the Culture
of Capitalism* (1999) elaborates on the rise of consumerism. He
believes that in order for this to happen in the United States, the
buying habits of the population needed to be transformed. He
points out that what used to be considered as luxuries and vanities had to come to be perceived as necessities, and he identified
ways through which this could be accomplished.[3] Exploring the
powerful role of advertising as another 'revolutionary development' in the promotion of a consumer culture, Robbins writes:

> The goal of advertisers was to aggressively shape consumer
> desires and create value in commodities by imbuing them
> with the power to transform the consumer into a more desir-
> able person . . . In 1880, only $30 million was invested in
> advertising in the United States; by 1910, new businesses,
> such as oil, food, electricity and rubber, were spending $600
> million, or 4 percent of the national income, on advertising.
> Today that figure has climbed to well over $120 billion in the
> United States and to over $250 billion worldwide.[4]

In modern times 'possession' has became a 'virtue'. One of the
most popular expressions of this 'virtue' is the fashion industry. The temptation to be fashionable has prompted millions of
people to buy things not because they need them but because of
style and image.

People today live in an environment influenced by a culture of
consumption linked to materialistic desires and lifestyle. Marketing is aimed at reshaping human desire and the gratification of
instinctual needs and appetites. To elicit a response from custom-
ers, the material desires are overrated and excessively glamourized.

Likewise, a person's worth is measured by how much he or she possesses (or seems to possess) in material terms, for example 'looking like a million dollars'.

In his classic book *To Have or To Be?* (1976) Erich Fromm exposes the false perceptions of this mentality. He identifies two different kinds of character structure or fundamental modes of existence in society. In the 'having' mode a person's relationship with the world is one of possessing and owning. In the 'being' mode of existence the person relates to the world in an authentic way that reflects his/her true nature and reality. Fromm also states that 'God, originally a symbol for the highest value that we can experience within us, becomes, in the having mode, an idol' – something to possess.[5] The having mode is a by-product of the materialistic mindset which seeks security and satisfaction through material power and possession. In contrast, moderation and detachment characterize the being mode.

Consumption itself is influenced by the need for profit. As a major component of free market economics and its variations, the search for profit is the driver of ever-increasing consumption in societies based on capitalism. This connection between materialism and economics constitutes an integral part of human dependency on material means as a source of satisfaction and survival.[6] But consumption also includes a vast array of leisure activities, and our senses are constantly bombarded with publicity for these through the mass media. In such a society, individuals internalize habits and influences toward material attachment, which are culturally encouraged. This phenomenon shapes individuals' attitude, behaviour, and expectations in their day-to-day lives as they embrace a new identity based on the culture of pleasure and self-indulgence.

Although with the advancement of science and technology there has been significant refinement and sophistication in the market economy and the approach to consumption, the basic attitude of appealing to the human mind and instinct to maximize the need for happiness is not new. The utilitarian concept of life and happiness described in Chapter 1 is consistent with modern-day consumerism and advertising marketing practices. The approaches of the latter are aimed at people's interest in happiness and pleasure, which is rewarded or maximized through the acquisition of more and more material goods. Thus, with the help of modern technology, consumerism in the 20th century became a practical embodiment of an 18th-century utilitarian and empiricist philosophy.[7]

In recent years there have been an increasing number of research studies examining the relationship between human well-being and consumption. According to Ahuvia (2002), research on consumption and subjective well-being (SWB: a term meaning the belief that one is happy) shows that people in rich countries, on average, enjoy significantly higher levels of SWB as compared to people in poor countries. This is consistent with a link between one's overall level of consumption and one's SWB. But when a comparison is made between individuals within the same country, there is very little relationship between income and SWB once basic needs are met. This also supports the notion that 'higher levels of consumption may not be linked to higher levels of SWB'.[8]

According to Rosenberg (2004) most consumer behaviour is automatic because people examine neither their consumption actions nor the real needs that are only temporarily satisfied by buying things. She believes that the advertising industry uses this non-conscious process to lead us to believe that we want to consume by capitalizing on our tendency to be automatic (not mindful) in buying advertised goods. When this type of behaviour continues, people begin to think that what they see in advertisements is what they need and that the fulfilment of these 'needs' will bring happiness. Thus they develop a conditioned response to material possessions, with the false assumption that possessions will be a source of inner contentment.[9]

The enormous sensory overload of advertising messages by marketing companies has become a daily distraction. From early morning when one gets up in western cities to bed time one faces hundreds if not thousands of all sorts of publicity messages generated by the marketing industry. These include unsolicited phone calls from marketers as well as media messages on radio, television and the Internet, bombarding listeners and viewers with countless advertisements. Outside the home, ads in public places, on billboards, in busy subways and other means of public transportation, in shopping centres and at the beginning of movies, target consumers for all kinds of products. Using mind-influencing psychology, these messages designed to attract people's attention are becoming increasingly sophisticated and enticing.

With the advancement of cell phones, ipods and social media such as Twitter it is hard to find a moment's peace. The explosion of new information has thus created a dilemma: technology and communication science have become a powerful instrument for the expansion of capitalism, but consequently life has become a struggle for survival.

In our busy lives we often miss opportunities to stop and evaluate the messages we receive from the media or from our personal encounters which might go against our inner convictions and logic. This is the price we pay for becoming so occupied with technology and progress that we lose out on those moments of reflection so precious to our mindfulness and survival.

Children and the marketing industry

The pervasive nature of the marketing industry has an impact not only our minds but our family relationships too. These impacts can have a long-term effect on children who, in some parts of the world, spend more time in front of the television and on the Internet than at school.

Children are by nature highly impressionable, and their way of processing information is different from that of adults. They try to make sense, in their own way, of messages they receive from the world around them. This makes them particularly vulnerable to promotional marketing. Levin and Linn (2003) point out that children below the age of 8 are more vulnerable to this kind of exploitation than older children because their ability to reason and to think in abstract terms is not yet fully developed. When they see advertisements they have a tendency to believe what they see rather than question the message. And advertising corporations make no realistic distinction between desire and need when they launch the promotion of certain foods or games for children. Their strategy is to expand and multiply human wants for consumption, and is psychologically devised to produce maximum effect in young children. The proliferation of electronic media and other factors have also contributed greatly to the transformation of children into a consumer group. Children between the ages of 2 and 14 influence the purchase of almost US$500 billion worth of goods each year – a huge business. Levin and Linn note that money spent by corporations on marketing goods for children had increased to $12 billion a year by 2002. For example, in 2000 Burger King spent $80 million on advertising to attract children.[10]

This bombardment by extensive marketing campaigns and advertisements means that the average child sees 40,000 commercials each year. Using their sophisticated technology and psychological expertise, many large corporations have created powerful advertising strategies to influence children though TV, movie characters, websites and computer games. These large-scale advertising activities naturally influence children's minds, suggesting what they should desire. Given the emotional vulnerability of children, such exploitation raises questions about the ethics of such a practice and how to protect children in a world engulfed in consumerism.[11]

The exposure of children to television advertising was prohibited in the early days of television. Some countries, including Sweden and Norway, still prohibit advertising directed toward children under 12 years of age. But in the United States, such a policy is not followed; television is seen as a media whose purpose is entertainment, not education.[12]

As Levin and Linn indicate, 'by conceptualizing childhood as a market segment, corporations focus on making progress, often at the expense of what is best for children'.[13] These ethically questionable aspects of targeting children for commercial advertisement involve marketing violent media programmes and encouraging junk foods. This is particularly serious at a time when nearly a third of American children (and an increasing percentage of British children) are overweight or obese.[14] An article 'Underage, Overweight' published in May 2010 in the journal *Scientific American* suggests that the United States federal government 'needs to halt the marketing of unhealthy foods to kids'. It points out that through commercial advertisement on television and in other media such as movies and video games, the food and beverages marketing industry is promoting the consumption of sugar- and fat-laden foods to children. Researchers at the University of California in Los Angeles who reported that children who view more television are more likely to become fatter found that this condition is not correlated with television per se, but comes about as a result of watching more commercial programming aimed at children which promote foods that can cause obesity.[15] Advertising these products in such an environment is unethical; it risks the development of cardiovascular disease, diabetes or other weight-related problems.

Researchers in cognitive psychology have recently reported that words, objects and faces learned in early childhood have a lasting effect and are recognized more quickly than similar items learned later in life. Based on these observations they have stated that early acquired brand names are more rapidly recognized than brands acquired later. This finding has implications for the advertising industry.[16]

For example, children too young even for kindergarten can be led to a lifelong recognition of brands primarily aimed at adults. Marketers who want to promote the sale of adult-oriented products such as cosmetics and perfumes target children under the age of 5. This early exposure to such products can have unhealthy consequences in later life. It empowers marketers to influence and exploit young minds in order to enhance impulse-buying and consumption in the future. The earlier children are exposed to brands or are aware that their role models choose certain brands, the more likely they are to use them as they grow older.[17]

It is evident that the advertising industry should not use psychology as a tool to manipulate children. Such actions not only promote an unhealthy lifestyle with the risk of mental and physical disorders, but also undermine children's ability to make proper judgements that will be in their best interest. Such psychological manipulation will also have bearing on the social and spiritual development and well-being of young children.[18]

The above research studies and critical observations underline the insidious role of the materialistic mindset, promoted through the media, which makes children a market for business promotion and exploitation. Especially in families where both parents work outside the home, there is little time to closely observe or discuss with one's children the hazards and the unhealthy role of commercial advertising. Consequently, the impression left in the minds of the young children can have far-reaching effects. The Universal House of Justice, the international governing council of the Bahá'í Faith, even goes so far as to say that the alienation of children, whether living in conditions of wealth or poverty, has its origins in materialism: 'This alienation has its roots in a selfishness that is born of materialism that is at the core of the godlessness seizing the hearts of people everywhere. The social dislocation of children in our time is a sure mark of a society in decline . . .'[19]

Materialism and youth

Today our young generation faces the powerful influence of relentless advertising and marketing, which affects young minds. It is to be noted, however, that not all of the barrage of publications is harmful or intended to cause adverse effects; some of it is educational, promoting better health and well-being. Parents should help their children and youth by their counsel and example to recognize and avoid messages which are toxic and detrimental to health. The following is based on psychosocial and scientific research and observations on the subject.

Jean Kilbourne (2004) in his review of literature noted that companies spend more than $200 billion per year on advertising. The average American is exposed to more than 3,000 ads every day. 'Far from being a positive mirror of society, it [advertisement] is an effective and pervasive medium of influence and persuasion and its influence is cumulative, often subtle and primarily unconscious.'[20] Young people, particularly during their period of adolescence, are vulnerable to the seductive influence of marketing and advertisement. This is a period in their lives during which they acquire their values, examine their options and develop their concepts of life. During this period many adolescents are influenced by peer pressure and may not resist the cultural marketing messages which are reinforced by the media. 'A cigarette provides a symbol of independence. Designer jeans or sneakers convey status. The right perfume or beer resolves doubts about femininity or masculinity. Most young people are vulnerable to these messages.'[21]

A research study on the influence of media on the minds of young women was conducted in 1999 in the island of Fiji.[22] The study explains that before television was available in Fiji there was little talk about dieting. In fact, saying that someone had gained weight was traditionally a compliment, while weight loss was viewed as a sign of a problem. Within three years of television being introduced into Fiji in 1995, the number of teenagers at risk for developing eating disorders had more than doubled; 74 per cent of Fijian adolescents said that they felt too fat or too big and 62 per cent said that they had dieted during the previous month. The researchers commented that although this did not prove that there was a direct causal link between television and teens' eating disorders, since Fiji was experiencing a cultural transition during that period, nevertheless in view of the fact that Fijian girls were heavy viewers of television, it was reasonable to postulate that many of them were affected by images of thinner individuals seen on TV.

It is to be noted that not all advertisers and marketers intend to manipulate their target populations, or to cause unacceptable consequences. However, some advertisements are aimed at arousing fear and anxiety related to self-esteem in young people. The intention is to create a need to compensate through the acquisition of the advertised product to address the perceived problems such as weight gain and negative body image.

It is important that children and youth learn to appreciate and value themselves for who they are as persons, rather than how they look or how much they own. Psychologists Tim Kasser and Allen Kanner have criticized the use of psychology in marketing to attract children's attention toward an overdependence on products. For instance, Kasser writes: 'Psychologists who help advertisers are essentially helping them manipulate children to believe in the capitalistic message when all the evidence shows that believing in that message is bad for people. That's unethical.'[23] In February 2008, BBC News in the United Kingdom stated that 'the selling of lifestyles to children creates a culture of material competitiveness and promotes acquisitive individualism at the expense of the principles of community and cooperation'.[24]

In addition to psychosocial, ethical and economic parametres of materialistic influences on children and youth, it is helpful to reflect on the spiritual aspects of challenges in today's society. The Universal House of Justice analyses these in the following statement:

> The forces at work on the hearts and minds of the young, to whom the Guardian directed his appeal most fervently, are pernicious indeed. Exhortations to remain pure and chaste will only succeed to a limited degree in helping them to resist these forces. What needs to be appreciated in this respect is

the extent to which young minds are affected by the choices parents make for their own lives, when, no matter how unintentionally, no matter how innocently, such choices condone the passions of the world – its admiration for power, its adoration of status, its love of luxuries, its attachment to frivolous pursuits, its glorification of violence, and its obsession with self-gratification. It must be realized that the isolation and despair from which so many suffer are products of an environment ruled by an all-pervasive materialism. And in this the friends must understand the ramifications of Bahá'u'lláh's statement that 'the present-day order' must 'be rolled up, and a new one spread out in its stead.' [25]

Thus it remains the sacred task of parents, family and community to guide and assist children and youth to overcome the seductive forces of attraction to materialism, through both words and actions.

CHAPTER 3

MATERIALISM AND DISCONTENT

Contentment is natural wealth, luxury is artificial poverty.
Socrates[1]

In the first two chapters of this book we have seen that materialism and the consumer society are inextricably linked with the
pursuit of happiness. But does materialism make people happy?
Increasingly, people in the rich developed countries are discovering that it doesn't.

Studies on the relationship between wealth and well-being
suggest that, especially in developed countries, the relationship
between material success and well-being is complex and unclear.[2]
According to David Myers (2000) the number of Americans
reporting themselves as 'very happy' actually declined slightly
between 1957 and 1998 despite the doubling of income in real
terms. During the same period, the divorce rate doubled and teen
suicide tripled. 'We are twice as rich and no happier,' he notes;
the 'American Dream' has become 'life, liberty and the purchase
of happiness'.[3] This negative relationship between wealth and
well-being is replicated in studies covering diverse cultures – in
Australia, Germany, Norway, Romania, Russia, South Korea and
the United Kingdom, for example – but the relationship cannot
be generalized because a state of well-being also necessitates a
certain degree of wealth and financial sustenance. Being hungry
and sick without material resources to respond to these needs is
not a happy and healthy situation. Poor people too are distressed
and dissatisfied. But in research studies carried out in Europe it

was noted that once a level of income greater than the poverty level was achieved, happiness and money ceased to have anything to do with each other.[4] In other words, after the basic needs are met, happiness does not necessarily increase proportionately with increasing money and wealth. Gregg Easterbrook, a fellow of the Washington think tank The Brookings Institution, comments:

> . . . there is a final reason money can't buy happiness: the things that really matter in life are not sold in stores. Love, friendship, family, respect, a place in the community, the belief that one's life has purpose – these are essentials of human fulfillment, and they cannot be purchased with cash. Everyone needs a certain amount of money, but chasing money rather than meaning is a formula for discontent. Too many people today have made materialism and the cycle of work-and-spend their principal goals. Then they wonder why they don't feel happy.[5]

Ottar Hellevik (2003) explored the level of happiness in relation to income in the Norwegian population. This research examined why, in spite of substantial increases in income from 1985 to 2001, the level of happiness did not increase in the population during the same period. The analysis of data based on several large representative surveys of the Norwegian population showed that some of the subjective indicators did not reflect the improvement of the objective economic conditions. One of the factors implicated in the process is value orientation. The Norwegians' increasing tendency to give priority to income and material wealth appears to have resulted in an adverse effect on levels of happiness during that period.[6]

In the 1980s a survey conducted at the University of Michigan asked people what would improve the quality of their lives. The first and foremost answer given was 'more money'.[7] However, in 1985 another study showed that the possession of significant wealth does not translate into happiness. In that study of a group of the wealthiest individuals in the United States, it was noted that their level of happiness was barely above that of people with average income.[8] Clearly having more money has not been found to be associated with greater contentment and well-being. This was also shown in a study of lottery winners in 1999,[9] while a longitudinal study of a representative sample of approximately 1,000 American adolescents showed a consistently low negative relationship between material wealth and the subjective feeling of well-being.[10]

So is material reward conducive to happiness? Csikszentmihalyi (1999) identified three reasons which support the notion that material reward does not necessarily result in happiness:*

1. *Escalation of expectations.* After attaining a certain level of affluence, people rapidly become attached and habituated to possessions. They then begin to desire a higher level of wealth, property, reward or pleasure. As an example, he cites a 1987 poll conducted by the *Chicago Tribune.* According to this poll, people who earned less than $30,000 a year said they needed $50,000 to fulfil their dreams. Those with a yearly income of over $50,000 stated that they would need to earn $250,000 to be satisfied.[11] Research confirms that the initial goals are moved upward once the lower levels of expectation are achieved.

2. *Contentment is relative.* Variations in contentment are dependent on human expectations and extrinsic needs. Some people may never be content. When resources are unevenly distributed, people view their possessions as compared with those of others who have more, and not in terms of what they really need to live. 'Thus the relatively affluent feel poor in comparison with the very rich and are unhappy as a result.'

3. *Other factors.* Although the experience of being rich and famous is satisfying, hardly anyone has noted that material

---

* The following critical analysis of the reward paradigm is not intended to discount the usefulness of reward so much as to underline the seriousness of overdependence on material reward as a source of happiness.

rewards alone are sufficient to render happiness. There are other factors involved, such as a fulfilling family life, close friends and other contributing elements. Sometimes rewards are not tangible or material but occur spontaneously as a result of an inner enlightenment or the discovery of a truth.

The escalation of expectations: A cycle of neediness

The global domination of attachment to material things and a materialistic way of life is so pervasive as to leave little room for reflection on life beyond materialism. It seems that the more we are drawn into materialistic behaviour, the less we are interested in qualitative aspirations or seek positive alternatives which would give a true meaning to life. As Kasser et al (2004) note, 'the culture of consumption . . . not only degrades psychological health, but spreads seeds that may lead to its own destruction. Materialistic values not only heighten our vulnerability to serious social and environmental problems, but also undermine our ability to work cooperatively in finding solutions to these problems.' They destroy altruism, leading people to be more interested in rewards than in the inherent qualitative nature of their activities. This, in turn, can undermine their intrinsic aspirations and motivation.[12]

An excessive attachment to material things and the notion that these will bring happiness can therefore lead to a perpetual struggle to have more and more, in satisfaction of a neurotic need. But once a material goal is achieved the feeling of satisfaction does not last – rather, it may lead to another goal with higher expectations, as we have seen. For example, someone may have been longing to own the latest model of a deluxe car. Once he has it, he may be temporarily satisfied but will then compare it with a better or newer model. This new expectation dampens his excitement and a new journey of longing begins.

The same applies to the amassing of money. Easterbrook comments: '. . . it is the very increase in money – which creates the wealth so visible in today's society – that triggers dissatisfaction.

As material expectations keep rising, more money may engender only more desires.'[13] It is very interesting to note how in a materialistic society, the achievement of a goal does not lead to a sustained sense of contentment and gratitude, as though nothing is enough to quench the perpetual thirst of desire and need for satisfaction. This underlines the undercurrent of greed which prevents humans from experiencing enduring gratification and contentment. In such a climate, life becomes a chain of struggle for material prosperity, which is destined to engender disappointment. 'People seem conditioned to think they do not have enough,' writes Easterbrook, 'even if objectively their lives are comfortable.'[14]

The kindling of desire to have more, often fuelled by a sense of jealousy and comparison with others, is one of the insidious by-products of the accumulation of wealth. It becomes an obsession in a life which is joyless, despite its apparent glamour, wealth and comfort.

But this analysis is not a condemnation of the pursuit of wealth or a glorification of poverty; it simply demonstrates the critical need for self-evaluation, for moderation and contentment.

Contentment

Although achievement and success are abundant, true contentment is rare. At the peak of modern civilization and material advancement there are many reasons to be content, and yet people seem to find so many reasons to be discontented or miserable. Mind seems to have lost its contact with feeling and, as Archibald MacLeish wrote, when 'the fact is dissociated from the feel of the fact . . . that people, that civilization is in danger . . .'[15]

According to 'Abdu'l-Bahá,

> Contentment is real wealth. If one develops within himself the quality of contentment he will become independent. Contentment is the creator of happiness. When one is contented

he does not care either for riches or poverty. He lives above the influence of them and is indifferent to them.[16]

'Abdu'l-Bahá's words so befittingly apply to the affairs of humanity today. For instance: '. . . all the sorrow and the grief that exist come from the world of matter – the spiritual world bestows only the joy!'[17] So the more we are attached to and dependent on material things or possessions as our prime source of security, the greater is our vulnerability to their loss.

When contentment becomes merely a by-product of success, failure to succeed becomes a source of pain and discontent. Yet a highly competitive lifestyle and a perpetual struggle for higher and higher material gains are hallmarks of the industrialized countries. Such a pattern of behaviour often results in isolation, while sharing and cooperation is conducive to fellowship and prosperity. In a survey of 644 Harvard alumni in 1983 it was reported that over 40 per cent of them were not content with their lives despite an average annual income of US$300,000.[18] This finding shows that neither a distinguished academic post nor a high level of income can bring true contentment. Many less fortunate people, including those who live in poverty, may yet possess inner peace and contentment.

The words 'detachment' and 'wealth' – which strike us as being poles apart in meaning – are in their spiritual essence quite similar. Bahá'u'lláh explains that the essence of detachment is for a person to turn his face toward God and enter His Presence. Then He remarks that the essence of wealth is love for God: 'whoso loveth [Him] is the possessor of all things'.[19] In both cases the essence is love for God and being attracted to His threshold. When we reflect on the above statements carefully and look around ourselves in society at large, we realize how joyless life can be, whether with wealth or without it, if there is no love for divine reality to give it a deeper meaning. We are therefore reminded, with these words of 'Abdu'l-Bahá: 'If thou art seeking after spiritual tranquillity, turn thy face at all times toward the Kingdom of

Abhá. If thou art desiring divine joy, free thyself from the bands of attachment . . .'[20] Likening this material world to a garden, 'Abdu'l-Bahá deplores undue attachment to it in these words:

> These few brief days shall pass away, this present life shall vanish from our sight; the roses of this world shall be fresh and fair no more, the garden of this earth's triumphs and delights shall droop and fade . . . And therefore is none of this worth loving at all, and to this the wise will not anchor his heart.[21]

Spirituality and material interests, however, are interrelated; they are not to be perceived as two mutually exclusive phenomena. Likewise, spirit and matter, or soul and body, are interconnected; their relationship is complementary. One cannot judge one as good and the other evil. Although desire is seen in some religious communities as the source of evil, a complete elimination of desire is not possible. What is important is mastery over one's desires and temptations and the development of the insights and skills of self-discipline and self-regulation. Furthermore, extremes of attachment either to spirituality or to material interests are best avoided; moderation is required. Neither the reclusive lifestyle of a hermit nor excessive indulgence in pleasure is ideal.

The pursuit of happiness

As elusive as it is mysterious, the idea of happiness has been pursued throughout the ages. To discover such an elixir, every herb, plant and medicine known to man has been tried; incredibly diverse forms of art, music and drama have been explored. From traditional tribal rituals to the most sophisticated neuroscience laboratories, people are in an intense search to discover a panacea that will satisfy their thirst for happiness. The pursuit of happiness has become a timely subject of extensive studies, debate and discussion around the world, particularly in the West.

Researchers, writers, novelists, humanists, psychologists and even chemists are working on this 'hot' topic in their desperate search to find a recipe, an elixir or a drug which would bring about a temporary or a lasting happiness.

Thus, 'happiness' in an intensely materialistic society can often be perceived as a form of commodity to be found in different shapes and forms available in the market. This is the only kind of happiness which can be planted on a farm, grown on mountains or synthesized in a lab! It can be carried home in a bottle and served at a party. It can be mailed to a friend or sold on the black market. It can be consumed, disposed of, or stored in a cellar.[22] This kind of happiness has many faces and many names; it can be called ecstasy, mescaline, champagne, cocaine, angel dust, and many others. It can render instant joy and rapture or cause tragedy and sorrow. People celebrate the most cherished moments of their lives and toast their anniversaries with these 'happiness' products.

For example, the discovery of ecstasy, an amphetamine derivative, resulted from a chemical search for a product to bring about happiness. It is hailed by millions of youth as a potion to deliver them from a joyless life and to transport them into a world of illusion for the sake of a temporary 'happiness'. It is interesting to see that people are so desperate for happiness that they are willing to embark on a dangerous excursion into a world of unreality and, in the process, lose their minds in order to find some glimpses of happiness. Unfortunately what they find is nothing but an illusion and it is far from lasting. For true happiness is essentially an experience; it is not something one can obtain at any price or borrow from anyone. In its deepest sense it is profoundly spiritual, with emotional manifestations.

Speaking about human honour and happiness in 1912, 'Abdu'l-Bahá explained that

> The honour of man is through attainment of the knowledge of God; his happiness is from the love of God; his joy is in the

glad tidings of God; his greatness is dependent upon his servitude to God. The highest development of man is his entrance into the divine Kingdom, and the outcome of this human existence is the nucleus and essence of eternal life. If man is bereft of the divine bestowals and if his enjoyment and happiness are restricted to his material inclination, what distinction or difference is there between the animal and himself?[23]

'Abdu'l-Bahá also makes it 'abundantly clear' that

the Divine religions, the holy precepts, the heavenly teachings, are the unassailable basis of human happiness, and that the peoples of the world can hope for no real relief or deliverance without this one great remedy. This panacea must, however, be administered by a wise and skilled physician, for in the hands of an incompetent all the cures that the Lord of men has ever created to heal men's ills could produce no health, and would on the contrary only destroy the helpless and burden the hearts of the already afflicted.[24]

Research into the mysteries of 'happiness' in whatever shape, form or feeling has intensified in recent years. In the year 2000, 50 books were published on happiness in the United States, while in 2008 there were 4,000 books published on the same subject. Courses such as positive psychology and happiness are the most popular ones at Harvard and many other universities, according to Flora Carlin (2009). Yet apparently the United States as a nation has grown 'sadder and more anxious' during the same years that the happiness movement has flourished.[25]

Can inner joy be detected and measured by technology? The answer partly depends on how we define joy or happiness. It may be possible to find and measure joy if it is perceived as a biological entity. But if you take it in the context of a spiritual or any other non-physical experience, material measurement may fail to detect it, or if it does, the finding may be merely the physiological ripple effects. Still, just as there have been extensive studies on depression and the role of neurotransmitters, scientists have considered themselves compelled to explore the opposite feelings of joy and happiness.

Researchers, therefore, have been exploring the biology of joy. In 2005 Richard Davidson reported the following observation in a laboratory experiment at the University of Wisconsin. Using functional magnetic resonance imaging (fMRI) and electroencephalograms (EEG) he began to record the brain activity of a Buddhist monk as the monk entered a state of 'blissful meditation'. While he was observing the electrical activity of the brain, Davidson suddenly noted the emergence of something very unusual which initially he found difficult to believe. He rushed to double check the data streaming into his computer. The brain's electrical activities were accelerating at a tremendous rate – unexpected in a monk who was in a serene state of meditation. Davidson was very excited by this paradoxical observation; he had been exploring the link between the brain's pre-frontal lobe activity and the deep serene state of meditators and found these results confirmed his findings that happiness is not just a vague and ineffable experience, but a physical state of the brain. He also came to believe that happiness is something that one can deliberately induce.[26]

Although this is a very interesting study, can one equate a serene state of meditation with happiness? What characterizes these electrical brain activities which are equated to happiness? Is the state of meditation always a happy experience, or can there be deep meditation during which, although one is calm and serene, one is not necessarily in a state of joy and delight? One explanation could be that the brain's electrical activities, in a state of obvious happiness, are similar or identical to those of the state of contentment and this similarity justifies such a conclusion. But how do we know that the same brain activities wouldn't occur in another person who is not clearly happy? What is happiness and what is not? Is a feeling of pleasure the same as true happiness or can pleasure also be a joyless experience?

Happiness is more than a smiling face or laughter. True happiness has a quality of contentment, a sense of fulfilment, finding life meaningful and in harmony with the purpose of creation and the universe around us. People who look for a quick fix after a break-up or failure may lose the chance to work through their sad experience for greater personal growth in the long term. Helen Keller is often quoted as saying: 'When one door of happiness closes, another opens, but often we look so long at the closed door that we do not see the one which has been opened for us.'[27]

Sometimes, however, it may not work that way. People who have a genetic predisposition to depression may find it harder to snap out of their loss or other disappointment. These are individuals who will need active treatment of their depression. However, the support of family, friends and community can have an empowering effect. A spiritual perception of life and its challenges also has an empowering effect, as it makes life experiences more meaningful. It helps us to understand happiness in the larger context of human destiny in the universe. Why were we born and what is the purpose of this life? Why do we suffer in this world and what is the meaning of death? Why do wealth and material satisfaction not bring lasting happiness? These are some thought-provoking questions worth exploring

Human beings are by nature adaptable; they usually adjust to both the positive and negative experiences of life. Sometimes a life crisis may enhance our appreciation of happiness which otherwise is taken for granted. If there is no darkness, how can we appreciate the light? and if there is no winter, how can we look forward to the warm summertime? Paradoxical life experiences provide us with rich learning opportunities.

'Abdu'l-Bahá makes a clear distinction between true happiness and material happiness. People worldwide, and particularly in the West, have failed to recognize this difference. In the following statement He elucidates the difference between these two types of happiness:

Know thou that there are two kinds of happiness – spiritual and material. As to material happiness, it never exists; nay, it is but imagination, an image reflected in mirrors, a spectre and shadow. Consider the nature of material happiness. It is something which but slightly removes one's afflictions; yet the people imagine it to be joy, delight, exultation and blessing. All the material blessings, including food, drink, etc., tend only to allay thirst, hunger and fatigue. They bestow no delight on the mind nor pleasure on the soul; nay, they furnish only the bodily wants. So this kind of happiness has no real existence.

As to spiritual happiness, this is the true basis of the life of man because life is created for happiness, not for sorrow; for pleasure, not for grief. Happiness is life; sorrow is death. Spiritual happiness is life eternal. This is a light which is not followed by darkness. This is an honour which is not followed by shame. This is a life that is not followed by death. This is an existence that is not followed by annihilation. This great blessing and precious gift is obtained by man only through the guidance of God . . .

This happiness is the fundamental basis from which man is created, worlds are originated, the contingent beings have existence and the world of God appears like unto the appearance of the sun at midday.

This happiness is but the love of God . . .

Were it not for this happiness the world of existence would not have been created.[28]

CHAPTER 4

MATERIALISM AND MENTAL HEALTH

It must be realized that the isolation and despair from which
so many suffer are products of an environment ruled by an all-
pervasive materialism.
The Universal House of Justice[1]

Exploring a possible relationship between modernization and depression, Brandon Hidaka (2012) asks: if modernization is related to a higher risk of developing depression, then what are the specific components of modern society, including western culture, which contribute to this phenomenon? He suggests that a decrease in physical well-being in a lifestyle characterized by a sedentary life with less physical activity and exercise, as well as poor diet leading to obesity, contribute to depressive mood. Moreover, a 'toxic social environment characterized by increasing competition, inequality and social isolation may also contribute to a depressiogenic milieu. Each of these aspects of the contem-porary environment is associated with diseases of modernity and affects the incidence of depression and its treatment.'[2]

The modern social environment in industrial countries has become intensely competitive, insecure and isolating. Moreover, capitalist values have contributed to a decline in the social and emotional well-being of societies in the western world. When freedom – in itself laudable –becomes a pervasive and obsessive preoccupation, it can generate high expectations and stress with a shift toward a narcissistic need for satisfaction. But modernity and modern life should not be perceived as all negative, fraught with disease and discontent. There are also many positive aspects including progress in family life and in the health of society as a result of scientific discoveries. This progress has brought prosperity, prevented diseases and alleviated human suffering.

Other studies also suggest a relationship between depression and modernization. For example, there is a higher prevalence of depression among Mexican Americans born in the United States who have adopted the American lifestyle, as compared to new immigrants from Mexico. On the other hand, minorities, especially migrants and refugees, on arriving in a new country may find the challenge of adapting to a new environment and culture very stressful.

Another example of this relationship between depression and modernization has been observed in metropolitan China, which during recent decades has experienced significant cultural transformation. People are facing greater risks of depression and its prevalence has risen significantly in that country. Hidaka reports that Chinese people born in 1966 are 22.4 times more likely to suffer a lifetime depression episode compared to those born in 1937.[3] It has also been noted that in developing countries urban dwellers have a higher prevalence of psychiatric disorders, particularly mood and anxiety disorders, as compared to their rural counterparts.[4]

Related to these findings about modernization and depression is that in the Amish culture, where there is a strong sense of community combined with a coherent religious perspective and shared values, the rates of major depression and bipolar disorder are very low – approximately 1 per cent for each of these disorders.[5] In brief, there remains little doubt that assuming a predominately materialistic perspective and way of life, characterized by an overdependence on material means to satisfy intrinsic needs, produces a climate in which depression is much more likely to develop; whereas a society or community life characterized by an emphasis on the development of spiritual values and support-ive cooperation among its members creates an atmosphere where depression and other related disorders are less likely to occur.

It is counterintuitive to think that suicide, which is the most extreme outcome of depression, is associated with happiness in some parts of the world. It contrasts darkly with what has been believed for centuries. However, researchers Stephen Wu and Andrew Oswald reported, surprisingly, that the happiest coun-tries possess the highest suicide rates. Their study used US and international data, including comparisons of a random sample of 1.3 million Americans who were asked to indicate their subjective well-being, and another set of data on suicide decisions among a random sample of approximately one million Americans. The results showed that 'the happiest countries . . . tend to have the highest suicide rates' and 'people judge their well-being in com-parison to others around them'.[6]

The observation of this prevalence had already been known for individual nations such as Denmark, and the above study revealed that a number of nations, including Canada, Iceland, Ireland, Switzerland and the United States, which enjoy a relatively high degree of happiness, are also beset with high rates of suicide. The researchers wondered whether, because each nation has its own cultural attitudes and suicide reporting systems, the results of the study might reflect these differences and therefore be less defini-tive. However, having then conducted the same study across the United States, i.e. in a single relatively homogeneous (according to the authors) country, they were able to produce results that confirmed those obtained from the international data. That is to say, in the American study, in states where people were satisfied with their lives they also tended to have higher rates of suicide. For example, the state of Utah was ranked first in life satisfaction, but also had the 9th highest suicide rate in the country. On the other hand, New York was ranked as 45th in life satisfaction, but had the lowest suicide rate.[7]

Although the researchers recognize that this phenomenon is

counterintuitive (that happiness and suicide are correlated), they feel that this comparison is useful as it may indicate that those with low self-esteem, who are more likely to become discouraged, are less likely to thrive in an environment where many around them are happy and satisfied since human beings have a tendency to compare themselves with others and feel less fortunate. This may be especially the case if they have unrealistic expectations, as I have written elsewhere.[8]

Depression and society

In both industrialized and developing countries there has been a rise in sadness and clinical depression since the mid-1960s, associated with a decline in social support, social bonding and mutual trust. Is it because priority has been assigned to commodities over love and friendship? Does the market society inhibit enduring friendship in society?

In exploring an answer to these thought-provoking questions, political scientist Robert E. Lane (1994)[9] examined deficits in friendship as a contributing factor to the appearance of depression. He also explored the growing incidence of depression in economically advanced and affluent societies. A caring and supportive interpersonal relationship, as well as a social network of friends, may reduce the impact of stress and isolation and consequently provide a protective environment against loneliness and depression. This underlines the influence of friendship and family support as compared to the availability of material wealth and commodities. While material means are necessary for providing medical care, friendship is also important for the prevention of isolation and depression. Unfortunately, during depression the social networking of individuals is diminished. Lane argues that the decline of family cohesion and also the weakening of close friendships or social networks since the end of the Second World War has contributed to the rise of depression.[10] During the same period, the rise of individualism in North America has further influenced the decline of friendship networks, resulting in isolation and loneliness. A decline in social support and integration, whether as a cause or consequence of depression, has been widely noted.

Like the affluent, the poor are not free from unhappiness and depression. They are affected by poverty, stress, inability to cope with different life circumstances and worries about survival. In that respect they are at a disadvantage as compared to those with a higher income and better socio-economic status, who have more economic opportunities for dealing with problems. But increases in socio-economic status and affluence do not necessarily bring happiness.

As to whether depression causes lower socio-economic status (social drift hypothesis) or, conversely, it is socio-economic status which leads to depression, is worth exploration. A study carried out in the 1950s and 60s showed that socio-economic status seems to be a contributing factor in depression.[11] But on the other hand, the more depressed an individual is, the more he or she is likely to be dysfunctional unless treated, and consequently is more likely to drift into loss of productivity, poverty and a lower socio-economic condition. Research observations showed that 'economic growth is unlikely to be a solution since precisely those countries that have experienced or are currently experiencing rapid economic growth have the highest incidence of depression'.[12]

This report can be challenged by the financial crisis of 2008–2009 which precipitated despair and depression in many of those who lost their jobs and income; however, as shown later in this chapter, economic recession in rich countries tends to lower the mortality rate and have an overall positive effect on physical health. Nevertheless, during recessions the pressure of low income may lead some people to neglect their health or to suffer from depression or other emotional disorders. In poor countries the impact of economic crisis can have devastating effects, especially if people are already in a vulnerable situation. A broad perspective is necessary, therefore, on the positive and negative aspects of economic impacts on health and daily life.

Elaborating on the difference between acquiring commodities and acquiring friendship in relation to attaining happiness, Lane suggested the following points. First, the pleasure achieved from acquiring commodities is more momentarily satiable than the pleasure of friendship. However, commodities, while easily acquired, seem never to deeply satisfy, in contrast with the pleasure of friendship which expands with experience. The second point is that friendship is usually infinitely expandable to a larger number of friends without increase in the price of friendship, while in the economics of commodities there is always fear of scarcity. Third, self-esteem is closely associated with friendship and contributes to the prevention of depression. Fourth, the reward of the market is money, while the reward of friendship is praise, although there are drawbacks such as favouritism and the fear of exclusion. Fifth, friendship is a protective factor against depression, while accumulation of wealth is only positive among the poor.[13]

Moving from a commodities orientation to a friendship values orientation, Lane concludes, is a positive step in a culture of individualism in which people have become isolated entities, over-dependent on objects and commodities which serve them as substitutes for people.

Other research studies, such as that by Kasser and his associates,[14] show that people who overrate the importance of extrinsic and materialistic values also report a lower quality of life in terms of self-actualization and vitality, as well as more anxiety and depression. This suggests that a higher materialistic orientation will not bring contentment and may correlate with narcissism, combined with low self-esteem and drug use. These researchers note that people who place a high priority on being rich often encounter many psychological problems. Their review shows that materialism is consistently associated negatively with happiness and life satisfaction. They note that a materialistic lifestyle may be partly due to the need for security, as discussed in Chapter 1, but may also lead people to engage in activities which result in unsatisfactory psychological experiences.

For example, the friendship and love relationships of those with a strong materialistic value orientation (MVO in Kasser's terminology) tend not to last, and are characterized more by emotional extremes and conflicts than by happiness and trust. This may be due to the tendency of materialistic people, with a low sense of empathy, to place less value on affiliation and benevolence. Moreover, they are more likely to compete than to cooperate. As a result of these and other factors, people with a high MVO have difficulties in establishing warm and trusting interpersonal relationships.

A study using data from 2004–05 among American adults found that 6 per cent of them have a lifetime prevalence of narcissistic personality disorder.[15] Bridget Grant and associates conducted a survey on 35,000 Americans aged 18 or over. The results of these interviews showed that narcissistic personality dysfunction is prevalent among Americans. This disorder is characterized by a pattern of unusual grandiosity as well as a need for admiration. Individuals who suffer from narcissism lack empathy and have a tendency to exploit others for their own interest. Grant found that this type of personality disorder is linked with substance abuse and other psychological problems.

One of the very intriguing findings in this study was that narcissistic men and women were significantly less likely to suffer from mild to moderate chronic depression, as compared to non-narcissistic men and women. One explanation could be that narcissistic individuals protect their fragile self-esteem through substance abuse; according to Grant, then, substance abuse may shield them from depression.[16]

Fear and anxiety

One of the most prevalent fears in the western world is the fear of death. This kind of fear is viewed as one of the 'four existential fears that are present implicitly and explicitly in every person's life'.[17] Death is one of life's critical experiences that we have no control over. In a world in which we strive to have control over whatever comes our way, this total and absolute inability to defy the finality of death creates a sense of helplessness. The inevitability of death as a sign of cessation of this earthly life brings about a profound insecurity if we fail to comprehend its deeper meaning as a portal to a spiritual world. In a society in which 'death denial' and the search for the fountain of eternal youth shape people's attitudes and concepts of life, individuals find it hard to accept the reality of mortality. In such an environment, bereavement becomes like a disease giving rise to the endless agony of anxiety, due to the reluctance to accept the reality of death.

A materialistic conception of life, especially in an individualistic culture, deepens the fear of death as total annihilation. In cultures where there are more extended families and greater bonding and unity within the family, this fear is less frequent. Children are more exposed to illness and the death of loved ones, especially the elderly, which provides family members with opportunities to be prepared for the inevitability of the death.

In modern western society some people become less tolerant of their relatives as they grow older, preferring to place them in institutions rather than care for them themselves. Yet the presence of the elderly in a family can be viewed as a rich experience with opportunities for children to learn about existential challenges and the art of compassion and caring. And separating the elderly from their families deprives children and the rest of the family from the opportunity to be present during the final stages of their loved ones' lives and the possibility to say goodbye and bring their relationship to a meaningful close. The more we rely on technology and a materialistic lifestyle, the less we are inclined to extend compassionate care and a loving touch to those who are unable to take care of themselves.

Margaret Somerville, a renowned ethicist and professor at McGill University, believes that 'our society is highly materialistic and consumeristic. It has lost any sense of the sacred . . .' She relates the effects of materialism to a permissive attitude toward euthanasia (in objecting to its legalization), stating, 'a loss of the sacred fosters the idea that wornout people may be equated with wornout products; both can then be seen primarily as "disposal" problems.'[18]

Many elderly people in what is often perceived as an unfriendly and unwelcoming institutional environment, or even in their own home environment, may feel guilty that they are a burden on their family, especially if they suffer from chronic or disabling illnesses. Some may wish that their death could be hastened or attempt suicide; others may resort to drinking or misusing narcotic prescription drugs and become addicts. Alcoholism and substance abuse among the elderly population is high.[19]

In recent years there have been reports of elderly people who have been asking for physician-assisted suicide. What is very unusual is that this request may come from individuals who don't necessarily suffer from fatal or disabling afflictions and who enjoy seemingly reasonable good health and have financial resources. The following anecdote was reported in a Canadian magazine.

In February 2010 a 95-year-old apparently healthy woman wrote a letter to her local newspaper, the *Time Colonist* in western Canada, beginning with these words: 'I am tired and I am ready to die now.' Mrs. P....... presented a carefully considered argument suggesting a change to the Criminal Code to allow physician-assisted suicide. Stating that 'I have decided, after much reflection, that I wish to end my life now before my mind and body deteriorate further so I am incapable of making that decision', she asked if Parliament could give her the right to assisted suicide. In conclusion, she noted, 'I could then have my family and friends around me to say goodbye as I die with dignity.' She was surprised by the extent of debate and publicity that her letter created in the media. When interviewed by *Maclean's* magazine she said that her letter was also about the importance of making a will, noting that people generally don't make a will because of their refusal to face their mortality. During the interview she admitted, 'I am in good health. I'm not suffering from an illness that will be eventually fatal . . . I am tired and I do suffer from congestive heart failure.' On the other hand, she had had a stroke in the past from which she recovered, but she feared that she might have another one that would incapacitate her. That fear, she said, filled her with horror.[20]

We perceive our bodies in various ways, depending on our concept of the meaning and purpose of the journey of life. For some, the body is sacred in creation because it serves as an instrument for the progress of the soul and its development. For others, it may be perceived as a machine or an object which can be disposed of whenever it loses its lustre and utility and no longer serves a purpose. There is also an intolerance toward suffering which may relate to a materialistic view of life and one's relationship with one's body. Imagine that one is travelling on a train toward a destination. In order to reach the destination one may need not only to enjoy delightful new experiences and all their blessings but also to endure countless unpleasant trials and tribulations as one longs to reach the ultimate goal. Jumping from the train before it arrives at its destination will prevent the soul from completing its natural journey.

Anxiety is more often reported than the common cold by people in different walks of life. But are we truly living in an 'Age of Anxiety', or has anxiety always been with humanity throughout history? The dramatic rise of the consumption of tranquillizers since the 1950s, particularly in the United States, has been perceived to be associated with a high prevalence of anxiety. In her book *The Age of Anxiety* Andrea Tone asks,

> Is anxiety socially constructed (largely a by-product of a particular cultural milieu) or biologically driven? . . . In one sense, anxiety has always plagued us. History is replete with narratives of those who have suffered under its spell. 'No Grand Inquisitor has in readiness such terrible torture as has anxiety,' wrote Danish philosopher Søren Kierkegaard in 1844.[21]

But she admits that anxiety may be more pronounced in this period of history. It has been described, interpreted and treated in many different ways. She concentrates less on subjective experience of anxiety than on the ways in which people have addressed and alleviated anxiety throughout history. 'Today', she writes, 'drugs for anxiety are a billion-dollar business in the United States.'[22]

The first minor tranquillizer was produced in 1955 in the United States and called Miltown. By 1957, 36 million prescriptions for this medication had been filled for Americans, with over a billion tablets manufactured. In the 1950s tranquillizers were referred to by patients as 'peace pills' and 'emotional aspirins'. The widespread popularity of Miltown boosted the perception of anxiety as an emotional disorder serious enough to require pharmacological treatment:

> The rise of a far-reaching tranquilizer culture and the medicalization of anxiety it galvanized were largely patient driven. For countless users, the decision to take tranquilizers was a seemingly cheap, fast (and many thought, harmless) way to cope with suboptimal circumstances beyond one's immediate control.[23]

Aside from the role of pharmacological and medical institutions in promoting the use of tranquillizers, their consumption also flourished in response to public interest in meeting the needs of a modern lifestyle. The discovery of minor tranquillizers coincided with post-war social conditions that were filled with both uncertainty and growing prosperity. But the upward trend in the consumption of tranquillizers continued, leading to drug dependency and other challenges.

Of course, in discussing this subject it is not my purpose to be critical of medical progress in discovering new diseases, with new remedies to relieve human suffering, but rather to put in perspective who we are, beyond our mental and physical nature and needs – to gain a deeper understanding of the reality of our existence.

Violence and self-destructiveness

The general loss of faith and spiritual conviction in the purpose of creation – to know God and to worship Him – is a contributing factor in the rise of violence and destructive behaviour. The home, traditionally a safe and sacred place where children are born, educated and raised as the most valued fruits of family life, has sadly sometimes turned into a destructive venue where a father kills his young children or a mother destroys her newborn infant. Why is this happening? What turns a gentle, loving father or mother into a monster?

In May 2009 CNN reported that in the United States a man from Maryland 'wrote six suicide notes expressing his love and sorrow for his family and then shot his wife and three children before killing himself with a shotgun'. In the same month another man killed his wife and two sons in their home in Florida. He then shot himself. The CNN reporter went on to write that in some of the most disturbing cases of family violence that year, 'fathers have turned against their own flesh and blood – asphyxiating and beating teenagers, firing shots into sleeping children tucked in bed, slaying grandparents and shooting infants in diapers'.[24] People have heard of suicide and homicide; now they have to get used to the term 'familicide', a carnage that shocks everyone.

One may wonder in what psychological state of mind the perpetrators must have been before acting upon their violent impulse to murder and commit suicide. What triggers their minds to slay their own loved ones and then destroy themselves? Is it out of hate, or an act of twisted love? The CNN report suggested that in some cases of mental illness, wives and children are perceived by mentally sick fathers as possessions, so that no one else may take care of them once the father is dead. Thus he takes them with him to the grave.

According to the Violence and Injury Prevention Program at the University of South Florida, it was estimated in 2009 that out of 1,500 to 2,000 murder/suicides each year, 70 per cent had two victims and 10 per cent involved familicides. Although many of the perpetrators of familicides were also unemployed, there have been others who were not in a hard financial crisis and who committed their carnage during times which for them were economically favourable. It is also possible that because of the stigma of suicide in the family, these perpetrators don't want the family left to face that humiliation. Hate and revenge are often other factors in such tragedies.[25]

Individual care, compassion and empathy are essentially based on a spiritual belief and understanding of human nature and the meaning of life. Such a conviction often has a protective role against the destruction of self and others. Can greed, insecurity, or lack of contentment in the material means of life be a factor? It is quite possible. In many cultures people are in deeper poverty than those in North America, yet the extent of murder and suicide is not as high. The poor of these countries are protected by their belief in contentment and their reliance on higher forces in creation. The following words of Bahá'u'lláh resonate in these circumstances:

> Thou art My dominion and My dominion perisheth not; wherefore fearest thou thy perishing? Thou art My light and My light shall never be extinguished; why dost thou dread extinction? Thou art My glory and My glory fadeth not . . .[26]

A major part of the fear and anxiety engulfing many people stems from their excessive attachment to a materialistic lifestyle, together with the expectation that material goods will bring about true and lasting contentment. This imbalance, brought on by an extrinsic preoccupation with riches and an intrinsic spiritual poverty, has created a crisis in human conscience. This may be related to lack of faith in the Creator and the influence of materialism. Shoghi Effendi commented:

. . . pervading all departments of life – an evil which the nation, and indeed all those within the capitalist system, though to a lesser degree, share . . . is the crass materialism, which lays excessive and ever-increasing emphasis on material well-being, forgetful of those things of the spirit on which alone a sure and stable foundation can be laid for human society.[27]

A materialistic philosophy of life relies on the primacy of matter over mind and the human spirit, which are not products of material processes. Through such a notion, material well-being and satisfaction not only is over-idealized in daily life but 'the satisfaction of everyday economic needs is the primary reality'.[28] This concept has led to a system of social relations which is devoid of a spiritual foundation. In this materialistic framework, the innate or instinctive drives are the motivating force for human conduct. Based on this hypothesis, aggression is considered to be an innate and integral part of individual behaviour; thus war and violence become inevitable in human society. This notion by implication undermines or denies the important role of education in the development or modification of an individual's behaviour.

Proponents of this line of thinking such as Charles Darwin, Konrad Lorenz and Sigmund Freud believed that there is a kinship between the human species and other animal species and that the former are driven by the same instincts as the latter. However, as Ashley Montagu pointed out, 'our kinship with other animals does not mean that if their behaviour seems often to be under the influence of instincts, this must necessarily also be the case in humans'.[29] Erich Fromm, who also explored the subject of human aggression, states that 'the thesis that war is caused by innate human destructiveness is plainly absurd'. He argues that human behaviour cannot be reduced to the animal equivalent and that from the time of the Babylonians and the Greeks to the present day, wars have been planned. The motivation for them has been the acquisition of land for cultivation or the exploitation of valuable minerals, the expansion of territory, and defence. In other words, warfare is not an 'uncontrollable biological activity, but requires planning and careful execution'. Violent behaviour is not genetically programmed into human nature; it is bad science to assume that humans have 'inherited a tendency to make war from our animal ancestors'.[30]

On the other hand, the question has been raised as to whether by an innate sense of dignity human beings can prevent crime. 'Abdu'l-Bahá elaborates on this issue:

> There are some who imagine that an innate sense of human dignity will prevent man from committing evil actions and insure his spiritual and material perfection. That is, that an individual who is characterized with natural intelligence, high resolve, and a driving zeal, will, without any consideration for the severe punishments consequent on evil acts, or for the great rewards of righteousness, instinctively refrain from inflicting harm on his fellow men and will hunger and thirst to do good. And yet, if we ponder the lessons of history it will become evident that this very sense of honour and dignity is itself one of the bounties deriving from the instructions of the Prophets of God.

He continues:

> We also observe in infants the signs of aggression and lawlessness, and that if a child is deprived of a teacher's instructions his undesirable qualities increase from one moment to the next. It is therefore clear that the emergence of this natural sense of human dignity and honour is the result of education.[31]

He furthermore states that even if instinctive intelligence and innate moral quality prevent wrongdoing, individuals with such characteristics are very rare – 'as rare as the philosopher's stone'. And even if such a rare individual does exemplify instinctive intelligence and innate moral quality, his strivings will be strongly reinforced if he becomes 'an embodiment of the fear of God'. Briefly, 'It is religion . . . which produces all human virtues, and it is these virtues which are the bright candles of civilization.'[32]

Affluence and the 'Affluenza' phenomenon

The civilization, so often vaunted by the learned exponents of arts and sciences, will, if allowed to overleap the bounds of moderation, bring great evil upon men.
Bahá'u'lláh[33]

In recent years there has been a great deal of interest in exploring a possible link between affluence and emotional disturbances such as discontentment and depression. 'Affluenza' is a metaphorical term used to suggest 'an illness that occurs when people view the acquisition of material goods as a measure of their worth'.[34] Although it is not the author's intention to label certain populations, nor do all affluent people fulfill the above definition, evidence is emerging that many of them view their worth as being measured by money and wealth.

Affluenza is, reportedly, a common societal problem and a condition which is socially transmitted, like a contagious disease. British psychologist Oliver James states that a correlation exists between the rise in affluenza and an increase in material inequality which in turn leads to unhappiness.[35] This condition occurs in families of the affluent or privileged classes whose members are hard-working high achievers, and where the pursuit of wealth can become the central theme of life. Moreover, successful parents may also pressure their children to excel in the same manner, even if they are not always successful. A possible consequence of this lifestyle is that children raised in such an environment, and spoiled by indulgent parents who allow them easy access to money, may find life less challenging, and lose motivation to explore ways to overcome life crises and become self-sufficient. Their ability to solve problems at times of financial crisis may be inadequate and, as a result, they may become even more discontented and frustrated. In fact, in such an affluent family environment children are more likely to become vulnerable to anxiety, substance abuse, stress and depression.[36]

According to Suniya Luthar (2002), a professor of psychology at Columbia University, the primary causes of the above behavioural problems experienced by children are twofold: one is physical and emotional isolation from parents and the other is excessive pressure to achieve academic and non-academic goals. The obvious and material advantages of affluent life may obscure some psychological challenges of the well-being of these children and adolescents.[37]

Researchers have noted that some people who seek wealth and affluence, after attaining what they wish for, quickly thereafter get used to it and begin to strive for additional wealth, and this pattern may perpetuate. If their desire to have more does not materialize, frustration sets in, a process similar to that of addiction and withdrawal which compels a person to get more in order to maintain satisfaction. 'Wealth is addictive. It enticingly offers happiness, but it cannot provide satisfaction, so those who attain some of it keep thinking more of it will provide satisfaction . . . [Those] who have become addicted to it . . . can experience severe withdrawal when they can't get it. Withdrawal from wealth, and the hope of wealth, can be terrifying.'[38] Luthar (2003) believes that one of the impacts of the competitive structures of market economies is the promotion of distress through inhibiting supportive and cooperative relationships and networks. The result of this process is a decrease in shared goals and values and an increase in isolation and anxiety. In contrast to this scenario, and what society requires, is genuine and mutual relationships inspired by the spirit of love and generosity.[39]

Lack of empathy and a sense of indifference toward others characterize the lifestyle of those consumed by materialistic self-interest. On 28 January 2012 the *New York Times* published an article which reported that in China 'a 2-year-old girl was run over by a van. The driver did not stop. Over the next seven minutes, more than a dozen people walked or bicycled past the injured child. A second truck ran over her. Eventually, a woman pulled her to the side, and her mother arrived. The child died in a hospital. The entire scene was captured on video and caused an uproar when it was shown by a television station and posted online. A similar event occurred in London in 2004, as have others, far from the lens of a video camera.[40]

In December 2013 CNN reported that a 16-year-old teenager, too young to drive legally in Texas, had violated the laws of driving when he killed four people in a drunken driving accident. During the court hearing his attorney as well as a psychologist and defence witness testified that this adolescent boy suffered from a condition called 'affluenza' lifestyle. They claimed that the privilege of being wealthy had deprived him from experiencing any consequences of bad behaviour. The prosecution sought 20 years of imprisonment but the teenager received 10 years of probation and a mandatory stay in a high-class rehabilitation facility. Many expressed outrage over this light sentencing, saying that it would have been harsher had he been from a poor family and from a minority population.[41]

Two years later, in December 2015, CNN reported that the so-called 'affluenza teen' and his mother had been detained in Mexico. Earlier in the month the teenager had gone missing in Texas where he had received his 10-year probation sentence. He had allegedly violated his probation and authorities ordered his return to Texas.[42] This calls to mind these words of Helen Keller, American author and educator: 'Character cannot be developed in ease and quiet. Only through experience of trial and suffering can the soul be strengthened, ambition inspired and success achieved.'[43]

When youth in wealthy families continue to be distressed because of parental expectations and pressure with no relief or positive intervention, they may resort to self-medication and use of alcohol and illicit drugs. Luthar's 2003 study of wealthy sub-urban communities in the United States revealed that girls living in such communities experience depression at a rate almost three times higher than that of girls from less affluent families living in urban areas (22% vs 7%).[44]

It is important to identify children and youth with symp-toms of anxiety, depression, and substance abuse problems and to provide clinical intervention and counseling. Unfortunately, some parents may not seek treatment as they may underestimate the seriousness of the symptoms. More important is the preven-tion of developing emotional problems in affluent countries.

It is also to be noted that not all children and youth of affluent families experience psychological disorders. In a family where the material and spiritual needs of children and youth are fulfilled and they are valued not for what they have but for what they are, this moderation and harmony may have a positive effect on the development of the children in affluent communities.

The recession effect

Although the excessive accumulation of wealth and greedy attach-ment to it can be a source of psychological and social concern, research shows that economic recession in prosperous countries has paradoxically positive effects on health and mortality trends of the people living in these countries. Stephen Bezruchka (2009) examined the effect of economic recession on the health of people in rich countries. His analysis of economic downturns in the 20th century shows that in contrast to people's expectations, these meltdowns were associated with a decrease in mortality rates. Conversely, economic expansions are correlated with a rise in mortality.[45] This positive correlation of business cycles and mor-tality has been further confirmed recently.

In poor countries, however, the above correlation is reversed. For poor nations, economic growth – so long as it is shared with the wider population – is likely to improve the health situation, as it provides the means for the basic needs of people to be met, including clean water, food, shelter and access to essential healthcare services. However, this trend changes after the developing country reaches $5,000 or $10,000 gross national product (GNP) per capita, at which point few health benefits will arise with further economic growth.[46] The above observation and analysis may suggest that when poverty is lifted in a population and people enjoy sufficient financial gain to satisfy their basic needs, their life expectancy improves and they begin to follow the health trends of rich populations. However, this prosperity levels off at a certain point.

In another study in 2009, researchers José Tapia Granados and Ana Diez Roux at Michigan University reported that records of economic and mortality data from the period 1920–1940 showed that there was an increase in the life expectancy of Americans (white and non-white males and females) during periods of deep recession and economic downturns, but a decrease during strong expansion and economic upturns. It appeared that economic expansion was associated with higher mortality during the latter periods. The only exception was the increased suicide rate from 1930 to 1933 during the Great Depression; however, the number of suicides constituted less than 2 per cent of all mortalities during that period, but the overall mortality rate for all ages decreased as compared to preceding years. Although the Great Depression was a tragic, dark period in American history when millions of Americans lost their jobs and worldly possessions, there seems to have been a silver lining, according to these research findings: economic depression may be hard on mental health, but it is favourable for physical health.[47]

Why then, when rich populations get richer, do they pay the price in higher mortality rates? In my opinion, unless there is moderation and a spiritual perspective in life, an increase in wealth will result in an increase in the temptation to find avenues of pleasure-seeking behaviour and self-neglect. In such circumstances overindulgence will dominate, resulting in the breakdown of families, the neglect of personal health and well-being, and life stress.

Not all societies follow this trend, however. Some may concentrate on the accumulation of wealth for philanthropic and humanitarian public services. In some countries, the distribution of wealth and economic growth is aimed at reducing the burden of poverty and at expanding public and health delivery services. Japan has emerged as a modern-day example because it has used its economic growth to reduce poverty and to raise the quality of healthcare, which is now one of the best in the world.[48] Cuba, although basically a poor country which has suffered from economic embargos for the past 50 years and has not seen noticeable economic growth, has made significant progress in healthcare and medicine by concentrating its limited resources on this vital area of community life. It has also promoted healthcare with an equitable approach toward its Afro-Cuban and white populations.[49] On the other hand, in the United States, one of the richest countries of the world, the overall health of the population was reported in 2006 to be on a par with that of Cuba.[50]

In view of the above research, economic growth cannot always be taken as a marker of improved health. Indeed, research findings have shown that greater national wealth does not necessarily bring better well-being and human welfare unless governments spend a sufficient part of their wealth on the health and well-being of their population.[51] The United States has the highest GNP per capita in the world and yet the life expectancy of its population is lower than almost all other rich countries and even a few poor countries on earth. This is especially striking given the fact that its spending on health constitutes half of the total expenses of global healthcare.[52] It also has the greatest level of poverty as compared to any rich nation, with significantly poor health outcomes and immense health disparities.[53] Such deficiencies improved somewhat under the healthcare reform implemented by the Administration of President Obama. Still, the endemic materialism that is so widespread in the United States underlies its income inequalities, health disparities and other challenges.

Some other possible reasons for lower mortality rates and improved health during recessions in rich countries may include the following. Although there are financial disadvantages when there is a recession or an economic downturn, there is also more leisure time to spend with family, children and friends, and to engage in physical activities and sport. Since job stress and mental pressure lead some people to anxiety and despair and thus to overeating, drinking, misuse of drugs and other unhealthy behaviour, this lifestyle may decline during a recession. The impact of a stressful workplace, where there is little control over job pressure and competitive performance which may lead to cardiovascular and other physical or emotional disorders, may be mitigated.

A national survey of negative and positive health indicators in the United States[54] following the economic recession of 2008 showed the following. Although there was a sharp increase in anxiety, stress and frustration as a result of the recession and the economic crisis, over 75 per cent of women polled in the survey reported that they had engaged in one or more positive coping strategies, especially prioritizing family and financial responsibilities. Most of the women admitted that they had participated in more positive activities during the recession as compared to the six months before the recession began. They spent more time with family, friends, would pray and attend religious services (one of the benefits of religious devotional attendance is the presence of a warm social network and caring friendship), exercise, listen to music, and so on. The majority of them also acknowledged the benefit of receiving mental health support.

Recessions in rich countries can also stimulate more creative thinking about wealth distribution, or a search for sustainable business activities to overcome the economic downturn and its hardships. They provide an opportunity to reflect on the purpose of life and its spiritual meaning, and may bring people together in mutual support and cooperative relationships in order to cope during the difficult times. The rise of unity amidst adversity can buffer the impact of the material distress of recession. Also, some important and historic initiatives may be taken during economic recession, such as healthcare reform.[55]

Loneliness and materialism

Loneliness is a common phenomenon in modern society which may have a range of contributing factors. Besides being caused by depression and other emotional disorders, it can be due to cultural, psychosocial and other factors.

It is believed that materialism contributes to loneliness in society. This is based on the assumption that too much attachment to material possessions overshadows personal and social relationships. Kasser (2002) stated that a materialistic way of life may be harmful to 'the quality of connectedness and decrease the ability to satisfy needs for intimacy, closeness and connection'.[56] Rik Pieters (2013) tested, through research, the hypothesis that the 'material trap' of materialism fosters isolation and loneliness. He notes that loneliness probably contributes more to developing materialism than the other way around. It may be that materialism and loneliness form a self-perpetuating vicious cycle.[57]

Another problem which may occur due to leading a materialistic way of life is a feeling of emptiness and a void in consciousness which may or may not be associated with loneliness. In such individuals, consumption of food or drink which is unnecessary, or shopping for objects, needed or not, whose acquisition does not fill the inner void, are characteristic behaviours. Viktor Frankl in his well-known book *Man's Search for Meaning* elaborates on this existential vacuum and points out that a person may have everything one can dream of yet feel a void within that is unfillable.

Many individuals who become heavy drinkers or drug addicts acknowledge this feeling of inner void. In 2013 Kim Daul, a successful young South Korean model, was battling a sense of loneliness, emptiness and depression. She was reported to have stated, "The more I gain the more lonely it is. I'm like a ghost.'[58]

She felt nothing was worth living for and was trapped in an existential dilemma. Beauty, fame and wealth could not save her and she committed suicide.

Having a spiritual understanding of the meaning of life may alleviate the angst and distress of an existential vacuum within us. Addressing human beings, Bahá'u'lláh writes, 'With the hands of power I made thee and with the fingers of strength I created thee; and within thee have I placed the essence of My light. Be thou content with it and seek naught else, for My work is perfect and My command is binding.'[59]

Lifestyle choices influenced by materialism

Lifestyle by itself is not an indicator of mental illness. Individuals differ from one another depending on their upbringing, character and the lifestyle they choose. Culture, education and socio-economic factors can also influence people's behavioural patterns. Poverty or wealth can lead to emotional and adaptational challenges that may need to be overcome. As was discussed in the section on affluence in this chapter, obsession with wealth and lack of insight into the potential consequences of breaking rules and overstepping ethical standards can come with a high price. These failings may also lead to emotional isolation, substance abuse, drinking and other problems.

In their review of the development of psychosocial disorders from the past to the present, Wallace and Forman (1998) note a shift from biomedical to psychosocial factors contributing to disease. Historically, the leading cause of death in western society was infectious disease. But with the passage of time, especially in recent decades, the causes of morbidity and mortality have shifted to disorders precipitated by changes in lifestyle and reckless or self-destructive behaviours.[60] This has led researchers to explore alternatives which would lead to a healthy life devoid of such behaviour.

A significant number of diseases, injuries and mortality in the population are not necessarily the outcome of genetic disorders, infections or other medical diseases; rather they are the consequence of personal habits, lifestyle and social or environmental factors, many of which are preventable. They are precipitated by human will and personal choice in behaviour. Examples include diseases resulting from the smoking of cigarettes, the consumption of alcohol, substance abuse, and sexual promiscuity. AIDS and HIV infections, of which millions of people in the world are victims, are also often caused by lifestyle choices.

The issue that has caught media and public attention recently is the rise of obesity among children and adolescents. In the United States obesity was reported in 2008 as affecting 16–33 per cent of this population,[61] while in the United Kingdom around 27 per cent of children are overweight. With almost one in three children under the age of 18 overweight or obese, being overweight is now the most common medical condition during childhood. There is cause for alarm about the future of these children, because their weight increases as they grow into adulthood. They risk serious diseases, some of which can be disabling with life-threatening consequences. Also of concern is that two-thirds of the adult population, who are potentially role models for teaching children healthy eating habits, are themselves overweight or obese. It has been estimated that the cost of treating obesity-related diseases in the adult population of the United States was $147 billion in 2009.[62]

Research findings suggest that reduced exercise plays an important factor in the development of obesity in children. It is also noted that obese children tend to come from families where the parents are also obese due to family lifestyle.[63] In a world where thousands of children die from hunger and disease each day as a result of poverty, millions in the more prosperous countries overindulge in eating, binge drinking and spending long hours at their laptops or in front of the TV, and take little physical exercise. The rise in adult lifestyle diseases and mortality has been attributed to this pattern of physical inactivity developed during childhood and adolescence and persisting into adult life. Obesity can precipitate diabetes, high blood pressure, cardiovascular disease and death. Yet with some exceptions due to genetic or other biological factors, it can be prevented by healthy eating habits, proper exercise and an active lifestyle. Research indicates that approximately 300,000 deaths annually are caused by unhealthy and excessive eating habits and the inactivity of modern life.[64] On the other hand, there are some individuals in developed countries who voluntarily submit themselves to restrictive diets for aesthetic purposes or, in the case of those wishing to go into certain careers, to please the fashion or entertainment industries. Anorexic and bulimic disorders are largely cultural expressions of consumerism and the dictates of a materialistic society.

Modern science and technology have made life much easier than it used to be but have not succeeded in educating us about the adverse effects and costs of our modern-day easy, sedentary life. On the other hand, religious values and teachings have been found to have a beneficial impact on health. This is because religious education, in its original essence, seeks to edify the human soul with a resulting transformation in behaviour and thus helps to develop a positive attitude toward personal health and well-being. More than 300 research studies show a positive association between religion and human health across socio-demographic populations (gender, race, ethnicity).[65] In contrast, a lack of religiosity or a lesser degree of religiosity is believed to present a risk factor for developing a number of behavioural problems, including deviant or delinquent behaviour.[66]

The shift of paradigm toward behavioural and psychosocial disorders has been particularly evident in junior youth and youth populations. Among many contributing factors to these social morbidities, injury is the number one cause in the American adolescent population. Other factors are substance abuse and smoking, sexual promiscuity, unhealthy dietary habits and physical inactivity.[67] Motor vehicle accidents, drowning, fires and ingestion of poison are the main causes of unintentional injuries.

Approximately 60 per cent of injury-related mortalities among American teenagers are the result of these so-called unintentional injuries, and it has been estimated that 78 per cent of all unintentional injuries are the result of car accidents in the United States. The majority of these are due primarily to driving under the influence of alcohol or other substances of abuse or as a result of riding in a car driven by someone who was under the influence of alcohol or drugs, or to the non-use of a seat belt.[68] The passion for car racing and reckless drinking and driving is another example of lifestyles fuelled by consumerism, the media, and materialism.

It has been reported that intentional injuries, particularly homicide and suicide, are the second and third leading causes of death in youth.[69] However, as suicide is not always reported, and in view of the high suicide rate in some cultures, death due to suicide may be underestimated. Alcohol and illicit drugs are reported to be responsible for almost 20,000 deaths each year among adults of the United States.[70]

Promiscuous and precocious sexual activities have had serious impacts on the health and well-being of both adolescents and adults. This includes the consequences of extramarital sexual involvement: unwanted pregnancies and abortion, and sexually transmitted diseases including HIV/AIDS and HPV (human papilloma virus) infections. National health services in rich countries have now begun to advocate routine vaccinations for adolescent girls against HPV, which is contracted through sexual intercourse and can cause infertility or lead to uterine cancer. In one study among high school students in 1997, 53 per cent of them reported having had sexual intercourse.[71] This can help explain the alarming rates of teenage pregnancy in some parts of the world. All of this reflects a loss of control and self-discipline, resulting in the spread of gross immorality in human society. These are but a few symptoms of the excessive freedom and decadence of the permissive society. There seems to be no end to it except through a new system of knowledge based on spiritual and moral values.

A large number of people today live in the 'world of the senses'. Their goal is to satisfy the senses and engage in pleasure-seeking behavior, a goal that the entertainment industry worldwide helps them fulfill. By entertainment industry here is meant the markets that provide recreational opportunities, drugs, alcohol, access to sexual relations, gambling and other forms of activities to satisfy carnal desires.

According to Elliott Morss, an American academic who has worked in 45 countries with the International Monetary Fund (IMF), there is a huge worldwide market for such materialistic entertainment activities. In 2009 it was reported that the sale of recreational drugs (cannabis, cocaine and ecstasy) was estimated to be $546 billion. The income of three other entertainment industries, namely prostitution, gambling and pornography, totalled $507 billion a year. According to the United Nations Office of Drugs and Crime (UNODC) 2008 report, 3.9 per cent of the world's population (166 million people) used cannabis. This worldwide consumption of such a mind-altering substance generated $410 billion annually.[72]

Most of the above-mentioned consumption (especially alcohol and drugs) affects the emotional and mental states of consumers. In many cases there are tragic consequences such as mental disturbances, injury or death due to drinking and driving, as well as damage to personal and family life due to loss of income in gambling.

The above statistics reflect the sad reality of a humanity that is submerged in a 'sea of materialism'. In such cases consumption goes well beyond searching for goods and other basic necessities for survival. It extends to activities or substances that create an excursion to a temporary world of pleasure, sensory satisfaction, and artificial happiness.

Elaborating on true happiness, 'Abdu'l-Bahá stated:

Happiness consists of two kinds; physical and spiritual. The physical happiness is limited; its utmost duration is one day, one month, one year. It hath no result. Spiritual happiness is eternal and unfathomable. This kind of happiness appeareth in one's soul with the love of God and suffereth one to attain to the virtues and perfections of the world of humanity. Therefore, endeavor as much as thou art able in order to illuminate the lamp of thy heart by the light of love.[73]

Modernity and the advancement of science and technology have extended our level of comfort to the brink of sickness and destruction. But are science and technology to blame? Science is an invention and product of the human mind; it is an instrument which we can use for or against ourselves. Why is it that, in spite of amazing medical progress and discoveries, we have become prisoners of lifestyles which result in so much pain and sorrow? It seems that material civilization has got out of balance so that life has lost its meaning and purpose. The foundation of human prosperity is based on a life enriched by both material and spiritual values.

CHAPTER 5

MATERIALISTIC SCIENCE AND BIOETHICS

Man is said to be the greatest sign of God – that is, he is the Book of Creation – for all the mysteries of the universe are found in him.
'Abdu'l-Bahá[1]

Materialistic science

As is mentioned in the Introduction to this book, materialistic philosophy does not recognize anything which is non-physical or non-material as reality. Therefore, when a scientific reductionist approach is applied to examine the nature of religious and spiritual reality, the argument and analysis is skewed toward the material aspects and physical relevance of the subject. During recent decades, for example, there has been a growing body of literature based on some research studies, including neurobiological exploration, which report that stimulation of certain segments of the brain can evoke a sense of religiosity.[2] Based on neurological laboratory experiments, some researchers have come up with theories which reduce the origins of religious faith to the activity of brain cells or through genetics.

The scientific reductionist view of human consciousness is that it is a purely physical phenomenon and that the brain, rather than the 'mind', is the source of human intellect, memory and power of discovery. This assumption has stimulated debate about the duality of brain and mind in scientific literature.[3]

As a scientific approach in research studies and analysis, reductionism has been widely used and has served as a method for scientific progress. But its application as an approach, combined with a materialistic concept, is often intended to de-emphasize or deny the existence of a metaphysical or abstract transcendental reality. This approach characterizes the work of many materialistic philosophers, writers and researchers today. Francis Crick, who together with James Watson unravelled and explained the structure of DNA, had a view of human nature as follows:

> 'you', your joys and your sorrows, your memories and your ambitions, your sense of personal identity and free will, are in fact no more than the behaviour of a vast assembly of nerve cells and their associated molecules.[4]

Reductionism can have many serious consequences in the behavioural sciences. Here, by reductionism is meant a conceptually narrow and deterministic view which ignores the importance of the human reality. Although by reduction it was hoped to gain a 'deeper insight into the phenomena of interest', it is all too easy to lose that bigger picture.[5]

In the opinion of many neuroscientists and psychiatrists, mental disorders are entirely manifestations of the brain function. Mind is perceived as a by-product of or identical with the brain and mental health is viewed in the same way. Ironically, in the background of this debate lies the word 'psychiatry' which in its Greek origin means 'healing of the soul or spirit'!

Psychiatry and neuroscience have made major progress in recent years but many questions still remain unanswered, including the cause of a number of psychiatric disorders. Yet because of the influence of the reductionist approach, many researchers tend to believe that everything can be explained through molecular biology and genetics. The proponents of reductionism claim that 'the mind is what the brain does', thus psychological phenomena are articulations of material and biological organization.[6] Critics of this approach hold a different opinion, for example:

> Neuroscience research has attempted to explain psychopathology at a cellular level . . . Mental symptoms are emergent phenomena that are a function of the mind, and cannot be reduced to the activity of neurons [brain cells].[7]

For these critics, the reductionist approach makes it difficult to unravel the mysteries of mental illness. How can issues such as mental health and human thought – as well as conscience and consciousness – be explained through the study of cellular neurobiology?

The emergence of neuroscience as the predominant paradigm of modern psychology was greatly enhanced when the 1990s were declared as the 'decade of the brain'.[8] Some scientists have been exploring the brain and the human genome in order to identify certain brain centres or mechanisms as the cause of religious experience. This viewpoint of religion is being studied by some scientists who are themselves 'militant' atheists.

According to Edward O. Wilson, 'if the brain has evolved by natural selection . . . religious beliefs must have arisen by the same mechanism'.[9] Through this statement Wilson suggests that religion is the product of an evolutionary adaptation of the brain. This materialistic perception has been reinforced by Alper, who believes that religion, like any behaviour which has been universally spread across historical cultures, must be 'genetically inherited'.[10] These views, although they may provide support for a materialistic notion of human reality in relation to God, have been criticized by other neuroscientists and researchers. Beauregard and O'Leary argue that the fact that a behaviour presents itself widely through historical cultures does not justify the position that it is genetically inherited. For these researchers, what an individual inherits is the capacity to appreciate abstract ideas like

God, ethics, death, the future and so on. Furthermore, religious beliefs may have intellectual associations with certain parts of the brain, but this association cannot be interpreted as meaning that an inherited brain mechanism governs religious ideas or beliefs.[11] Indeed, despite the opinion of many materialist neuroscientists that specific brain function can trigger religiosity, they have failed to provide an adequate neurobiological explanation of how mind and conscience can arise from the interaction of the various brain regions and cellular activities.[12] As the Dalai Lama has stated:

> The problem arises when reductionism, which is essentially a method, is turned into a metaphysical standpoint. Understandably this reflects a common tendency to conflate the means with the end, especially when a specific method is highly effective. In a powerful image, a Buddhist text reminds us that when someone points his finger at the moon, we should direct our gaze not at the tip of the finger but at the moon to which it is pointing.[13]

A recent discussion among academics and researchers about the essential construct for defining a psychiatric disease has given rise to conflictual debates and disagreements. Can a diagnosis be verifiable through laboratory measurement? Will the presence of biological markers become a requirement for a definitive diagnosis such as depression or psychosis? The current trend of requiring a biological basis for every psychological phenomenon raises interesting questions, such as: Are psychiatric disorders 'diseases of the brain'? Commenting on this question in 2010, one of the world's foremost neuroscientists, the psychiatrist Dr Herman van Praag, made this remark:

> . . . brain studies have little to offer in understanding the individual soul: how it is structured, how it came to be, how it responded to life's tribulations, what its hopes and expectations are – at least for the time being and probably for a very

long time. The soul is a derivative of the brain and, simultaneously, a territory in its own right. A territory to be studied by soul searchers, soul researchers, and soul healers. It would not be in the interest of psychiatry nor its clientele if the soul regresses into a mere appendage of the brain.[14]

Van Praag refers to the soul as a derivative of the brain which is a 'territory in its own right'. This reflects the fact that even an enlightened scientist who recognizes the existence of the soul and who makes a distinction between the functioning of the brain and the 'understanding of the individual soul' is unable to characterize the soul as a non-material entity. As discussed later in this book, the Bahá'í Writings offer an explanation about the reality of the soul and its relationship with the body.

The human mind is very complex; it cannot be broken down and reduced to a simple mechanism of brain function. Reducing the mind to the brain and considering it a product of neuronal brain activity is over-simplistic and reductionist and does not solve the question as to what the mind is. In fact, in spite of the tremendous progress of neuroscience, we still can't explain the nature of many mental and behavioural disorders. As Alan Wallace states in his book *The Taboo of Subjectivity*, 'If one were to study the brain alone, while totally ignoring human behaviour and subjective conscious states, one would never learn anything about consciousness or any other mental phenomena.'[15]

On a larger scale of thinking, mind and brain are instruments of the soul as the computer is an instrument of the programmer. Whatever a computer can produce is primarily the result of the art and creative design of the programmer. Likewise, mental faculties are connected to the soul in a special and mysterious way; they are, in the words of 'Abdu'l-Bahá,

> . . . of the inherent properties of the soul, even as the radiation of light is the essential property of the sun. The rays of the sun are renewed but the sun itself is ever the same and

unchanged. Consider how the human intellect develops and weakens, and may at times come to naught, whereas the soul changeth not.[16]

According to the Bahá'í teachings, science and religion are intertwined. Both are progressive and the truth in both is relative; religion progresses through revelation while science advances through research, methodology and observation.[17] According to 'Abdu'l-Bahá,

Religion is the outer expression of the divine reality. Therefore, it must be living, vitalized, moving and progressive. If it be without motion and nonprogressive, it is without the divine life; it is dead.[18]

On the other hand, 'Abdu'l-Bahá considers science to be

the first emanation from God toward man. All created beings embody the potentiality of material perfection, but the power of intellectual investigation and scientific acquisition is a higher virtue specialized to man alone.[19]

Harmony between science and religion is essential; otherwise the outcome of science will be materialism while that of religion will be fanaticism. As Farzam Arbab states:

Religion and science are two knowledge systems that hold together the foundations of civilization. They are two forces that propel the advancement of civilization. They are two sets of practices that draw upon the higher powers of the human soul and must be in harmony. Understanding the nature of this harmony is essential if humanity is to generate and apply the kind of knowledge that will advance civilization in both its material and spiritual dimensions.[20]

Who is a person? An ethical debate

Distinguishing human beings from animals and the notion of personhood, that is, who is a person and who is not, have been the subjects of heated debate in recent years. Some philosophers, including Peter Singer, argue that a human is just another animal. They also believe that not all humans are persons. In fact, in their view, certain animals should be regarded as persons and should have the same rights and protection as human beings. Some of these philosophers reject the notion that human beings are created noble and deserve special respect. They divide people into two categories: persons and non-persons and claim that a human being should possess certain attributes in order to be considered a person.[21] Such attributes include self-awareness, intelligence, sense of future and capacity to relate to others. Another group believes that animals that possess attributes comparable to human ones should be treated as non-human persons. Commenting on the debate about human beings and animals, Margaret Somerville, Samuel Gale Professor of Law at McGill University, writes, 'If there is nothing special about being human, there is no "essence of our humanness" that we must hold in trust for future generations . . .'[22]

In reality, the materialistic debate and the reductionist attitude toward what distinguishes a human being from an animal is lacking in depth. It is not sufficient to distinguish human beings from animals based on a few vague and general characteristics such as self-awareness, intelligence, and relating to others. What is in question here is human nature itself and the virtues and attributes that can emanate from it. The Bahá'í teachings explain that 'the reality of man is his thought, not his material body'.[23] Thus, while humans have certain features in common with animals such as the senses, and behaviour when it is governed by man's lower nature, animals are captives of nature, unlike human beings who are able to transcend its laws. Also, unlike the animal, the reality of a human being, as mentioned above, is his or her thought and soul. And it is through the creative power of the mind and soul that humans are able to harness nature, discover new galaxies and advance science and civilization. Although animals have existed for millions of years they have not been able to attain that creative capacity and station. Human beings are distinguished from animals by the 'most noble' virtue of science, 'the power of investigating and discovering the verities of the universe'.[24]

The notion of 'abortion after birth'

In an article published in the *Journal of Medical Ethics*, researchers discuss the contentious ethical issue of abortion after birth. The following is a summary of the case made by these authors:

> Abortion is largely accepted even for reasons that do not have anything to do with the fetus' health. By showing that (1) both fetuses and newborns do not have the same moral status as actual persons, (2) the fact that both are potential persons is morally irrelevant and (3) adoption is not always in the best interest of actual people, the authors argue that what we call 'after-birth abortion' (killing a newborn) should be permissible in all the cases where abortion is, including cases where the newborn is not disabled.[25]

They state that caring for children born with Down syndrome and those with severe disabilities can be an unbearable burden on the family and on society. Although they acknowledge that some people are willing to raise these children and often they are reported to be happy, nevertheless they make the claim that 'killing a newborn would be ethically permissible in all circumstances where abortions would be . . . we call such a practice "after-birth abortion" rather than "euthanasia" because the best interest of the one who dies is not necessarily the primary criterion for the choice, contrary to what happens in the case of euthanasia'. The authors conclude that if the costs (social, psychological, economic) for potential parents are good reasons for having an abortion even when the fetus is healthy, if the moral status of the newborn is the same as that of the infant and if neither has any moral value by virtue of being a potential person, then the same reasons which justify abortion should also justify the killing of the potential person when it is at the stage of a newborn.[26]

The above statement raises a number of questions. Essentially the authors seem to consider a foetus and a newborn infant as lacking any moral status or value because neither one of them 'can be considered a "person" in a morally relevant sense'.[27] Would this mean that since a foetus or newborn infant has not yet accomplished anything worthwhile it has no value as a person and is basically worthless? The authors acknowledge that the foetus and the newborn are human beings and are potentially persons, but they are not qualified to have a 'moral right to life', because they are not able to attribute any value to their existence and thus they are not persons.

The authors furthermore claim that 'Merely being human is not in itself a reason for ascribing someone a right to life. Indeed, many humans are not considered subjects of a right to life. . .'[28] This analogy is bereft of any spiritual dimension of human reality and may lead to the dehumanization of individuals.

Prenatal selection and abortion

In an article published in the *Canadian Medical Association Journal* in 2011, Hesketh, Lu and Xing explore the prevalence and consequences of sex-selective abortion across several countries in Asia.[29] The authors detail some of the reasons why sons are preferred: males having a higher wage-earning capacity as well as taking on responsibility for the care of parents in illness and old age. But there are additional local and cultural reasons for this preference. In India the expense of the dowry for the female plays a role, while in China and South Korea the patriarchal family system could be a reason. Although in countries where this occurs the preference for sons is deeply rooted in cultural beliefs, it may also be influenced by materialism, especially in the West.

For centuries the preference for having a son in the family caused post-natal discrimination against girls which resulted in neglect and infanticide of newborn females. More recently, progress in medical technology and the use of ultrasound starting in the 1980s has provided an easy and practical diagnostic tool enabling sex selection through the identification of female offspring during pregnancy. South Korea, followed by China, India and other countries have pursued sex selection to identify and decrease the number of female births. The ratio at birth (SRB) is defined as the number of boys born compared to every 100 girls. Normally this ratio is 105 male births to every 100 female births. But pursuant to the use of sex selection and the consequent rise in the number of males being born, the ratio began to rise, initially in South Korea in the mid-1980s to reach an SRB in 1992 of 125 in that country.[30] In China, because of the one-child policy, the situation was complicated, but the steady increase of SRB is reported to have spread to reach 121 in 2005, when 1.1 million 'excess' males were born in China. That meant that the number of males under 20 years of age exceeded the number of females in the same age range by approximately 32 million individuals. With the recent change in the one-child policy in China and the efforts of policy-makers, this imbalance between male and female may change, but it may take decades until the sex ratio at birth in countries such as China and India reaches normal rates.[31]

The practice of sex selection is not only an act of discrimination against girls which is contrary to medical ethics as well as an infringement on their right to exist; there are social consequences associated with this practice. One is the creation of an imbalance of males to females in the population, described above, which impacts the ability of males to fulfil traditional expectations of marrying and raising children of their own. Such an inability may lead to psychological consequences, including the feeling of being unfulfilled in life, low self-esteem, depression and frustration.

Technoscience has been used to identify not only the sex of unborn children but also their potential disabilities. Some of these tests are often in conflict with medical ethics. In July 2011 a Danish newspaper announced 'Plans to Make Denmark a Down Syndrome-Free Perfect Society'. The article reported, 'Denmark has decided to listen to people who may complain of human selection and have put their foot on the ground to promote increased abortion of foetuses suspected of having Down Syndrome.' It went on to state that a university bioethicist 'described it as a "fantastic achievement" that the number of newborns with Down syndrome is approaching zero', and then asked, 'What next? Is the child born with diabetes . . . [to] be discarded?' This kind of prenatal human selection goes on in other countries, but in Denmark it is openly and transparently discussed. It is presently estimated that in North America over 85 per cent of unborn babies with Down syndrome are aborted.[32]

With the advance in technology for prenatal screening, in addition to tests that identify the sex of the foetus and certain conditions such as Down syndrome, there will also be a range of tests for pregnant women that will be able to recognize various disabilities as well as how perfect and beautiful the baby will grow to be. Such progress in technoscience may open the door to unethical decisions regarding the elimination of selected newborns. This calls into question the notion of unconditional parental love and acceptance of children. Although carrying out such decisions may not be prevalent at present, the influence of materialistic philosophy may enhance such an approach for eliminating 'undesirable children' of the future. To end on a brighter note, however, in 2011 the Parliament of the Council of Europe passed a resolution urging its 47 Member States to prohibit sex selection unless there is a serious hereditary disease.[33]

CHAPTER 6

FINDING THE BALANCE: MATERIALISM AND INTRINSIC VALUES

. . . the honour and distinction of the individual consist in this,
that he among all the world's multitudes should become a source
of social good.
'Abdu'l-Bahá[1]

Intrinsic and extrinsic values

In their studies Kasser and Ryan (1996) suggest that there are two
types of goals and values: intrinsic and extrinsic. The intrinsic
values help people engage in activities and experiences which may
satisfy their psychological needs and improve their well-being;
they involve self-acceptance, affiliation and community feeling.
The extrinsic values emphasize a need for material achievement,
fame and social position which may slowly lessen the quality of
life and feeling of satisfaction. The authors noted that extrinsically
oriented teenagers, college students and adults expressed feelings
of low self-actualization, vitality and positive affect. Among this
group, they reported more depressive mood, anxiety, narcissistic
behaviour and substance abuse problems.[2]

Kasser and Ahuvia (2002) explored the relationship between
values aimed at money, image, popularity and well-being in participants who lived in an environment which was supportive of

those values, a group of 92 business students in Singapore. The results showed that those who strongly internalized materialistic values also experienced low self-actualization. This result, which was consistent with previous findings on the subject, indicated that certain values may be unhealthy for people's lives. The authors commented that these findings suggest that 'materialistic ambitions, even successfully pursued, are relatively empty in terms of potential well-being benefits'.[3]

Goldbart and associates (2004) have noted that especially since 1980 the driving force of American culture has been financial gain; this has dominated other aspects of well-being such as family, intimacy, aesthetics, and the pursuit of wisdom.[4] There is a need to maintain a balance between financial gain on the one hand and personal and family well-being on the other. Without such a balance, excessive reliance on material attachments can create a moral and psychological dilemma.

The expression 'sudden wealth syndrome' has been used to describe the emotional challenges and identity conflicts in individuals who suddenly receive a huge amount of money for which they are not prepared. Many of them haven't grown up with riches and are not well-equipped to deal with the benefits and challenges of suddenly becoming wealthy. They may experience anxiety, guilt and depression or, on the other hand, overconfidence and elation as they try to come to terms with their good fortune. The challenge is how to establish a balanced relationship with wealth in one's personal life.[5]

According to the philosopher Jacob Needleman (1991), balance occurs when money is used in the pursuit of life goals, values and meaning. If such a balance is achieved, the possession of money may be free from emotional conflict, but it is not easy to arrive at this state of equilibrium.[6] People's attitude toward wealth is very mixed. Wealth can lead to feelings of power and entitlement, but also to feelings of entrapment, guilt and isolation. It may have an impact on people's beliefs, values and core identity.[7] It can adversely affect one's motivation, sense of responsibility and pattern of personal life. But wealth is an essential necessity without which material progress would be impossible, as we shall see in the next chapter. It is not wealth that makes man selfish or insensitive – it is the human mind that can create a monster! Although attachment to wealth poses many challenges, money by itself is not the problem; the wealthy person determines his or her own degree of attachment to it:

> Clarity of values combined with a solid sense of identity enables people to effectively steward their wealth, making choices in service of a life filled with meaning and pleasurable purpose.[8]

This view of wealth is confirmed in the Writings of Bahá'u'lláh:

> Say: Pride not yourselves on earthly riches ye possess. Reflect upon your end and upon the recompense for your works that hath been ordained in the Book of God, the Exalted, the Mighty. Blessed is the rich man whom earthly possessions have been powerless to hinder from turning unto God, the Lord of all names. Verily he is accounted among the most distinguished of men before God, the Gracious, the All-Knowing.[9]

Consumption may also be viewed from a different perspective. Although it is often perceived as a physical experience, it can also be a form of psychological fulfilment. As we have seen, it can be an expression of the need to compensate for an inner emptiness: 'The empty self needs filling, so it is easy to influence and control. This is a major mechanism encouraging consumerism.'[10] As a result, consumption or the possession of objects in this context does not bring true and enduring joy and satisfaction. Consumerism preys on people's inner needs by offering material substitutes to compensate for what they don't have. This is often the case in patients with bulimic eating disorder.[11]

As Joe Dominguez and Vicki Robin wrote in their 2006 book

Your Money or Your Life: 'We have learned to seek external solutions to signals from the mind, heart or soul that something is out of balance. We try to satisfy essentially psychological and spiritual needs with consumption at a physical level.'[12] When the intrinsic needs are not properly satisfied, discontent continues.

In search of the true self

The literature on self and the psychology of gratification and fulfilment has become abundant in recent decades. The expectation of instant satisfaction has become a mindset, so that neither the high intensity nor the speed of gratification can ever be fast or good enough. Some become pleasure addicts, while others wonder what the real purpose of life is. Today over 200 million people in the world are involved in substance abuse and addiction.[13] If the number of alcoholics were to be added, this figure would skyrocket. Why do people use toxic substances to numb their brains when they know the dangers of doing so? Is it purely a drive for pleasure or a search for meaning in life?

Among those humanistic psychologists who have explored the subject of individual needs, self, and self-actualization is Abraham Maslow. In his research on the hierarchy of basic needs, Maslow identified five levels: 1) physiological; 2) safety and security; 3) love and belonging; 4) esteem; 5) self-actualization. In this hierarchy, needs are fulfilled according to their order of priority, i.e. from the most basic physiological needs to the highest – self-actualization. Only after the basic needs are gratified are individuals able to experience self-actualization; the fulfilment of needs follows an upward movement. Therefore, if the lower set of needs is not met, the higher needs are unlikely to be prioritized. The four lower levels of the hierarchy are referred to as 'deficiency needs'.[14]

Satisfaction of one or more of the lower needs in some individuals may follow a neurotic pattern which can affect the fulfilment of other needs. On the other hand, Maslow indicated that higher needs may occasionally emerge, not after gratification, but rather after forced or voluntary deprivation, renunciation, or suppression of lower basic needs and gratifications (asceticism, sublimation, strengthening effects of rejection, discipline, persecution, isolation, etc.) We know very little about either the frequency or the nature of these events, although they are reported to be common in Eastern cultures.[15]

Maslow goes on to say that such phenomena do not contradict his thesis about hierarchy because gratification is not the only source of strength. Indeed, in observing the lives of those who have suffered deprivation, persecution and injustice one cannot fail to note that the self-actualization process may advance in spite of the lack of satisfaction of the lower needs, to the point where some people are prepared to make sacrifices or even give their lives in defence of their beliefs or ideology. In some religions the practice of fasting, a voluntary and purposeful abstinence from food and drink from sunrise to sunset (or other variation of fasting depending on the religion) prescribed for believers, is a clear denial of gratification of the lower needs in order to focus on higher needs for the purpose of spiritual progress and self-actualization.

Biological or physiological needs are the most basic ones; they are essential for human survival and include the need for food, water, oxygen, sleep, sex, shelter, and so on. The other levels of needs in Maslow's original hierarchy – safety, love and belonging, esteem and the peak need of self- actualization which relates to human identity and purpose – have been extended to seven or eight stages by others on the basis of their interpretation of Maslow's work. Maslow believed that

human life will never be understood unless its highest aspirations are taken into account. Growth, self-actualization, the striving toward health, the quest for identity and autonomy, the yearning for excellence . . . must by now be accepted beyond question as a widespread and perhaps universal human tendency. And yet there are also other regressive, fearful, self-diminishing tendencies as well, and it is very easy to forget them in our intoxication with 'personal growth', especially for inexperienced youngsters . . . We must appreciate that many people choose the worse rather then the better, that growth is often a painful process . . . [16]

Einstein viewed human beings as part of the whole or the 'universe', but a part limited in time and space. He perceived himself, as a human being as well as his thoughts and feelings, as something separated from the rest of the universe. Such an impression of self, according to Einstein, is like a kind of 'optical delusion of his consciousness'; he comments that

> this delusion is a kind of prison for us, restricting us to our personal desire and to affection for a few persons nearest to us. Our task must be to free ourselves from this prison by widening our circle of compassion to embrace all living creatures and the whole of nature in its beauty . . . striving for such achievement is . . . a part of the liberation and a foundation for inner security.[17]

This statement echoes this well-known passage from the writings of 'Abdu'l-Bahá:

> . . . the honor and distinction of the individual consist in this, that he among all the world's multitudes should become a source of social good. Is any larger bounty conceivable than this, that an individual, looking within himself, should find that by the confirming grace of God, he has become the cause of peace and well-being, of happiness and advantage to his fellow men?[18]

And a letter written on behalf of Shoghi Effendi states:

The more we search for ourselves, the less likely we are to find ourselves; and the more we search for God, and to serve our fellow-men, the more profoundly will we become acquainted with ourselves, and the more inwardly assured. This is one of the great spiritual laws of life.[19]

Although learning about self, and self-knowledge, are important parts of life, becoming obsessed with self and its satisfaction can delay personal growth.

In a society in which cultural beliefs are based on a materialistic concept of life, these beliefs can have a powerful influence on the shaping of individual attitudes toward the self and others. Bahá'u'lláh noted a change of perception in human society:

In this day, the tastes of men have changed, and their power of perception has altered. The contrary winds of the world, and its colours, have provoked a cold and deprived men's nostrils of the sweet savours of Revelation.[20]

In the winter of materialism the 'contrary winds' and 'colours', and the dark clouds of desires, have created a climate which obscures the light of true life. People are wrapped in the blanket of self and passion, struggling against the chilling storms of those tests which may ultimately awaken their slumbering souls.

According to 'Abdu'l-Bahá:

Today, all the peoples of the world are indulging in self-interest and exert the utmost effort and endeavour to promote their own material interests. They are worshipping themselves and not the divine reality, nor the world of mankind. They seek diligently their own benefit and not the common weal. This is because they are captives of the world of nature and unaware of the divine teachings, of the bounty of the Kingdom and of the Sun of Truth.[21]

In this self-indulgent society, many people are characterized by a sense of greed and selfishness. There is an insatiable need for gratification – physical, emotional and intellectual. In spite of the fact that, especially in prosperous populations, there are so many choices available, this hunger persists and a feeling of emptiness often prevails. The problem is not purely material; there is also a spiritual thirst to discover true meaning in life. Unaware of this spiritual need, individuals become prisoners of their own selves. As the human mind and pleasure centres become saturated with materially rewarding experiences, gratification loses its effect and despair ensues.

The Bahá'í Writings indicate that 'life is a constant struggle, not only against forces around us, but above all against our own "ego"'.[22] This paradox of detachment from material vanities and attachment to divine reality sums up the Bahá'í attitude toward this world of existence. But, as indicated here, detachment is not only from material things, it also applies to detachment from our own ego, the dark side of our self.

In a prayer Bahá'u'lláh reveals our need of divine assistance for protection from the temptation of self:

> I implore Thee . . . not to abandon me unto mine own self and unto the desires of a corrupt inclination. Hold Thou my hand with the hand of Thy power, and deliver me from the depth of my fancies and idle imaginings . . .[23]

For, according to Shoghi Effendi:

> The materialistic civilization of our age has so much absorbed the energy and interest of mankind that people in general do no longer feel the necessity of raising themselves above the forces and conditions of their daily material existence.[24]

When the energies and interest of a population are controlled by the lower nature, the higher nature suffers as a result; efforts towards the acquisition of noble virtues are replaced by apathy and indifference. As 'Abdu'l-Bahá told an audience in New York in June 1912: 'The fountain of divine generosity is gushing forth, but we must have thirst for the living waters. Unless there be thirst, the salutary water will not assuage.'[25] Earlier that week he commented:

> Desire and passion, like two unmanageable horses, have wrested the reins of control from him [man] and are galloping madly in the wilderness. This is the cause of the degradation of the world of humanity . . . By devotion to the carnal, mortal world human susceptibilities sink to the level of animalism.[26]

When the mind goes out of control in its perpetual effort to satisfy the body, there comes a time when satisfaction loses its meaning; then emptiness prevails. Thus a dissatisfied body hosts a discontented soul!

Bahá'u'lláh uses the analogy of the soul as a bird:

> Know also that the soul is endowed with two wings: should it soar in the atmosphere of love and contentment, then it will be related to the All-Merciful. And should it fly in the atmosphere of self and desire, then it will pertain to the Evil One . . .[27]

Using the same metaphor in another place, Baha'u'llah writes about the release of this bird of the soul from the defilement of this nether world:

> Ye are even as the bird which soareth, with the full force of its mighty wings and with complete and joyous confidence, through the immensity of the heavens, until, impelled to satisfy its hunger, it turneth longingly to the water and clay of the earth below it, and, having been entrapped in the mesh of its desire, findeth itself impotent to resume its flight to

the realms whence it came. Powerless to shake off the burden weighing on its sullied wings, that bird, hitherto an inmate of the heavens, is now forced to seek a dwelling-place upon the dust.[28]

Human desire: Religious perspectives

In the *Encyclopedia of Religion* desire is described as volitional or emotional. In volitional terms, it is identified with willing, wanting, appetite, choice and motivation. When desire is understood more in terms of emotional or affective terms, it is associated with experiences such as passion, love, eros, attachment, craving, greed and lust. The volitional and affective aspects of desire are not necessarily incompatible, as in the case of willing and loving.[29]

Religious views of desire vary. Some people believe that, regardless of its nature, desire is spiritually destructive. For these, the primary objective of spiritual discipline is 'to wean themselves from all desire, even the desire for enlightenment, self-transcendence, liberation, salvation, nirvana, or mystical union with God'.[30] But in general, desire is not intrinsically problematic in itself; rather, it is essential for humanity. It is the appropriate or inappropriate direction which it takes that makes the difference.

Cultural and religious concepts of desire differ between oriental and occidental cultures. While in Asia desires are viewed in the context of stages of life, in the West they are evaluated more in relation to their objects and the quality of these objects. In addition, 'desire figures in human experience in many ways and becomes religiously valid or problematic under a variety of circumstances'.[31] In Hinduism, *kama* (Sanskrit: 'desire') is considered to be one of the four basic aims or drives which need to be either satisfied, restricted, or transcended during life:

While in Hindu mythology asceticism and eroticism revolve about each other in cycles of alternating ascendancy, chastity building into desire and the fulfilment of desire leading to chastity, the balance of these energies is found ideally through the control and transformation of desire.[32]

Selfish desire, greed and covetousness have been recognized by religion as among the causes of destruction and suffering. In Buddhism these desires are referred to as 'craving' in the second of the Four Noble Truths. Such craving is considered to be 'a fetter: Poisoning the heart, deluding the mind, and binding people to evil courses of action'.

Buddhism rejects all kinds of desires, viewing them as harmful and a source of bondage. In the monotheistic religions (Judaism, Christianity and Islam and to some extent Buddhism and Sikhism), a distinction is made between the evil of passions of the flesh and healthy ambition for goodness and the passion for God. In the Chinese religion, while excessive and selfish desire is condemned, desires by themselves can be considered good so long as they are in harmony with the Tao.

In Hinduism desire is viewed as an important manifestation of selfish craving and a cause of unhappiness, pain and sorrow. Humanity is surrounded by destructive desires, and desire is associated with pleasure, passion, lust, sensuousness and craving. Conquering all desires will bring joy, wisdom and the freedom of Nirvana. One should not have desire, either for this world or for another world.[33] This is expressed often in the Bhagavad Gita:

> Desire has found a place in man's senses and mind and reason. Through these it blinds the soul, after having overclouded wisdom.
>
> Set thou, therefore, thy senses in harmony, and then slay thou sinful desire, the destroyer of vision and wisdom.[34]

Finding a balance ('harmony') in one's life is dependent on the mastery of desire:

> When a man dwells on the pleasures of sense, attraction for

them arises in him. From attraction arises desire, the lust of possession, and this leads to passion, to anger.

From passion comes confusion of mind, then loss of remembrance, the forgetting of duty. From this loss comes the ruin of reason, and the ruin of reason leads man to destruction.

But the soul that moves in the world of the senses and yet keeps the senses in harmony, free from attraction and aversion, finds rest in quietness.

In this quietness falls down the burden of all her sorrows, for when the heart has found quietness, wisdom has also found peace.

There is no wisdom for a man without harmony, and without harmony there is no contemplation. Without contemplation there cannot be peace, and without peace can there be joy?[35]

In the many monastic orders of Christianity, mostly drawn from Benedict of Nursia, desires are renounced by the triple vow of chastity, poverty and obedience. The Benedictine rule required manual labour in an effort to control desire by diverting energy from physical desire toward the love of God. As a result, asceticism was encouraged and poverty was sought after as a way of freeing oneself from worldly attachments.[36]

Augustine attributed those desires related to heavenly themes (such as praise of God and His greatness) to the City of God, while in contrast, desires of an earthly nature (such as the desire for success or sexual desire) are viewed as belonging to the City of Man. He makes an important distinction between these two types of desire: desire directed upward which tends toward God, and desires directed downward which he considers as lust. All humanity is divided between the heavenly (the City of God) and the earthly (the City of Man). The former concerns the love of God; the latter, the love of self. In this sense desire can be categorized into the two types: spiritual or material. The first has to do with the higher nature of a human being, while the other relates to the lower nature.

The rigidity of Augustine's self-discipline and his renunciation of the pleasures of life raised many objections, particularly against his repudiation of sexual desire. Martin Luther departed from Augustine's strong position on the requirement of celibacy as an essential practice of priesthood and called for its abandonment. Another objection relates to Augustine's concept that human life is motivated by desire. If this is correct then he may be criticized for having identified the love of God with desire, although such a love differs from other desires.[37]

Christ is reported to have said, 'For what is a man profited, if he shall gain the whole world, and lose his own soul?'[38] And according to the Tao Te Ching: 'No calamity is greater than not knowing what is enough, no fault worse than wanting too much. Whoever knows what is enough has enough.'[39] In Confucius' judgement, the striving for wealth and power is less significant than the striving for virtue. He furthermore considered virtue as the root of which wealth is a branch.

The 12th-century Hindu poet–saint Allama wrote:

They say that woman is an enticement.
No, No, she is not so.
They say that money is an enticement.
No, No it is not so.
They say that landed property is an enticement.
No, No, it is not so.
The real enticement is the insatiable appetite of the mind,
O Lord Guheswara![40]

while in the Qur'án we read:

Have you seen him who makes his desire his god, and God sends him astray purposely, and seals up his hearing and his heart, and sets on his sight a covering? Who, then will lead him after God [has condemned him]? Will you not then heed?[41]

To the mystics, desire has still other meanings: it is generally equated with the search for the transcendent. In the language of a religious mystic, spiritual desire, joy, ecstasy and delight have much greater significance than mere worldly desires and ephemeral attachments. Likewise, to the Sufis, the pivot of their spiritual quest is union with God and all else in the world of existence is superfluous.[42]

The Bahá'í viewpoint on desire is different from that of many other religions in that it does not consider human physical desires as 'bad' or 'evil' in themselves. God has created humans as essentially noble beings. The body, with its physical and mental faculties and organs, has been created to serve as the temple of the soul. Since Bahá'í morality and ethics are based on the notion that the purpose of this earthly life is to progress spiritually, the body provides a vehicle for the fulfilment of this goal. The satisfaction of desires should therefore be seen in its proper context, which would align with the progress of the soul and the will of God for His creation. Whether a specific physical or mental desire is to be considered right or wrong depends on whether it will enhance or hinder that progress, and it is the individual who is responsible for the proper regulation or channelling of that desire.

'Abdu'l-Bahá, elaborating on human attitudes toward passion and desire, indicated that

> desire is a flame that has reduced to ashes uncounted lifetime harvests of the learned, a devouring fire that even the vast sea of their accumulated knowledge could never quench. How often has it happened that an individual who was graced with every attribute of humanity and wore the jewel of true understanding, nevertheless followed after his passions until his excellent qualities passed beyond moderation and he was forced into excess. His pure intentions changed to evil ones,

his attributes were no longer put to uses worthy of them, and the power of his desires turned him aside from righteousness and its rewards into ways that were dangerous and dark.[43]

The human will plays a decisive role in controlling, regulating and directing desire. The experience of desire arising from psychological or biological needs may be natural, but the manner of its treatment to sublimate or channel it into positive and morally appropriate behaviour will make the difference. The manner in which human will deals with various sorts of desires is influenced by one's values, education and upbringing. Religion plays an important role in this process by providing a guiding path for the development of the spiritual nature. Elaborating on the temporary and superficial nature of human desires, 'Abdu'l-Bahá writes:

> Every soul seeketh an object and cherisheth a desire, and day and night striveth to attain his aim. One craveth riches, another thirsteth for glory and still another yearneth for fame, for art, for prosperity and the like. Yet finally all are doomed to loss and disappointment. One and all they leave behind them all that is theirs and empty-handed hasten to the realm beyond, and all their labours shall be in vain. To dust they shall all return, denuded, depressed, disheartened and in utter despair.
>
> But, praised be the Lord, thou art engaged in that which secureth for thee a gain that shall eternally endure . . .[44]

The dynamics of material and spiritual nature

Human beings possess two powerful but opposing forces: a spiritual or higher nature and a material or lower nature. The spiritual nature is divine in origin; its attributes are praiseworthy virtues such as the capacity to love, to be merciful and compassionate, to be just, kind and trustworthy, and other noble human qualities. The material nature is characterized by behaviours which reflect greed, cruelty, injustice, selfishness, untruth and conduct of low quality. The spiritual attributes are signs of light and perfection while the material qualities are signs of darkness. To do good or evil is a choice which depends on human will. In daily life we all are confronted with such choices.[45]

Because we live in this material world, our inclination toward animal or physical forces is strong, so that we human beings are heavily influenced by and attracted to our lower nature. Therefore our lower nature needs to be subordinated to our higher or spiritual nature. But to develop spiritual qualities requires great effort and sacrifice; one has to rely on one's will, spiritual insight and education. If this effort fails, human beings descend to animal ways of life and become immersed in self-indulgence and carnal passion. Human life is a constant struggle between these two natures or two forces. When the spiritual powers and qualities gain strength and subdue the animal forces, detachment from the material world takes place. This spiritual empowerment and ascendancy is aided by the spirit of faith and divine education. Human will and effort are like the wings of a bird: without them, flight is impossible. This struggle between the spiritual and material forces is a lifelong process. It may be associated with pain and hardship, which will have the effect of an awakening that reinforces spiritual growth.[46]

The purpose of religion and divine education is to enable the spiritual qualities to dominate the material or lower qualities. Individuals with saintly and noble virtues have succeeded in this process of empowerment. 'Abdu'l-Bahá explains that 'all the perfections and virtues, and all the vices, are qualities of man'. For example, 'knowledge is a quality of man; and so is ignorance; truthfulness is a quality of man; so is falsehood . . .'[47]

Spiritual and material attributes are not abstract terms or vague ideologies; they shape and express human character. As society is formed of individuals, so it can reflect a peaceful, honest and just population or, on the contrary, one that is brutal, greedy and unjust. Civilization is based on the characteristics of the people and nations that contribute to its development, whether positively or negatively. It mirrors the perfections and imperfections of the people of its time. Thus, civilization develops along the lines of the mentality and behaviour of a people at a particular period of history, and consequently can be predominantly either a spiritual or a material civilization.

The world in which we live at present has descended into one whose characteristics are of the lower nature, where war and violence, greed, lawlessness and tyranny, bloodshed, deception, overindulgence in pleasure-seeking behaviour, and social and political corruption depict the gloomy environment. It is also a reflection of the dark side of human conscience, overshadowing the bright spiritual nature of humanity.

During the later years of His life 'Abdu'l-Bahá repeatedly warned about 'the severe mental tests that would inevitably sweep over His loved ones of the West . . . tests that would purge, purify and prepare them for their noble mission in life'.[48] This further underlines the challenge of living in the western world which is so influenced by materialism.

In such a time one needs to reflect on the true meaning and purpose of life. According to the Bahá'í teachings, this is to know and to worship the Creator and to strive for an ever-advancing civilization.

> . . . man is said to be the greatest sign of God –that is, he is the Book of Creation – for all the mysteries of the universe are found in him. Should he come under the shadow of the true Educator and be rightly trained, he becomes the gem of gems, the light of lights . . . Should he, however, be deprived of this education, he becomes the embodiment of satanic attributes, the epitome of animal vices, and the source of all that is oppressive and dark.[49]

In the Bahá'í view, this world is an illusion, 'a show, vain and empty'[50] or 'a mirage rising over the sands, that the thirsty mistaketh for water'.[51] The following are the words of Bahá'u'lláh admonishing those who pride themselves on the fame and riches of this world:

> Exultest thou over the treasures thou dost possess, knowing they shall perish? Rejoicest thou in that thou rulest a span of earth, when the whole world . . . is worth as much as the black in the eye of a dead ant? Abandon it unto such as have set their affections upon it, and turn thou unto Him Who is the Desire of the world. Whither are gone the proud and their palaces? Gaze thou into their tombs, that thou mayest profit by this example, inasmuch as We made it a lesson unto every beholder. Were the breezes of Revelation to seize thee, thou wouldst flee the world, and turn unto the Kingdom, and wouldst expend all thou possessest, that thou mayest draw nigh unto this sublime Vision.[52]

This quotation finds an echo in Christ's words:

> Lay not up for yourselves treasures upon earth, where moth and rust corrupt, and where thieves break through and steal: But lay up for yourselves treasures in heaven . . . For where your treasure is, there will your heart be also.[53]

In Christianity material attachment and materialism are related to the following four of the seven deadly sins: greed, pride, gluttony and envy.[54] All four have become characteristic of Christmas celebrations in the West. A study carried out among the US population about their Christmas experiences showed that the more their holiday tradition was associated with spending money, shopping and receiving gifts, the less it was characterized by spiritual activities. This study, which was replicated by other researchers, confirmed that when people concentrate their attention and behaviour on materialistic interests they are more likely to be distracted from their spiritual ideals and from acquiring spiritual virtues. Kasser and Sheldon, who conducted the study, noted that these findings also revealed that a conflict exists between materialistic and spiritual goals in life. There are also indications that a materialistic mindset interferes with the reduction of suffering and the promotion of human compassion.[55]

Consequently, according to Kasser, materialistic values are associated with a greater degree of suffering and lower levels of happiness. This is why people who have a predominantly materialistic orientation are less satisfied with life and express fewer pleasant emotions of a joyous nature. This negative association between individual well-being and materialistic characteristics has been reported in study samples from North America, Europe and Asia. It has been confirmed in children as young as 10 years old and in an adult population in their 70s.[56]

What about those who possess strong materialistic values as well as a high sense of religious identity? A study of adults who had a combination of both showed the following results: while materialistic characteristics were associated with a greater degree of anxiety regardless of people's religious values, those among them who demonstrated both strong religious and materialistic values reported much higher levels of stress.[57] It is possible that those who harboured a strong degree of materialistic attitude as well as religious adherence were more vulnerable to guilt because of their failure to live up to their spiritual ideal of detachment, a quality common to religious people.

A materialistic orientation that overvalues money and possessions may also increase the possibility of 'objectifying' other people – that is, treating others as objects that can be manipulated for personal gain. Moreover, a greater focus on the pursuit of money, power and status may lead to lower empathy, generosity, loyalty, true friendship and less perceptivity toward others, lessening the possibility of equality and social justice in interpersonal relationships. Materialistic individuals are less likely to engage in pro-social activities such as sharing, helping and caring for others; in contrast, they are more likely to engage in ethically questionable business activities.[58]

Cross-cultural research studies show that the more people value wealth and status, the less they tend to value protecting the environment and the weaker their sense of unity with nature or the feeling of being globally connected with other living creatures. This reflects a lower sense of compassion and less spiritual insight. It also reflects the influence of consumerism, where people are less interested in safeguarding the environment and promoting sound and sustainable ecological development. People with materialistic attitudes are less likely to engage in ecologically friendly activities such as recycling, riding bicycles or using public transportation to avoid adding more pollution to the environment. They are also less interested in being frugal in the use of the earth's natural resources and in re-evaluating their lifestyles to help counteract climate change and for the good of the future of the planet.[59]

A culture of pleasure

Human beings are in constant pursuit of a good life, which is only natural. But such pursuit may be taken to extremes in a world of abundance where pleasure-seeking behaviour can be intensified by other, culturally determined, behaviours such as excessive freedom. This again raises the question as to whether more money and leisure will bring true happiness; we have already seen in Chapter 2 that it will not. Although money is necessary to fulfil basic human needs, including food, housing, and education, some people are unable to attain higher levels of material fulfilment. Many people in this situation, living in a materialistic society and under the influence of the barrage of commercial advertisements from the media, may feel inadequate, unworthy of having their multiple physical and psychological needs satisfied. As a result, 'most Americans are trapped in Maslow's hierarchy of basic needs and are operating at levels very much below self-actualization'.[60]

Van Boven and Gilovich (2003) examined the hypothesis that happiness is achieved more by allocating discretionary income for the acquisition of life experiences than in investing it in material possessions. To carry out this study, they had to delineate the distinction between 'experiences' and 'possessions' in a meaningful way in everyday life. This presented challenges of interpretation: what is experience? and what is possession?. Intentionality in investing money to attain happiness might be an important factor. Using the intention-based distinction, the authors proposed two dichotomies.

One distinction has to do with consumer behaviours in relation to either 'hedonistic' or 'utilitarian' goods. Hedonistic goods are acquired with the primary intention of enjoyment, while utilitarian goods are acquired with the primary purpose of achieving practical objectives. The other distinction concerns the difference between extrinsic goals on the one hand and, on the other, intrinsic objectives which relate to desires congruent with self-actualization and personal growth. The results of this study confirmed that individuals who value the acquisition of material possessions and who also endorse material goals are less satisfied with their lives. This indicates that experiential acquisition is more likely to make people happy. Van Boven and Gilovich elaborated on the reasons for this by offering the following three possibilities:

- Experiences are more open to positive reinterpretation.

- Experiences are more central to one's identity – the accumulation of rich experiences creates a richer life.

- Experiences have greater 'social value' – these individuals foster successful social relationships more effectively.[61]

In 2007 Kashdan and Breen explored the effect of the pursuit of wealth and material possessions as a strategy to enhance pleasure and meaning in life. They found that individuals with stronger materialistic values reported 'more negative emotions and less relatedness, autonomy, competence, gratitude, and meaning in life'.[62]

Researchers in the behavioural sciences have long reflected upon the behaviours and attitudes of persons who are preoccupied with materialistic pursuits. They have pointed out that individuals who define their personal success in terms of their extrinsic values and possessions are vulnerable to a decline in well-being. An excessive reliance on materialistic gains for social approval, or as a measure of self-esteem and self-worth, can have undesirable consequences in negative circumstances, including a withdrawal of social support and material failure. This in turn can adversely affect personal and social well-being. In contrast, those with intrinsic values are more oriented toward personal growth and have more meaningful connections with others. They also tend to have a healthier lifestyle.[63]

People who live in industrialized societies are flooded with socio-cultural messages and publicity about the rich and famous – celebrities – and the pursuit of wealth and possessions in an attempt to increase their well-being and satisfaction. Individuals often equate 'self' with the immediate satisfaction of goals rather than with a long-term plan for self-actualization and fulfilment. As we have seen at the start of this chapter, at the heart of materialism lies the extrinsic or external orientation goal of fulfilling a desire for power or possessions, or both.[64]

When extrinsic orientation and dependence on material objects as a source of pleasure and pride dominate people's perception of intrinsic values, life takes on a different colour. The result is an exaggerated and overrated view of the importance of pleasure. Some have embraced indulgence in pleasure-seeking behaviour as a form of liberation or healing, with pronouncements such as 'Let pleasure be the cure!' or 'If anhedonia is the problem is hedonism not the remedy? . . . Pleasure Healing is all about the positive power of self-indulgence.'[65] As part of a new concept of 'psycho-spiritual cosmetology', a spectrum of products has been promoted for various sorts of emotional needs. Peace of

Mind lotion, Clear Head Shampoo, Happy Ending conditioner, Green Tea Therapy (also referred to as Soul Cleaning), Tangerine Therapy (Sunny Side Up), cream that promises 'Mind Repair', and the delightfully named 'Nerve Whacker or Hot Off the Stresses', are promoted for restoration of mind, body and soul. These and other prescriptions for Pleasure Healing come with detailed instructions on how to 'Lift your spirits, indulge your psyche, refresh your soles' [sic].[66]

Although nothing is wrong with natural herbal and aromatic therapy for physical relaxation to alleviate the tensions and stress of a distressing world, when overindulgence in such therapy becomes another form of religion it can distract attention from the ultimate and deeper purpose of life. For example, as described by Davis in her 2002 book:

> The spa has become enshrined, in many ways, as the new temple of Pleasure Healing – the land of saving grace . . . We make pilgrimages to spas for reasons that go far beyond the beautification of the body or even the luxury of sensual indulgence. We go to perform the ritual of renewal and to elevate the spirit . . .[67]

Even if the behavioural sciences have shown beyond doubt that wealth is not a source of true happiness, there is paradoxically always a tendency to seek happiness through material goods and to believe that '[t]hose who say that money can't buy happiness don't know where to shop'.[68] The chief aim of the advertising industry is to stimulate the desire – or even craving – for consumer goods. In such a climate of marketing for profit, the consumer is treated as a biological subject – a 'punter' without the capacity to judge or to be an agent of change and a contributor to the well-being of society.[69]

And some people become so enmeshed in materialistic self-indulgence that they lose sight of the meaning of life beyond immediate pleasure; like flies attracted to honey, they become prisoners of their own excesses. Some gather at the edge of the dish, take their fill and depart; others enter further and deeper; still others, motivated by greed, proceed to the centre where they get stuck and are unable to escape. There, prisoners of greed, need and desire, they perish.

Science and greed

When a fascination with money or possessions, and an emotional attachment to them, takes on obsessional dimensions similar to an addiction, the human brain reacts differently from the brain of a person who sees money as a tool for social well-being. Andrew Lo, a neuroscientist at the Massachusetts Institute of Technology (MIT) gave the following explanation of fear, greed and brain function in an article sparked by the Bernard Madoff fraud in 2009. Using magnetic resonance imagery (MRI), Lo's team studied the reaction of the pleasure centres of the brain toward monetary gain or financial profit, and found that they stimulate the same reward circuits as cocaine. Both monetary gain and cocaine increase the release of dopamine, a neurotransmitter, into the brain's nucleus accumbens. Dopamine is involved in pleasure-seeking behaviours. A perpetual and obsessional attachment to monetary gain may lead one to a form of addiction, due to frequent stimulation of the brain's pleasure centre. Gambling is an example of such an attachment.

On the other hand, financial loss was reported as activating those circuits of the brain responsible for responses to physical attack and fight-or-flight experiences. Both financial loss and physical attack lead to the release of the neurotransmitters noradrenaline and cortisol, which raise the heart rate and blood pressure. These physiological responses of the human body correspond with the degree of financial gain or loss in our daily business interactions. Not everybody has the ability to handle these biological reactions.[70]

According to Warren Bickel, a professor of psychiatry and

chair of Alcohol Abuse and Drug Dependence at the University of Arkansas, an excessively shortened view of the future among youth may explain impulsive and risk-taking behaviour such as substance abuse and many other self-destructive behaviours, including crimes. Bickel asks, 'Why do addicts make poor decisions when they clearly face bad consequences that would cost themselves severely?' He believes that these individuals' self-destructive behaviour is partly due to their inability to evaluate rationally the trade-off between instant satisfaction and future consequences.[71]

Aided by the modern technology of neuroimaging and behavioural economics for his research on addiction, Bickel uses a temporal discounting approach to explore how the human mind chooses the relative values of immediate reward as compared to delayed attainment of reward. For example, the individuals under study were asked to choose between two hypothetical rewards: (a) receiving $1,000 in a month's time; or (b) receiving a small amount now. Those who impulsively seek immediate gratification, such as addicts, show a severely narrowed view of the future, choosing to discount it in favour of the present even though the reward is very small.

Bickel and his coworkers had also previously found that those with opioid and cocaine dependence, alcoholism, gambling and smoking habits would discount a hypothetical future reward much more frequently than a non-addict control group. The lack of foresight of these individuals has been the subject of further research studies which have found evidence of a link between addiction and impulsiveness. As a result, it has been hypothesized that two systems compete in the temporal discounting process. One has to do with the 'impulsive system' which requires immediate reward; the other is the role of 'executive systems' which rationally restrain or regulate the urge for instant gratification in favour of a delayed reward.[72]

Whether addicted individuals have a genetic vulnerability of their executive neurocircuitry which makes them susceptible to substance abuse, or the disorder of the brain's executive function is the result of substance abuse, is a matter for debate. The evidence supports both hypotheses and also suggests that there is an interaction between the natural or innate predisposition and the environment. In fact, researchers at the National Institute of Drug Abuse (NIDA) in the United States suggest that long-term substance abuse can impair the cognitive and executive function of the brain.

As Bickel points out, these research findings have implications for public policies, advocating the promotion of a long-term view of gratification, and educating children and youth not to discount future reward as a trade-off for immediate satisfaction. There are also implications on a larger scale for society as a whole: people need to exercise moderation and maturity in their pleasure-seeking behaviour within a materialistic society. Religion has a role to play here, for religious teachings in general encourage self-regulation and control in the face of risk-taking behaviours that may be in conflict with moral values.

Science and technology have brought many choices into modern life which provide unlimited opportunities to satisfy our needs. But there can be too many choices: when we face multiple options we can be trapped by the forces of desire which make it difficult to decide, especially for those who are perfectionists.[73] As 'Abdu'l-Bahá is reported to have said:

> One who is imprisoned by desires is always unhappy; the children of the Kingdom have unchained themselves from their desires. Break all fetters and seek for spiritual joy and enlightenment; then, though you walk on this earth, you will perceive yourselves to be within the divine horizon.[74]

And the following passage from the Writings of Bahá'u'lláh dwells on the ephemeral nature of material attachment:

> The generations that have gone on before you – whither are

they fled? And those round whom in life circled the fairest and the loveliest of the land, where now are they? Profit by their example, O people, and be not of them that are gone astray.

Others ere long will lay hands on what ye possess, and enter into your habitations. Incline your ears to My words, and be not numbered among the foolish.

For every one of you his paramount duty is to choose for himself that on which no other may infringe and none usurp from him. Such a thing – and to this the Almighty is My witness – is the love of God, could ye but perceive it.

Build ye for yourselves such houses as the rain and floods can never destroy, which shall protect you from the changes and chances of this life. This is the instruction of Him Whom the world hath wronged and forsaken.[75]

CHAPTER 7

WEALTH, POVERTY AND MORAL VALUES

Economic life is an arena for the expression of honesty, integrity, trustworthiness, generosity, and other qualities of the spirit. The individual is not merely a self- interested economic unit, striving to claim an every-greater share of the world's material resources.
The Universal House of Justice[1]

We often view wealth and virtue as opposing phenomena. There is an impression that wealth is bad for human character and may bring calamity, while virtues are high qualities. Yet in reality, wealth and material endowments are not evil in themselves; on the contrary, they can be beneficial so long as they do not become a barrier between an individual and the Creator. The influence of wealth on the human mind and soul has long been a subject of debate. Society views the pursuit of money in two different ways: either it is the most important endeavour, or it is seen as 'the root of all evil'.[2]

In much religious scripture believers are exhorted against indulgence in material wealth and attachment to this ephemeral world of existence. In Christianity the acquisition of material wealth was traditionally considered to be a barrier preventing one from attaining the divine spiritual virtues manifested in Christ. To reinforce this interrelationship between spirituality and poverty, Christians emphasize that Christ was poor and homeless and that his early disciples were also poor. Christ warned his disciples that 'it is easier for a camel to go through the eye of a needle, than for a rich man to enter into the Kingdom of God'.[3] As a result of this concept in Christianity (and also in Buddhism) of wealth being in opposition to spirituality, many devout believers chose a celibate, reclusive life in monasteries and convents, detaching themselves from the material world and its temptations, reading prayers and chanting the verses of their sacred scripture – and some still do today. In Islam, especially among Sufis, the notion of attaining closeness to the Kingdom of God through renunciation of material interests and worldly desire is prevalent.

In the teachings of Bahá'u'lláh the interrelationship between wealth and spirituality has been redefined. Although indulgence in riches can be a major factor in impeding the development of spiritual virtues and a saintly character, the possession of wealth and material endowments is not by itself an indicator of materialism. Referring to 'the pious deeds of monks and priests among the followers of the Spirit (Christ)', Bahá'u'lláh counsels them: 'In this Day, however, let them give up the life of seclusion and direct their steps toward the open world and busy themselves with that which will profit themselves and others.'[4] Bahá'u'lláh is quite emphatic about this re-balancing of the dichotomy between wealth and spirituality, stating:

> Should a man wish to adorn himself with the ornaments of the earth, to wear its apparels, or partake of the benefits it can bestow, no harm can befall him, if he alloweth nothing whatever to intervene between him and God . . .[5]

On the other hand, He exhorts the people:

> O ye that pride yourselves on mortal riches! Know ye in truth that wealth is a mighty barrier between the seeker and his desire, the lover and his beloved. The rich, but for a few, shall in no wise attain the court of His presence nor enter the city of content and resignation. Well is it then with him, who,

being rich, is not hindered by his riches from the eternal kingdom, nor deprived by them of imperishable dominion.[6]

Instead of priding oneself on one's earthly riches, writes Bahá'u'lláh, one should reflect upon one's end.[7] He perceives this nether world as 'a show, vain and empty, a mere nothing, bearing the semblance of reality',[8] further explaining:

> By the righteousness of God! The world, its vanities and its glory, and whatever delights it can offer, are all, in the sight of God, as worthless as, nay even more contemptible than, dust and ashes.[9]

Material attachment must be weighed with spiritual insight. In this context, viewing excessive attachment as a state of mind, a person may be poor but harbour a materialistic mindset, while another person may be rich but not be so influenced by that mentality. However, it is rare to find a rich person who 'is not hindered by his riches from the eternal kingdom' as Bahá'u'lláh writes in the Hidden Words quoted above. One such was Phoebe Hearst, one of the wealthiest women in the United States, about whom 'Abdu'l-Bahá wrote: 'Present my best greetings to the honourable and spiritual women; to those who are very much attracted toward God, and particularly to that one who has proved that it is possible for a camel to pass through a needle's eye.'[10]

Elsewhere, 'Abdu'l-Bahá describes the human condition thus: 'Man is in the ultimate degree of materiality and the beginning of spirituality . . .'[11] As creation is under 'a law of progression', individuals are endowed with 'powers of advancement toward spiritual and transcendental kingdoms'.[12] All created things, according to 'Abdu'l-Bahá, are 'captives of nature and the sense world' – except human beings, who are created in the image of God.[13] Although man can become 'emancipated from the captivity of the world of nature' through 'the ideal Power', until he becomes detached from that world 'he is essentially an animal' and it is the teachings of God which transform him into a human soul.[14]

In the Kitáb-i-Íqán Bahá'u'lláh recounts the following story about a believer and the Imám Ṣádiq:

> . . . one of the companions of Ṣádiq complained of his poverty before him. Whereupon, Ṣádiq, that immortal beauty, made reply: 'Verily thou are rich, and hast drunk the draught of wealth.' That poverty-stricken soul was perplexed at the words uttered by that luminous countenance, and said: 'Where are my riches, I who stand in need of a single coin?' Ṣádiq thereupon observed: 'Dost thou not possess our love?' He replied: 'Yea, I possess it, O thou scion of the Prophet of God!' And Ṣádiq asked him saying: 'Exchangest thou this love for one thousand dinars?' He answered: 'Nay, never will I exchange it, though the world and all that is therein be given me!' Then Ṣádiq remarked: 'How can he who possesses such a treasure be called poor?'[15]

Attachment to material things and desires, thus depriving oneself of the spiritual reality of existence, is among the forces of captivity in the physical world. 'Abdu'l-Bahá likens this force of the captivity of worldly desires to 'assaults' and 'shackles' in one of His prayers: 'Free me from the assaults of passion and desire, break off from me the shackles of this nether world . . .' He supplicates: 'Fill up for me the cup of detachment from all things, and in the assembly of Thy splendours and bestowals, rejoice me with the wine of loving Thee'.[16] Breaking off the 'shackles' is part of our daily struggle for personal transformation and freedom from the captivity of the material world and the current culture of self-indulgence.

Self-indulgence of different kinds has become part of today's lifestyle, yet Bahá'u'lláh exhorts the people of the earth to 'arise and gain victory over [their] own selves' so that the whole earth may 'be sanctified from its servitude to the gods of its idle fancies – gods that have inflicted such loss upon, and are responsible for the misery of, their wretched worshippers'.[17] Identifying these idols as obstacles on the path of human perfectibility, He cherishes the hope that through divine assistance humankind may be delivered from this 'state of grievous abasement'.[18] In today's sea of materialism one can clearly discern the images of this state of 'servitude' in those who worship the 'gods of idle fancies'. They have their own substitute faith, complete with temples, devout worshippers and high priests at their altars; they adore and revere these market-temples of materialism. In today's world, so advanced in science and technology, people in their search for 'freedom' have fallen into such abasement that they have virtually become 'prisoners of their own selves' – a situation that calls to mind these words of Bahá'u'lláh:

O Son of Man! Thou dost wish for gold and I desire thy freedom from it. Thou thinkest thyself rich in its possession, and I recognize thy wealth in thy sanctity therefrom. By My life! This is My knowledge, and that is thy fancy; how can My way accord with thine?[19]

Yet in a world where it is so easy to 'go with the flow', breaking the shackles of materialism demands from us qualities of vision, steadfastness and determination, as Bahá'u'lláh describes in a Tablet to one of His followers: 'Sharp must be thy sight . . . and adamant thy soul, and brass-like thy feet, if thou wishest to be unshaken by the assault of the selfish desires that whisper in men's breasts.'[20]

To subjugate our lower or animal nature to our higher or spiritual nature, the teachings of Bahá'u'lláh provide spiritual and material discipline. Fasting, daily obligatory prayer and payment of Ḥuqúqu'lláh (the Right of God) are a few examples. The latter, although it involves material substance, has a profound spiritual effect on the transformation of the human soul and detachment from material captivity. It is one of the most important laws revealed in the Kitáb-i-Aqdas; Bahá'u'lláh states that it is conducive to 'prosperity', 'blessing', 'honour' and 'divine protection', and is the source of 'all good'.[21] This law of the Bahá'í Faith will be discussed further in Chapter 12; one of its benefits is that it allows people to re-examine their attitude toward material things and grow spiritually. Ultimately, it will create in the world a spiritual economy in which prosperity has a different meaning from the one we now know. We shall see later in this chapter how desperately the world needs such a change.

Egotism vs. humility

Psychologically, the power of possession (ownership of wealth, estate, position, knowledge, and so on) brings with it a degree of entitlement, pride and self-importance which when excessive becomes very unhealthy. Should we, therefore, avoid any and all possessions? What are the consequences of an excessive tendency to possess? But possession, whether of wealth or position, is not an impediment in itself. What makes it a problem is the role of the human ego which invests in the possessing a sense of superiority. So the problem is embedded in our use of wealth – the purposes to which we put it. 'Consider', says 'Abdu'l-Bahá, 'to what a remarkable extent the spirituality of people has been overcome by materialism so that spiritual susceptibility seems to have vanished, divine civilization become decadent, and guidance and knowledge of God no longer remain. All are submerged in the sea of materialism.'[22]

The subjects of self and ego are explored extensively in the Bahá'í Writings. Bahá'u'lláh refers to 'the evil of egotism' and those who are 'captives of egotism',[23] and counsels, 'Tear asunder, in My Name, the veils that have grievously blinded your vision . . . Suffer not yourselves to be wrapt in the dense veils of your selfish desires . . .'[24] He further points out that 'so long as one's nature yieldeth unto evil passions, crime and transgressions will prevail'. 'Abdu'l-Bahá elaborates further on 'the rust of egotism', stating that the human ego is 'the Tempter (the subtle serpent of the mind), and the poor soul not entirely emancipated from its suggestions is deceived . . .'[25] The Bahá'í teachings also acknowledge that only the Prophets are truly free from the 'dross of self', because complete freedom from the ego is a hallmark of perfection and as human beings we can never attain that stage in this world. Still, through obedience to God and living our life according to the Bahá'í teachings, as well as through prayer and struggle, we can subdue our ego. Indeed, '. . . the ego can and should be ever-increasingly subordinated to the enlightened soul of man. This is what spiritual progress implies.'[26] Those called 'saints' are people who have achieved 'the highest degree of mastery over their ego'.[27]

Working in reciprocity with the spirit of love and unity is an expression of maturity in human society. In a materialistic society the opposite is the case: self-pride, arrogance and the priority of self over others is a common trait. This can be commonly observed in politics and business dealings and can be a source of conflict and division. The Bahá'í Writings clearly indicate that if a person is rendering a service with pure intent and his love of God and his behaviour does not show the 'slightest trace of egotism or private motives', that person is aided by eternal grace. But if such a person harbours 'the slightest taint of selfish desires and self love', his efforts will lead to nothing and he will be 'destroyed and left hopeless at the last'.[28]

In another statement 'Abdu'l-Bahá exalts the virtue of humility: 'If thou art seeking everlasting glory, choose humility in the path of the True One.'[29] The true state of being humble before God can be discerned from this statement of Bahá'u'lláh in the Hidden Words: 'O Son of Man! Humble thyself before me, that I may graciously visit thee.'[30]

It is moving and humbling to read the following words of 'Abdu'l-Bahá in His Tablet of Visitation: 'Make me as dust in the pathway of Thy loved ones . . .', or these by Bahá'u'lláh where he exhorts human beings to conduct themselves in such a manner that the earth upon which they tread may never be allowed to address to them such words as these: 'I am to be preferred above you. For witness, how patient I am in bearing the burden which the husbandman layeth upon me. I am the instrument that continually imparteth unto all beings the blessings with which He Who is the Source of all grace hath entrusted me. Notwithstanding the honour conferred upon me, and the unnumbered evidences of my wealth – a wealth that supplieth the needs of all creation – behold the measure of my humility, witness with what absolute submissiveness I allow myself to be trodden beneath the feet of men . . .'[31]

Moral challenges in present-day society

A deterioration in moral conduct in human society is a symptom of a crisis within the individuals who form that society. We tend to treat moral issues independently of physical and mental health; but in reality moral behaviour can have a profound influence on the appearance or prevention of various ailments and disorders.

One of the most pervasive problems today is an over-idealization of sexuality, which has led to a breakdown in chaste and moral character, and to the rise of marital infidelity, separation and divorce, promiscuity, sexual abuse and perversions of sexual conduct. These developments have increased the spread of sexually transmitted diseases such as HIV/AIDS disorders and other afflictions. Millions of children are born out of wedlock or are affected by diseases of which they had no knowledge nor the choice or power to refuse. The generally materialistic approach to life has become fertile ground for the expansion and dissemination of laxity in self-control and self-discipline in other areas too; there has been a massive increase in the consumption of alcohol and substances of abuse.

Bahá'u'lláh warned over a hundred years ago that 'the civilization . . . so often vaunted by the learned exponents of arts and sciences, will, if allowed to overleap the bounds of moderation, bring great evil upon men . . . If carried to excess, civilization will prove as prolific a source of evil as it had been of goodness when kept within the restraints of moderation.'[32]

Shoghi Effendi links purity and chastity – two words which many people today would find hard to define, so far have they fallen into disuse – with justice in a global society in his groundbreaking work *The Advent of Divine Justice*. Shoghi Effendi defines them as follows:

> Such a chaste and holy life, with its implications of modesty, purity, temperance, decency, and clean-mindedness, involves no less than the exercise of moderation in all that pertains to dress, language, amusements, and all artistic and literary avocations. It demands daily vigilance in the control of one's carnal desires and corrupt inclinations. It calls for the abandonment of a frivolous conduct, with its excessive attachment to trivial and often misdirected pleasures. It requires total abstinence from all alcoholic drinks, from opium, and from similar habit-forming drugs. It condemns the prostitution of art and of literature, the practices of nudism and of companionate marriage, infidelity in marital relationships, and all manner of promiscuity, of easy familiarity, and of sexual vices. It can tolerate no compromise with the theories, the standards, the habits, and the excesses of a decadent age. Nay rather it seeks to demonstrate, through the dynamic force of its example, the pernicious character of such theories, the falsity of such standards, the hollowness of such claims, the perversity of such habits, and the sacrilegious character of such excesses.[33]

Bahá'u'lláh challenges His followers to demonstrate high standards of behaviour and purity of motive in chastity:

> He is My true follower who, if he come to a valley of pure

gold will pass straight through it aloof as a cloud, and will neither turn back, nor pause. Such a man is assuredly of Me. From his garment the Concourse on high can inhale the fragrance of sanctity . . . And if he met the fairest and most comely of women, he would not feel his heart seduced by the least shadow of desire for her beauty. Such an one indeed is the creation of spotless chastity . . . They that follow their lusts and corrupt inclinations. . . have erred and dissipated their efforts. They indeed are of the lost . . . Purity and chastity . . . have been, and still are, the most great ornaments for the handmaidens of God. God is My Witness! The brightness of the light of chastity sheddeth its illumination upon the worlds of the spirit, and its fragrance is wafted even unto the Most Exalted Paradise. God . . . hath verily made chastity to be a crown for the heads of His handmaidens. Great is the blessedness of that handmaiden that hath attained unto this great station.[34]

Shoghi Effendi explains, however, that the above statements should not be misconstrued to suggest that one should adopt an ascetic lifestyle. He clarified his meaning in the following comments:

It must be remembered, however, that the maintenance of such a high standard of moral conduct is not to be associated or confused with any form of asceticism, or of excessive and bigoted puritanism. The standard inculcated by Bahá'u'lláh seeks, under no circumstances, to deny anyone the legitimate right and privilege to derive the fullest advantage and benefit from the manifold joys, beauties, and pleasures with which the world has been so plentifully enriched by an All-Loving Creator.[35]

Global poverty and wealth

Despite unprecedented progress in science and technology as well as the discovery and utilization of vast natural resources, economic power and globalization have not been able to resolve the large-scale problem of poverty and homelessness in different parts of the world. The wide gap between the 'haves' and the 'have-nots' is shocking: almost half the inhabitants of our planet are poor. Millions of people die each year from hunger, disease and deprivation of some of the most basic necessities of survival. The majority of the victims of these preventable tragedies are children and the sick, who die quietly without making the headlines. In 2005 when the tsunami struck in Asia, people around the world responded with much generosity; they dug into their pockets as they watched the grieving victims on their TV screens. This was a heart-warming response and was recapitulated in 2010 after the Haiti earthquake. But when there are no major reported disasters people tend to become stingy; they don't pay attention to the much larger number of people who die because of 'normal' deprivations. The *New York Times* reported that as compared to the 150,000 fatalities of the tsunami and an estimated similar number of Haiti earthquake victims, there are approximately two million people who die annually of malaria, most of whom are children – yet there is no outpouring of generosity for this insidious disease.[36]

The minority of the world's population who live in the wealthy industrialized nations tend to overindulge in a materialistic lifestyle, turning (with notable exceptions) a blind eye to those less fortunate in other parts of the world. Natural disasters on the one hand, and wars and violence with disease on the other, have created a climate of fear and despair in the many countries where they take place, shattering the lives and dreams of millions before they see their 10th or 15th birthday.

Statistics emerging from recent studies conducted by international organizations are a testimony to the consequences of these disparities. The poorest 40 per cent of the world's population accounts for only 5 per cent of global income, while the richest 20 per cent accounts for three-quarters of it.[37] According to UNICEF, 26,500–30,000 children die each day as a result of poverty. They 'die quietly' in some of the poorest villages on earth, far from the scrutiny and awareness of the people of the world. As these children are basically meeker and weaker in life, their death goes unnoticed.[38]

Statistics over the first decade of the 21st century include the following:[39]

- Nearly a billion people in the world entered the 21st century unable to read a book or sign their names.

- Less than 1 per cent of what the world spends every year on weapons would have been sufficient to put every child into school by the year 2000 – and yet this did not happen.

- Almost half the world's population (nearly three billion people) live on less than US$2 per day.

- Nearly half the population in developing countries suffers at any given time from health problems caused by a lack of safe water and adequate sanitation.

- Poor people worldwide pay a heavy price in infectious diseases. It is estimated that 40 million people are living with HIV/AIDS. Every year 350–500 million persons suffer from malaria. About 90 per cent of malarial deaths occur in Africa, with African children accounting for over 80 per cent of malarial victims worldwide.

- Of the 2.2 billion children in the world, one billion live in poverty – that is, every second child. A large number of children in developing countries have no adequate shelter

(1 in 3), no access to safe water (1 in 5) and no access to health services (1 in 7). About 121 million children of the world are deprived of education. About 2.2 million children die each year because of lack of immunization. Over 700 million people of Southern Africa have no electricity.

♦ It is estimated that the total wealth of the richest 8.3 million people worldwide (0.13 per cent of the world's population) rose 8.2 per cent to US$30.8 trillion in 2004, which gave them control of 25 per cent of the world's financial assets. In addition, the 20 per cent of the population that lives in the developed nations consume 86 per cent of the world's goods! This extreme disproportion of income and consumption compared to that of poor countries is an indication that the present world economy and social justice are breaking down.

Against this backdrop of vast and devastating poverty among millions of the world's population stands the stark reality of overindulgence and excesses in non-essential spending. This has increased immensely over the past decade. Here are some figures from 1998:

	$US (billions)
Cosmetics in the United States	8
Ice cream in Europe	11
Perfumes in Europe and the United States	12
Pet foods in Europe and the United States	17
Business entertainment in Japan	35
Cigarettes in Europe	50
Alcoholic drinks in Europe	105
Narcotic drugs worldwide	400
Military spending worldwide	780

The estimated additional costs for universal access to basic social services in all developing countries during the same period were:

	$US (billions)
Basic education for all	6
Water and sanitation for all	9
Reproductive health for all women	12
Basic health and nutrition	13

In 1998 the combined expenses of just three items in the first list of global priorities (ice cream, perfume and pet foods in Europe and the United States) would have been sufficient to wipe out the deficit of the four global priorities (US$40 billion) according to the Millennium Development Goals: basic education, water and sanitation, reproductive health for women and basic health for all!

The same amount (US$40 billion) was only 10 per cent of the sale of narcotic drugs used worldwide, and just over 5 per cent of global military spending. These shocking expenses for destructive goals, seen in the light of the desperate needs for education and saving lives, was an indication of the spiritual poverty of our materialistic world.

A decade later, by 2008, these figures had greatly increased, emphasizing the serious conflict between the amount of goods people want to consume or possess and what they really need to sustain their day-to-day lives. As the Bahá'í International Community pointed out in its statement *Rethinking Prosperity* (2010):

The unfettered cultivation of needs and wants has led to a system fully dependent on excessive consumption for a privileged few, while reinforcing exclusion, poverty and inequality, for the majority. Each successive global crisis – be it climate, energy, food, water, disease, financial collapse – has revealed new dimensions of the exploitation and oppression inherent in the current patterns of consumption and production. Stark are the contrasts between the consumption of luxuries and the cost of provision of basic needs: basic education for all would cost $10 billion;[40] yet $82 billion is spent annually

123

on cigarettes in the United States alone.[41] The eradication of world hunger would cost $30 billion;[42] water and sanitation – $10 billion.[43] By comparison, the world's military budget rose to $1.55 trillion in 2008.[44]

The narrowly materialistic worldview underpinning much of modern economic thinking has contributed to the degradation of human conduct, the disruption of families and communities, the corruption of public institutions, and the exploitation and marginalization of large segments of the population – women and girls in particular . . . [T]he shift towards a more just, peaceful and sustainable society will require attention to a harmonious dynamic between the material and non-material (or moral) dimensions of consumption and production.[45]

Without that 'harmonious dynamic', the gap between rich and poor will grow wider and access to the rightful fulfilment of basic needs of millions of people will be denied. According to the *Human Development Report 2007/2008* (HDR) of the United Nations Development Programme, there are approximately one billion people who barely survive (at the margin of survival) on less then US$1 a day, while an estimated three billion live on less than US$2 per day. This is a reflection of social injustice towards the large portion of humanity who are struggling to survive.

The statistical information above is a testimony to the fact that the contemporary socio-economic system is unable to bear the load of disparity which it has created between the wealthy minority of the world's population and the large majority of the inhabitants of the planet who suffer poverty and despair. The problem with the system is simply its materialistic foundation: in such a climate salvation is thought to occur in this life, here and now, so that notions of shame, guilt and sin are dismissed as irrelevant. Likewise, values such as thrift, modesty and self-denial are ignored, as is the notion of global solidarity. In a society obsessed with money and a materialistic lifestyle, corruption is everywhere

– and it is not limited to rich people; it also occurs among the poor. It is a cause as well as a result of poverty; and in whatever type of society, the poorest are those most affected. In the current stage of globalization, if the economic system is not carefully scrutinized corruption is bound to flourish and continue to exert a negative impact on the condition of the people.[46] As the Bahá'í International Community stated more than a decade ago,

> This unprecedented economic crisis, together with the social breakdown it has helped to engender, reflects a profound error of conception about human nature itself . . . Unless the development of society finds a purpose beyond the mere amelioration of material conditions, it will fail of attaining even these goals. That purpose must be sought in spiritual dimensions of life and motivation that transcend a constantly changing economic landscape and an artificially imposed division of human societies into 'developed' and 'developing'.[47]

World health and poor nations

The disparity between rich and poor nations affecting the whole globe has severe impacts on several aspects of the well-being of humanity. There is presently a serious shortage of health professionals worldwide: about 4.3 million doctors, nurses, midwives, community health workers and pharmacists are needed to respond to the public demand for healthcare. This shortage of health professionals is expected to rise by 20 per cent within the next two decades.[48]

A number of factors are contributing to this increase in the shortage of medical and health-related personnel:

1. A change in the landscape of healthcare needs and inadequate availability of sufficient health professionals.

2. The appearance of diseases such as HIV/AIDS or SARS,

which medicine had never encountered previously. These exemplify the changing disease pattern and the consequent greater need for trained health professionals. For example, 60 per cent more healthcare workers will be required in Tanzania, while Chad will require a 300 per cent increase.

3. The increased use of modern technology and financing, together with consumer demands and preferences for new procedures, have added to the healthcare worker deficit.

4. Long life expectancy and ageing, as well as increased chronic illness, are adding to the burden of healthcare delivery worldwide.

5. There is a large gap between countries in training physicians, due to limited resources. For example, while Ethiopia can train 200 new physicians per year for a population of 75 million, the United Kingdom trains more than 6,000 doctors for a population of 60 million. On the other hand, and especially with the increasing globalization of the health workforce, there is a serious shortage of medical human resources in poorer countries because their trained physicians opt for more prosperous countries where salaries are more attractive. Consequently, the loss of the poor countries becomes the gain of the richer countries for healthcare resources.[49]

Because a materialistic lifestyle generates self-indulgence in pleasure-seeking behaviour, it contributes to the risk of excess drinking, using psychoactive drugs such as ecstasy, and similar behaviour which can lead to car accidents and medical complications requiring skilled professionals. Also, permissiveness, including sexual promiscuity, may lead to HIV/AIDS and its complications. Another area of increased demand is that of aesthetic reconstructive surgery for purely cosmetic purposes, which often requires highly specialized surgeons. The income from such medical practices can be lucrative, so it should surprise no one that some physicians choose these sub-specialities over other fields where there is much demand but less financial compensation – such as working in poverty-stricken populations who suffer from malnutrition or malaria or providing chronic geriatric services in the public sector.

All the above have an impact on poorer populations who struggle with a shortage of medical workers. They have another major common factor: the increased financial burden in response to the recruitment, training and specialization of health professionals. In addition, financing the rapid increase of new and expensive medications and medical technology for the treatment of patients puts additional stress on the system. When these changes occur in tandem with a deficiency of compassionate care and healthcare provision, the outlook for the medical system is dim.

The result is that while in some parts of the world there are people fortunate enough to be able to spend thousands of dollars on not-so-essential aesthetic procedures, in poorer parts of the world thousands of children die of malnutrition and infectious diseases because of poverty and the extreme poverty gap in human society. For example, the continent of Africa, which suffers the most from this economic disparity, has 24 per cent of the burden of diseases, but only 3 per cent of health workers and less than 1 per cent of world health expenditure.[50] If our society had a more compassionate and spiritual perspective on life and suffering, wouldn't this burden on the health system be lessened? How can we raise society's consciousness of the pressing need for empathy and compassion in a world in which self-indulgence is rampant?

The above challenges demonstrate that there is a need to rethink the distribution of wealth and to re-evaluate the current economic system. Such an objective calls for dialogue and collaboration, not only between rich and poor nations but also between science and religion. Such a close relationship will help people to have access to broader knowledge and to develop greater skills in resolving the crisis in human affairs. Let's take the example of poverty, which will be further discussed in Chapter 9. As explained in a statement by the Bahá'í International Community:

> ... material resources exist, or can be created by scientific and technological endeavour, which will alleviate and eventually entirely eradicate this age-old condition as a feature of human life. A major reason why such relief is not achieved is that the necessary scientific and technological advances respond to a set of priorities only tangentially related to the real interests of the generality of humankind. A radical reordering of these priorities will be required if the burden of poverty is finally to be lifted from the world. Such an achievement demands a determined quest for appropriate values, a quest that will test profoundly both the spiritual and scientific resources of humankind. Religion will be severely hampered in contributing to this joint undertaking so long as it is held prisoner by sectarian doctrines which cannot distinguish between contentment and mere passivity and which teach that poverty is an inherent feature of earthly life, escape from which lies only in the world beyond. To participate effectively in the struggle to bring material well-being to humanity, the religious spirit must find – in the Source of inspiration from which it flows – new spiritual concepts and principles relevant to an age that seeks to establish unity and justice in human affairs.[51]

CHAPTER 8

GLOBAL WARMING, CLIMATE CHANGE AND ENVIRONMENTAL DEGRADATION

The deepening environmental crisis, driven by a system that condones the pillage of material resources to satisfy an insatiable thirst for more, suggests how entirely inadequate is the present conception of humanity's relationship with nature.
The Universal House of Justice[1]

Climate change and man-made pollution

The impact of climate change is an issue of international concern. Global warming and climate change are considered to be a mainly human-made phenomenon which threatens the future life of the planet, the natural adaptation of ecosystems and the life of the species and their habitats on the planet.

For decades many were afraid to tackle the problem of climate change, fearing that it would be very costly. A large number of governments, influential businesses and rich companies tried to undermine climate change action. But as significant scientific research findings emerged over the years, governments and large corporations became concerned about the disastrous consequences of neglecting environmental pollution and climate change. As a result, the United Nations Environment Programme (UNEP) created agencies to evaluate scientific knowledge on global warming which led to the Rio Earth Summit on climate change in 1992.

Growing numbers of people agree that 'climate change may be one of the greatest threats facing the planet. Recent years show increasing temperatures in various regions, and/or increasing extremities in weather patterns.'[2] In an article on capitalism and climate change in 2009, Servaas Storm asked, 'Can climate change be stopped while fossil fuel capitalism remains the dominant system?' citing research finding that 'the rising heat is caused by growing atmospheric concentrations of carbon dioxide (CO_2) and other greenhouse gases (GHGs)'.[3] If unabated, the result of these developments will raise the earth's temperature by about 3-4 degrees by the end of this century.

The United Nations Climate Change Conference in Paris in 2015 reached an historic global agreement on the reduction of climate change. Based on this agreement, the goal will be to limit global warming to less than 2 degrees Celsius compared to pre-industrial levels.

Many argue that since industrialized countries have produced much more greenhouse gas than developing nations, these countries must support developing countries to adapt in such a way as to avoid polluting the atmosphere. Anup Shah, for instance, views this as "climate justice", which has been ignored by the rich countries as well as their mainstream media. Shah wrote in 2012: 'Global warming is primarily a result of the industrialization and modernization levels in the OECD countries, on whom the main onus for mitigation presently lies'.[4]

According to the Global Footprint Network, the population of our planet uses the equivalent of 1.6 planets to provide the renewable resources we use and absorb the CO_2 waste. In other words, it takes the Earth one year and six months to generate what we use in a year: 'Moderate UN scenarios suggest that if current population and consumption trends continue, by 2030 we will need the equivalent of two Earths to support us. And of course, we only have one.'[5]

In light of the above it is evident that at present there is an ecological overshoot on the planet where turning resources into waste is occurring faster than waste can be turned into resources. This causes a depletion of the renewable resources upon which human life and biodiversity depend:

> The result is collapsing fisheries, diminishing forest cover, depletion of fresh water systems, and the build up of carbon dioxide emissions, which creates problems like global climate change. These are just a few of the most noticeable effects of overshoot. Overshoot also contributes to resource conflicts and wars, mass migrations, famine, disease and other human tragedies – and tends to have a disproportionate impact on the poor, who cannot buy their way out of the problem by getting resources from somewhere else.[6]

Excessive global consumption of resources not only by governments and industrial corporations, but also by the general population, can damage ecological capacity and cause it to exceed its limits. Therefore individual and collective action by the inhabitants of the planet is needed to achieve moderation and to take care of our ecological assets in a resource-constrained world in order to preserve its sustainability and to ensure human survival.

Paul Hanley (2014) gives the following analogy about the sustainability of ecological capacity:

> . . . let's imagine a grove of 1,000 fast-growing tress, where 100 trees mature each year and 100 new trees are planted. A forester would be able to log 100 trees a year sustainably, without ever decreasing the stock of trees. If, however he cuts 200 trees a year, his income doubles but the forest will disappear within 10 years, reducing his income to zero thereafter . . . Humanity will somehow have to reduce its consumption of resources and emission of waste by some 60 percent overall.[7]

What leads to global warming and climate change?

Climate is the pattern of weather measured for several decades. During the past 30 years there has been a pattern of rising temperatures worldwide. The first decade of the 21st century was reportedly the hottest decade on record since the late 1800s when reliable record-keeping began. According to the Union of Concerned Scientists, global warming amplifies the risk of extreme weather changes, and the rise in global temperature is caused primarily by an 'increase of heat-trapping emissions in the atmosphere created when we burn coal, oil, and gas to generate electricity, drive our cars and fuel our businesses'.[8]

As a result of global warming there is an increase in the rate of evaporation of water from the ocean and the soil into the atmosphere, and the amount of water vapour in turn creates conditions conducive to heavy precipitation in the form of severe rain and snow storms. This pattern on the one hand and the periods of drought on the other have become the 'new normal' and people are having to adapt to the likelihood of severe climate change.

Change in climate and global warming are attributed to a number of factors both natural and manmade. There is strong evidence from global warming observations during the last 50 years that human activities have played an important role in this phenomenon. Materialistic overconsumption is part of the footprint. It will require drastic and sustained action by governments and people worldwide to reduce the heat-trapping emissions through increased use of renewable energy, reduced deforestation and other means.[9]

Scientists also believe that the ice cores and sheets which took tens of thousands of years to build up and thousands of years to recede may now, with the dramatic changes in global temperature, take as little as a decade to undergo a series of changes.[10] These major shifts in the pattern of the global climate and its temperature will have an impact on ecosystems, people and the environment. The footprint of climate change and global warming produced by the inhabitants of planet Earth which has occurred during the last century has become more evident during the last two decades. In recent years the catastrophic results of some of these changes due to global warming have become evident. We are confronted with climate volatility and human vulnerability in the face of unprecedented storms with disastrous consequences. Some regions which were previously safe from severe flooding are increasingly threatened or affected by flash floods and river flooding with large numbers of fatalities, as in March 2017 in Colombia. The frequency and severity of tornadoes has also increased in some regions. Scientists predict that if the emissions which cause global warming continue unabated, the amount of rainfall during the season will increase by more than 40 per cent in the United States by the end of this century. Even if emissions are dramatically reduced, the downpours are likely to increase, but by only about 20 percent. Therefore, regardless of efforts to cut emissions, people will have to adapt to the likelihood of the occurrence of severe storms. They will need to improve local infrastructure to withstand floods and prepare houses for emergency situations.[11]

Climate change and global warming are also adversely affecting the reduction of poverty. Global warming has an impact on agricultural production and water resources, resulting in food shortages, as well as irrigation and power generation in some parts of the world, especially in coastal cities which are more exposed to violent storms.[12]

Environmental degradation

Over 80 years ago Shoghi Effendi wrote the following prescient words:

> We cannot segregate the human heart from the environment outside us and say that once one of these is reformed everything will be improved. Man is organic with the world.

His inner life moulds the environment and is itself also deeply affected by it. The one acts upon the other and every abiding change in the life of man is the result of these mutual reactions.[13]

Among the results of climate change is degradation of the environment. Erratic climate and weather extremes are affecting the availability of fresh water, human habitats, the productive capacity of soil and melting of the planet's snow pack and glaciers. The warming atmosphere of the planet increases water evaporation which, in the words of the Environmental Defense Fund (2017) is 'like fuel for storms, exacerbating extreme weather events, such as hurricanes. Rising sea levels make coastal flooding events worse. In more naturally arid areas droughts and wildfires intensify.'[14]

Alterations in ecosystems and water supply lead to changes in natural habitats. More specifically '[a]s climate patterns rapidly shift, habitats on land and in the sea are changing, making them inhospitable for some species, while letting others move in and take over. In some cases entire ecosystems are at risk of collapsing.'[15]

The changes occurring in the natural world are extensive, affecting ocean coral and shellfish and increasing the risk of deadly infestations in forests. As a result of milder winters and longer summers, tree-killing insects thrive so that trees are weakened with lower defence mechanisms because of prolonged droughts. 'This cycle of warmer weather, weak trees and thriving insects is likely the culprit behind the massive die-off of 70,000 square miles of Rocky Mountain conifers.' Likewise, animals such as the polar bear that are used to the Arctic climate and ice will struggle to survive and become an endangered species.[16]

Yet another group of consequences are those which become a burden and danger to health and society. Atmospheric changes endanger the life of the human race. Extreme weather and higher global temperatures are becoming a risk factor, causing stress and pressure on well-being, infrastructure and the economy.

Moreover, as already mentioned, climate change seriously affects agriculture, the source of food. Farmers around the world are struggling to keep up with erratic changes in the weather and the unpredictability of water supply for production. Man-made pollution combined with warmer temperatures and unpredictable weather are becoming harmful to health: 'A warmer atmosphere increases chemical reactions that form ground-level ozone, also known as smog. Smog is a well-known lung irritant and a major trigger of asthma attacks. Smoke from wildfires further degrades the air. Extreme summer heat will mean more deaths during heat waves, and warmer freshwater makes it easier for pathogens to grow and contaminate drinking water.'[17]

At the International Environment Forum (IEF) Conference on Education for Sustainibility in December 2004, the Center for a New American Dream discussed the following questions: 'Can Americans enjoy a high-quality life while consuming less?' and 'How much is enough?' It was stated that 'the average American every week uses the equivalent of 300 shopping bags filled with natural resources for food, shelter, energy and transportation. Americans end up paying about $200 billion a year on clean-up of resource extraction, pollution and wastes.' According to the Center, materialism, greed and selfishness have become the dominating passion of American life, overshadowing a more important and meaningful set of values based on family life, responsibility and community. People feel strongly that there is a need for a balance in the lives of individuals, that is to say, to raise the proportion of non-material values in life as compared to that of material gain and interest. 'The American dream of having more and more is killing us and our environment. People are hungry to talk about their disappointment with the work-and-shop consumer treadmill.'[18]

These excesses in the exploitation of natural resources have affected the ozone layer and the climate and will impact the well-being of future generations. The United Nations Environment and Development Committee noted that the North American tteeffortnenert

pattern of excessive consumption has been responsible as the primary engine driving global environmental problems. As Brown and Brown write, when 'have not' countries want to imitate the same standard of living as those who 'have' material wealth, the result will be a recipe for disaster: 'It has been estimated that if everyone on the planet used the same amount of resources as the "western/developed" world, we would need four more planets!'[19]

CHAPTER 9

CONSEQUENCES OF
MATERIALISM

*Mankind is submerged in the sea of materialism and occupied
with the affairs of this world. They have no thought beyond
earthly possessions.*
'Abdu'l-Bahá[1]

Material wealth and spiritual poverty

In Chapter 7 we discussed the 'poverty gap' between rich and
poor nations and the disastrous consequences of the current lack
of global solidarity. But to comprehend fully the issue of poverty
in the world we need to have a deeper understanding of the nature
of human beings and the purpose of civilization.

Poverty has a broad and multidimensional meaning. It is not
strictly confined to those who are poor and destitute; it affects
humanity as a whole. Central to understanding poverty is the
recognition of the true meaning and purpose of life. Poverty is
associated not only with deprivation of material resources and
opportunities; it can also be a state of mind, such as being unaware
of one's potential and capacity to create a condition which would
be conducive to a dignified society and one's rightful place in it.
Therefore,

poverty can be described as the absence of those ethical,
social and material resources needed to develop the moral,

intellectual and social capacities of individuals, communities and institutions . . . The concept of knowledge now needed to guide poverty alleviation efforts must be adequate to address both the poverty of means and the poverty of spirit.[2]

Poverty can be viewed as a symptom of economic inequity and injustice in social relationships:

While poverty is the product of numerous factors: historic, economic, political and environmental, there is also a cultural dimension, which manifests itself in individual values and attitudes. Some of these – such as the subjugation of girls and women, the lack of value of education or of an individual's right to progress – can exacerbate conditions of poverty.[3]

Non-material or moral and spiritual poverty can manifest itself in different people in different ways. It may appear in some as poverty of love and compassion as well as of other intrinsic values such as empathy, forgiveness, caring and justice. Poverty of altruism may lead to excessive self-centredness and indifference to the plight of those who are destitute. This kind of poverty is often very subtle.

Material poverty is more tangible and can appear in individuals with or without moral poverty. Sometimes one can lead to the other. A global economic crisis or financial breakdown, although technically a material downturn, is not entirely independent of moral and psychosocial decline.

Financial losses lead to unemployment which, if occurring on a large scale and unresolved, can bring about demoralization, social unrest and violence. When families break down, the education of children can be cut short or seriously compromised; domestic violence and other abuses can increase. Everything becomes a struggle for survival, so that adherence to moral values may no longer be a priority. The rise of drunkenness to numb the consciousness of things that are too painful to face, drug abuse and trafficking, gambling, robbery, sexual promiscuity, crime and chaos and confusion can prevail amidst hopelessness and despair. Rich and powerful leaders of society, instead of exercising generosity and compassion, may resort to force, taking advantage of the vulnerability of those who have become impoverished by exploiting them as workers, often violating their human rights.

In such a climate of oppression one may wonder how moral values can be conducive to the empowerment of a population in the grip of hunger and poverty. But what brought the people down to abject poverty and despair in the first place? In the case of the global economic crisis that began in 2008, was it not the greed and selfishness of those in power who could have acted differently to prevent this catastrophe? Prior to the crisis the World Bank and other international and civil society organizations had warned of a 'human catastrophe' in the poorest countries of the world unless the global economic situation was dealt with. Such a crisis is not purely a financial breakdown; it is also a crisis of human consciousness, morality and social justice. It is a sad demonstration of the state of affairs in a humankind which refuses to see each other as members of one family and to cherish all with the same love and unity that everyone in a family should enjoy.

Among the flagrant consequences of material and moral poverty in the world today are the injustices of child labour, human trafficking as well as organ trafficking, conflict and exploitation in countries rich in minerals or precious stones, and the fear and despair generated by not knowing how to feed one's family, often leading to violence at both individual and political levels.

Child labour

During the pre-industrial period with its predominantly rural economy, as well as through much of the Industrial Revolution, young children were treated as producers from an early age. They laboured many hours a day, often working beyond their ability; this was seen as normal by the culture.[4] During the worst excesses of the Industrial Revolution, in 1843 Elizabeth Barrett Browning captured the effects of child labour and suffering in her poem 'The Cry of the Children', written on reading the report of a parliamentary commission in England on the condition of child workers in coal mines:

Do ye hear the children weeping, O my brothers,
    Ere the sorrow comes with years?
They are leaning their young heads against their mothers,
    And they cannot stop their tears.
The young lambs are bleating in the meadows,
    The young birds are chirping in the nest,
The young fawns are playing with the shadows,
    The young flowers are blowing toward the west —
But the young, young children, O my brothers,
    They are weeping bitterly!
They are weeping in the playtime of the others,
    In the country of the free . . .

By 1848 legislation had been introduced to restrict the employment of children. Gradually, industrialized societies witnessed a transformation in social attitudes toward children, so that today child labour is seen worldwide as a stain on the character of a nation. Although child labour continues to thrive in many countries – usually because the children's meagre wages may be the only source of family income – most governments have ratified the ILO Convention on the Elimination of the Worst Forms of Child Labour. It is recognized not only that children are human beings who should enjoy certain rights and privileges in common with adults, but that they should be protected from harms that interfere with their education and development. Yet although there has been significant improvement in the lives of children worldwide, there are still many serious concerns and also some emerging ones. Among these are the expansion of commercial pressure on children's minds and the exploitation of their interests through the kind of extensive marketing and advertising described earlier in this book.[5]

Human trafficking and forced labour

One of the tragic evidences of moral and economic decadence is the trafficking of human beings and its devastating consequences on the lives of millions of victims. Many people, especially children and women, have been deceived, lured or coerced, removed from their homes and sent to another region or another country to carry out forced labour under the most deplorable and degrading conditions. Over 12 million people around the world are trapped in forced labour, at an estimated cost to them ('the cost of coercion') of over US$20 billion per year.[6] Meanwhile, the traffickers enjoy a lucrative global annual income of approximately US$42.5 billion. According to the United Nations, '4 million people a year are traded against their will to work in a form of servitude. The majority of them come from South-East Asia, Eastern Europe and Latin America.'[7] According to the Coalition to Abolish Slavery and Trafficking (CAST), 'every 10 minutes a woman or child is trafficked into the United States for forced labour'. This practice, which is referred to as 'trade or commerce in people', is basically slavery; it is an illegal and unethical exploitation of human beings.

The victims of trafficking are found in various deplorable situations such as prostitution, forced labour, or as child soldiers. The International Labour Organization (ILO) says there are eight main forms of forced labour in the world today: slavery, farm and rural debt bondage, bonded labour, people trafficking, abuse of domestic workers, prison labour, compulsory work and military forced labour.[8] Sometimes the young victims are kidnapped, or even sold by their own parents to traffickers to pay off a debt or for income.

It has been reported that human trafficking is the fastest-growing criminal industry around the world. The criminal organizations responsible usually aim at the most vulnerable and minorities, offering hope through the pretext of a job opportunity. Most of the victims are very poor or from deprived backgrounds, or are refugees belonging to persecuted ethnic minorities who are unaware of the real intention of the traffickers.

A recent UN report suggests that human trafficking is likely to escalate as the result of the worldwide economic crisis which is fuelling the causes of such exploitation – poverty, unemployment, the need for cheap labour, and gender inequality. The Council of Europe has indicated that it has reached 'epidemic proportions' during the past decade. And UNICEF has reported that every year over one million children enter the sex trade across the world. In the past 30 years approximately 30 million children have lost their childhood through sexual exploitation.

These developments depict a worldwide blatant abuse of human rights: the commercial abuse of human beings against their will. It also shows that slavery, which we might have assumed was abolished long ago, is still alive. Slave markets have become a modern economic enterprise investing in the exploitation of the more vulnerable human populations worldwide. In spite of the efforts of the United Nations Office on Drugs and Crime (UNODC) and the membership of 155 countries around the world for global assessment of the scope of human trafficking, according to the Executive Director of UNODC, 'many governments are still in denial. There is even neglect when it comes to either reporting on or prosecuting cases of human trafficking.'

Human organ trafficking

The growing demand for human organs has been taking its toll on poor people in developing countries. As the need for organs for transplant in rich and developed nations increases, so does the temptation for people in other countries who are in desperate need of money to willingly offer a kidney or other organs for sale on the black market. Such is the plight of poverty-stricken or destitute people, who endanger their lives through the risk of infection, haemorrhage or death on the operating table in order to pay their debts and feed their hungry children. According to the World Health Organization (WHO), five 'hotspots' have been identified as sources of organ trafficking on a large scale: Pakistan, China, the Philippines, Colombia and Egypt. Traffickers in these countries also have strong ties to organ traffickers in Nigeria, Brazil and Iran. In Iran there are 137 agencies and 23 legal clinics functioning with the specific task of kidney transplants. In the 2008–2010 financial crisis and through family pressure, increasing numbers of people were allowing their kidneys to be removed and sold in exchange for money to pay their debts. As a result, organ sale has become a growing business known as 'transplant tourism'.[9]

Donors who are subject to this emotionally and physically painful procedure need to match with patients, who are willing to travel long distances for organ transplants. The report of the 2006 World Transplant Congress reveals that patients receiving a transplant from countries other than their own experience a high incidence of infection and other complications from the transplant. Many of those who seek out illegal organ traders for organ transplant come from developed countries. They choose this approach for two reasons: to get a lower-cost transplant, and to have a shorter waiting period. Organ brokers who handle these kinds of cases usually require a one-time payment of up to US$120,000, which includes travel expenses and the organ transplant. But those who give up their organ for cash are not only denied proper medical care after the operation; they often receive less money for their organ than was initially promised. Because of the illegal nature of the transaction, the donors have no legal recourse to justice. This is a double disappointment for poverty-stricken donors. Deceived and missing a vital part of their body, they must be content, under the threat of the middlemen, with what they receive.[10]

The following heartbreaking story made headlines in the news media in 2005. A 26-year-old Bangladeshi mother put a classi-fied ad in a Bengali-language newspaper, *Ittefaq*, offering one of her eyes for sale. This single mother of a two-and-a-half-year-old daughter had found herself penniless after her husband, who was her only source of income, left her. Destitute, she decided to sell her eye as the only option available in order to find money to pay her rent and to feed her daughter. As she informed the reporters: 'I have no education, so it's not possible for me, a single mother, to get a decent job. All I want is some money so that I can buy a piece of land for my daughter. I would not repent (sic) if that causes me blindness.' Her story caused a public outcry and international news coverage to the point that the then Bangla-desh Prime Minister Khaleda Zia reacted with concern over her plight. She called the young woman to her office and pledged her a package of government assistance including a home, free food rations and educational expenses for her daughter. Although this particular story ended happily, there are millions of other people whose living conditions are as deplorable as this woman's or even worse. According to the World Bank, Bangladesh has 'the highest levels of poverty in South Asia and among the highest levels of malnutrition in the world'.[11]

'Blood diamonds' and 'conflict minerals'

Diamonds, one of the precious stones most coveted as a symbol of wealth, beauty, love and happiness in many parts of the world, are now recognized in some countries as a symbol of conflict, hardship and poverty. The following is a brief examination of how diamonds and other precious minerals are being greedily exploited in the struggle between wealth and poverty.

A distinction should be made between 'conflict diamonds' and legitimate diamonds which are mined in government-controlled areas with certificates of origin: 'The high value that society places on diamonds allows the shift of wealth from the world's richest countries to some of its poorest.'[12] On the other hand, 'blood' or 'conflict' diamonds are diamonds which originate from 'areas controlled by forces or factions opposed to legitimate and internationally recognized governments, and are used to fund military action in opposition to those governments, or in contravention of the decision of the Security Council [of the United Nations].'[13]

Africa is a major global producer of diamonds, a fact which should prove a source of economic wealth for the continent. Botswana is reported to be the world's largest diamond producer, but also has the highest incidence of AIDS with about 37 per cent of its adult population HIV-positive. In Sierra Leone, which according to the United Nations Human Development Index is the world's poorest country, diamonds account for approximately 94 per cent of its exports while about 70 per cent of its people live on less than one dollar a day. Due to corruption and lack of good governance, people are enslaved by the diamond trade while the profit goes to buy arms to subdue them. As a result, Sierra Leone, a country so blessed with natural resources such as diamonds, gold, titanium and bauxite, is cursed with corruption and conflicts which have claimed the lives of 50,000 people and forced millions to flee from the conflict zones.

> O my mountain in the field
> I will give thy substance and all thy treasures to the spoil,
> And thy high places for sin,
> Throughout all thy borders.[14]

The exploration, mining and marketing of diamonds have become a source of painful strife and civil war because of greed and rivalry for wealth and power. Since the beginning of the 20th century many diamond-rich regions of the world, especially in Africa, have become the site of terrible struggles between armed rebels and central government, causing bloodshed and extensive devastation. Human obsession with power and motivated by greed has led to attempts to control this natural wealth through cruel methods resulting in human rights abuses. The diamond trade has fuelled tragic conflicts, violence, amputation of hands by rebels and other human rights violations. It has funded devastating civil wars, caused environmental damage and imposed cruel child labour. The hallmark of these cruel atrocities is greed.

In December 2000 the United Nations General Assembly unanimously adopted a resolution on the role of diamonds in fuelling the violence and armed conflict which have resulted in these ruinous wars. This measure was to prevent a worsening of these conflicts, but has been only partially successful. The terms 'blood diamond' and 'conflict diamond' have recently come to public attention through calls for further intervention by the United Nations.

The condition of workers in the mines of the conflict diamond areas is deplorable. They are subjected to poor wages and harsh labour conditions. The workers are often children who are recruited to work in the smaller and more dangerous areas of mines where adults cannot get through; they are given risky mining tasks. According to one recent study in Angola, 46 per cent of mine workers were children under the age of 16 who worked in these mines because of war, poverty and lack of education. In India, where more than half of the world's diamonds are processed, child labour is common and labour abuse and degradation of the environment are also common. Children are expected to work in dangerous conditions for years with little or no pay until they are replaced, usually by their younger siblings.

Increasing information has come to light concerning the use of other precious natural resources such as titanium, which provides materials used in cell phones and other electronic gadgets common in the industrialized world. The Democratic Republic of Congo (DRC) has been the scene of countless atrocities and suffering as a result of the exploration and mining of this mineral. In shocking reports published worldwide since 2009[15] it has been revealed how consumers of electronic products have been unaware of the complex chain of events which connects widespread forced labour and sexual violence in the DRC with minerals which are used to help power cell phones, laptops, MP3 players, video games and digital cameras.

Because of pressing demands in the industrialized world for ever-newer electronic gadgets with increased capacity and 'must-have' applications which nobody really needs, the DRC's protracted wars have produced the horrific and widespread violence and cruelty perpetrated by the many armed groups in the country. It has been reported that the war in the DRC in the first decade of the 21st century was 'the deadliest since World War II' and that sexual violence in particular has become a 'tool of war and punishment on a large scale. The war has the highest rate of violence against women and girls in the world'.[16] This terrible sexual violence is often triggered by militias fighting for control of the conflict minerals (ores containing tantalum, titanium and gold, among others) for their special uses in industry. Although reports on this heinous violence are not consistent because there are untold numbers of women who have chosen not to report this crime, there are nevertheless indications that hundreds of thousands of them have been brutally raped. The armed groups finance their affairs through illegal trade of these conflict minerals.

To prevent the fuelling of these atrocities some companies, according to the television news channel CNN, have decided to avoid such minerals; they are attempting to bar suppliers from selling ore containing tantalum from the DRC. Moreover, there have been strong warnings to the industrialized world to avoid trade with the DRC in these conflict minerals. So it is that through greed and corruption, a resource that could benefit the population of a country is transformed into a source of suffering.

Ivory and the exploitation of elephants

Each year thousands of elephants across Africa are slaughtered for their tusks. This tragic exploitation and destruction of animals for the wealthy is another demonstration of the extent of cruelty motivated by greed. According to one report, elephants are being killed at the rate of approximately 100 per day. It is difficult to determine exactly how many elephants have been slaughtered for their tusks, but figures range from over 4,000 to as many as 60,000 per year. Traditionally, African people, especially the Masai of southern Kenya who coexist with their wild life, rarely kill elephants because they revere them and regard them, like humans, as having souls. However, because of the need for money in the past few years, even the Masai have engaged in this practice.

It is reported that a pound of raw ivory, which sells originally for $20, is purchased by customers in Asian countries for about $700 after passing through a number of middlemen. While it is difficult to know how much ivory is being smuggled to Asia, it has been reported that over the last ten years about 45,000 pounds have been seized annually in or en route to Asia.[17] It is heartbreaking to see these socially-conscious animals, who mourn for their dead, being exterminated so that newly rich individuals living in another part of the world can display parts of them as a symbol of wealth and status.

All this shows that there is an urgent need for a transformation of human conscience and character in order to change the dire condition of the masses of humanity. This will not be possible, according to the Bahá'í Writings, without the healing message of the Divine Physician – a message which provides insight into the causes of this devouring flame of materialism engulfing the very fabric of human society worldwide.

The medicalization of life challenges

There have been heated debates in some medical circles about the advertising of lifestyle drugs for less serious health problems or conditions which lie at the boundary of illness and lifestyle wishes. Some researchers find the expression *lifestyle drug* an enigma. As David Gilbert and his associates state, 'It is difficult to define what we mean by the term lifestyle drug since the perception of what is illness and what is within the sphere of personal responsibility rather than health care may depend on whether one is a potential patient or a potential "payer".'[18] There are also social and cultural issues which influence our perception of ordinary life challenges and diseases.

It is not always possible to draw a clear line between lifestyle wishes and illness. A lifestyle problem may develop into a health problem because of medical and genetic factors. For example, neglecting care of a simple wound may lead to a severe inflammation or gangrene, a serious disease. In other circumstances, when a treatment is discovered for a lifestyle problem (e.g. smoking), the problem then may develop into a disease (i.e. lung cancer) requiring medical intervention which may remove responsibility for controlling smoking.

In an article entitled 'Selling Sickness', Ray Moynihan and his associates criticize a growing tendency of some forms of 'medicalizing' ordinary life problems as 'disease mongering'. The authors maintain that pharmaceutical companies influence this widening of the boundaries of treatable disease in order to expand markets for new products. Moreover, the media are used to framing conditions as more seriously widespread and damaging than they really are.

Moynihan believes that medical establishments portray ordinary processes or ailments as medical disorders requiring treatment. For example, baldness – which is an ordinary process of life – is transformed into a medical condition. When a treatment for baldness, Finasteride, first appeared in Australia, newspapers published new information about the emotional trauma experienced as a result of hair loss. A newspaper article indicated that, based on a new study, a third of all men suffer some degree of hair loss and suggested that hair loss may lead to panic and impact well-being and job prospects. It turned out that the study and the establishment were funded by the manufacturer of the product.

Using knowledge to 'shape' medical opinions to sell a sickness is unethical. The above authors make this point in connection with the promotion of certain newly developed medications to treat what they consider personal or social problems in Australia. For example, in 1998 a newspaper article entitled 'Too shy for words' suggested that two million Australians were affected by the condition of shyness.[19] Media coverage led to widespread discussion which moved this personal problem of under-assertiveness and shyness to the domain of psychiatric disorder requiring medication.

Another case was the suggestion that medication be used for 'social phobia' as a modern psychiatric disorder requiring treatment. Although social phobia with severe anxiety symptoms does exist in clinical terms as an illness, it is not as rampant as was publicized in the media, which reported that one million Australians had been under-diagnosed with this disease. Many of these so-called cases of social phobia may simply be shy people who prefer to be alone and remain productive. The announcement described the condition as 'soul destroying' and requiring antidepressants for treatment.[20] This underlines the excesses of a materialistic reframing or reinterpretation of normal life challenges as diseases in order to medicalize ordinary problems and create a market for profit. There are ethical issues in labelling certain physical or behavioural problems as diseases without clear scientific justification.

Beyond material attachment

We often think of attachment in material terms because material things are tangible. In reality, attachment embraces a host of other dependencies which are not material but which we over-idealize in our lives. Attachment applies not only to the possession of material goods and wealth, but to self, social status or position, glorification of one's achievements and self-centred pride in them, and popularity. One can even be too attached to the acquisition of knowledge, a means by which humankind unravels the mysteries of the universe, if one's knowledge is used for self-promotion rather than for the well-being, peace and prosperity of other human beings. In the former case knowledge can be nothing but a hindrance, a barrier in the path of true personal development. In the latter, it leads to a sense of altruism and service for the good of mankind.

Non-material attachment can be very difficult to discern or acknowledge in oneself. Self-deception and self-centredness under the influence of the ego often go unnoticed and may lead one to believe that nothing is wrong with one's own behaviour. In a materialistic society, self-love and pride are often the norm rather than the exception. Our system of education and the academic requirements for excellence often encourage young academics to be self-centred and to adopt an air of superiority. Such a sentiment is reinforced through the predominant climate of greed and competition instead of sharing and collaboration.

Selfishness is very common in human society, but individuals are not born evil, greedy or selfish. Although there is potential for such behaviour in a large number of people, its development depends on the nature and quality of one's education and childhood upbringing. And there is a difference between self-interest and selfishness. The former is generally perceived as an acceptable way of looking after oneself and maintaining well-being through an interest in personal health, diet, education, and so on. But the latter goes beyond this and becomes exclusive; selfishness is a state of self-centredness and greed. Although genetics plays a role, I believe that its impact on daily behaviour has been exaggerated. We live in a time when the thrust of scientific interest is towards genetic implications, and this trend has overshadowed the roles of environment, socialization and learning as well as the effects of education and attitudes.

Life can be a struggle between the forces of selflessness and altruism on the one hand and narcissistic selfishness on the other. The worst cases occur when people go to extremes. For example, to sacrifice one's own comfort and interests in service to humanity is a noble and altruistic act. But when one sacrifices to the point where one's health or family life is seriously compromised, one has gone too far. In the short term, such selflessness and sacrifice may evoke admiration, but in the long run it impedes further opportunity to render service: self-neglect will eventually bring about illness or disability, which will themselves cause problems for those who have to look after the person concerned.

Some behaviours stemming from self-centredness intensify into a materialistic lifestyle. Indifference or estrangement is one of these:

> When the souls become separated and selfish, the divine bounties do not descend, and the lights of the Supreme Concourse are no longer reflected even though the bodies meet together.[21]

Another is envy, or jealousy. This can affect anyone, especially when the environment is very competitive and self-orientation is common.

> Know, verily, that the heart wherein the least remnant of envy yet lingers, shall never attain My everlasting dominion, nor inhale the sweet savours of holiness breathing from My kingdom of sanctity.[22]

Backbiting is another divisive behaviour which 'quencheth the light of the heart, and extinguisheth the life of the soul'.[23]

These behavioural deficits all stem from the passion of self-love and self-centredness. The materialistic family or social environment is especially fertile in disseminating these vices, which impede individual growth, spiritual susceptibility and the progress of society.

A South African-made comedy film released in the 1980s, *The Gods Must Be Crazy*, demonstrates how greed and jealousy can destroy the calm, peaceful life of a tribal population. A tribe of Bushmen living off the land in a remote part of the Kalahari Desert are content because the 'gods' have provided for all their needs. They are completely unaware of civilization and technology. One day a pilot, passing overhead, tosses a Coca-Cola bottle out of his plane. It lands near the tribe. Thinking that this object is a gift from the gods, the tribe is at first delighted. Up to this point in their lives, the concept of property has never been an issue because there has always been enough of everything they need. But the bottle poses a problem because there are several tribe members and only one bottle. The intense desire to possess the new object creates a struggle; people began to experience emotions they have never felt before, such as envy, greed, jealousy, anger and hatred. Violence erupts, causing the tribe's leader, Xi, to decide that the bottle is 'evil', that the gods are crazy and that he needs to get rid this evil object. With the bottle in hand, he sets out to find the edge of the earth so that he can drop the bottle off it. In his quest to get rid of the bottle he encounters western civilization, and the film goes on to show his struggle in a new world he has never dreamed of before. The comedy exposes human temptation and desire to possess at all costs, even at the cost of a peaceful life.

Making the right choices

In light of the above, how, in a world so full of economic disparities and the afflictions that stem from them, are even the most basic survival needs of all the world's peoples to be met? How – on what basis – will we choose to meet the multiple challenges outlined in the last two chapters? A critical and yet enlightening analysis is made by Jeffrey Sachs in his article 'Common Wealth' (2008), which takes the example of malaria and its impact as a killer disease in Africa:

> Three hundred million antimalaria bed nets are needed to protect impoverished Africans from the disease. Each net costs $5 and lasts five years, for a total cost of $1.5 billion over five years. Yet that is less than one day's Pentagon spending!

Add in the costs of medicines and ongoing delivery services, and we find that comprehensive malaria control would cost less than two days' Pentagon spending each year . . .[24]

Sachs explores the changing character of the global economy and the challenge that human society has to face in making the right choices in terms of sustainable development. 'The 21st century', he writes,

> will overturn many of our basic assumptions about economic life. The 20th century saw the end of European dominance of global politics and economics. The 21st century will see the end of American dominance too, as new powers, including China, India and Brazil, continue to grow and make their voices heard on the world stage. Yet the century's changes will be even deeper than a rebalancing of economics and geo-politics . . . The defining challenge of the 21st century will be to face the reality that humanity shares a common fate on a crowded planet. We have reached the beginning of the century with 6.6 billion people living in an interconnected global economy producing an astounding $60 trillion of output each year. Human beings fill every ecological niche on the planet, from the icy tundra to the tropical rain forests to the deserts . . .[25]

He argues that we face a momentous choice. Either we continue our current course, which will mean that the world in which we live will likely experience growing conflict between the rich and the poor, as well as environmental catastrophes and a breakdown in the living standards of humanity from crises in energy, water, and food supplies, and disturbances caused by violence. An alternative to this is that through cooperation we harness technologies for better living, with reliable food supplies, clean energy, disease control and elimination of poverty:

That's why the idea that has the greatest potential to change the world is simply this: by overcoming cynicism, ending our misguided view of the world as an enduring struggle of 'us' vs. 'them' and instead seeking global solutions, we actually have the power to save the world for all, today and in the future. Whether we end up fighting one another or whether we work together to confront common threats – our fate, our common wealth, is in our hands.[26]

It is clear, then, that the issue of wealth and poverty requires much more in-depth reflection. At the heart of the matter is our attitude toward money and its wise spending. As to whether we should fear money or wealth, the following statement by the Universal House of Justice clarifies the matter:

As to your fear over money, the acquisition of wealth is not in itself a fearsome objective, it is a practical necessity. The problem with wealth arises from inappropriate attitudes toward possessing and using it . . .[27]

In addition, Shoghi Effendi emphasizes 'the social function of wealth, and the consequent necessity of avoiding its over-accumulation and concentration in a few individuals or groups of individuals'.[28]

As to whether it is possible to establish material equality for all people of the planet, this subject requires in-depth evaluation of the distribution of wealth and the feasibility of such a notion. According to an analysis by the Bahá'í International Community,

material equality is neither achievable nor desirable. Absolute equality is a chimera. At various points along the way, there will nevertheless be the necessity for the redistribution of some of the world's wealth. For, indeed, it is becoming increasingly obvious that unbridled capitalism does not provide the answer either. Some regulation and redistribution is necessary to promote material justice . . . Equal opportunities for economic advancement and progress, however, must be woven into the very fabric of the new order. Ultimately, the most important regulation on any economic system is the moral regulation that begins in the hearts and minds of people.[29]

Economic justice and the equitable distribution of wealth are of paramount importance in the social teachings of the Bahá'í Faith. According to Shoghi Effendi, Bahá'u'lláh 'provided for the essentials of a Divine Economy' which in his view was an 'inestimable gift to mankind'.[30] It will breathe new life into and transform economics by applying spiritual principles to the material condition of humankind.[31]

In the Bahá'í teachings, the spiritualization of work as an act of worship has elevated the significance of work and its contribution to humanity. Such spiritual acts of service, imbued with purity of motive and honesty of purpose, will stand in contrast to the selfish greed and competitive behaviour so rampant in the present-day economic system whose primary objective is the accumulation of wealth, and its consequent injustice.

Writing in 1944 about the admonitions of Bahá'u'lláh, Shoghi Effendi stated:

> Through the warnings He sounded, an unheeding humanity, steeped in materialism and forgetful of its God, had been apprized of the perils threatening to disrupt its ordered life, and made, in consequence of its persistent perversity, to sustain the initial shocks of that world upheaval which continues until the present day, to rock the foundations of human society.[32]

Many of the current social ills and crises of humanity – including those discussed above – are related to material discontent. People don't seem to ever be content or feel that they have enough. Many suffer from the illusion that if they had a little more income, they would be content and happy. But it is not material gain which will bring the satisfaction they seek. What is needed is deeper than that – a spiritual fulfilment within the heart. The next chapter will further explore Bahá'í perspectives on these matters.

Bahá'u'lláh states: 'Every created thing in the whole universe is but a door leading into His knowledge, a sign of His sovereignty, a revelation of His names, a symbol of His majesty, a token of His power . . .'[33] And again,

> every time I turn my gaze to Thine earth, I am made to recognize the evidences of Thy power and the token of Thy bounty. And when I behold the sea, I find that it speaketh to me of Thy majesty, and of the potency of Thy might, and of Thy sovereignty and Thy grandeur. And at whatever time I contemplate the mountains, I am led to discover the ensigns of Thy victory and the standards of Thine omnipotence.[34]

With this beautiful and mystic illustration of the earth and its environmental forces, Bahá'u'lláh expands our consciousness of the world in which we live and gives new meaning to it.

CHAPTER 10

BAHÁ'Í PERSPECTIVES ON MATERIALISM

The future civilization envisaged by Baha'u'llah is a prosperous
one, in which the vast resources of the world will be directed
towards humanity's elevation and regeneration, not its debase-
ment and destruction.
The Universal House of Justice[1]

The Bahá'í teachings are optimistic about the future of the world.
They look towards a peaceful global civilization characterized
by the spiritualization of mankind, the 'coming of age' of the
human race. But also, in the Bahá'í view, the world today is 'sunk
in materialism';[2] people are affected by the forces of a 'rampant
and brutal materialism'.[3] Shoghi Effendi pointed out that 'the
most precious fruits of civilization are undergoing severe and
unparalleled tests'.[4] In a letter to Bahá'ís in the United States he
wrote:

> The gross materialism that engulfs the entire nation at the
> present hour; the attachment to worldly things that enshrouds
> the souls of men; the fear and anxieties that distract their
> minds; the pleasure and dissipations that fill their time, the
> prejudices and animosities that darken their outlook, the
> apathy and lethargy that paralyze their spiritual faculties –
> these are among the formidable obstacles that stand in the
> path of every would-be warrior in the service of Bahá'u'lláh,

obstacles which he must battle against and surmount in his
crusade for the redemption of his own countrymen . . .⁵

Today, this 'crusade for the redemption' of the human race is ever
present in our minds and souls as the world of humanity enters its
darkest hours of a crumbling and corrupt civilization.

Shoghi Effendi explains that Bahá'u'lláh likens materialism to
a 'devouring flame' and regards it as 'the chief factor in precipitat-
ing the dire ordeals and world-shaking crises that must necessarily
involve the burning of cities and spread of terror in the hearts
of men . . .'⁶ At a time when 'terror' and 'terrorism' are expressions which evoke the fear of religious extremism, they also call
to mind their other roots in godlessness. The Universal House
of Justice (the international governing body of the Bahá'í Faith)
has described this particularly twentieth-century phenomenon as
follows:

Early in the twentieth century, a materialistic interpretation of
reality had consolidated itself so completely as to become the
dominant world faith insofar as the direction of society was
concerned. In the process, the civilizing of human nature had
been violently wrenched out of the orbit it had followed for
millennia. For many in the West, the Divine authority that had
functioned as the focal centre of guidance – however diverse
the interpretations of its nature – seemed simply to have dis-
solved and vanished. In large measure, the individual was left
free to maintain whatever relationship he believed connected
his life to a world transcending material existence, but society
as a whole proceeded with growing confidence to sever dependence on a conception of the universe that was judged to be at
best a fiction and at worst an opiate, in either case inhibiting
progress. Humanity had taken its destiny into its own hands.
It had solved through rational experimentation and discourse –
so people were given to believe – all of the fundamental issues
related to human governance and development.⁷

Yet materialism and its offspring cult of individualism have contributed to the process of separation of people from one another. The result has been a widespread sense of loneliness in the industrialized world, even in heavily populated areas such as London, New York and Chicago. The materialistic attitude to life, with its craving for wealth, social status and luxury, leads to a lifestyle that fosters isolation and self-centredness.

Within the family, the interaction of parents and children has also been affected by the climate of preoccupation with material things. In common with so many others, Bahá'ís are concerned about their children:

> Our children need to be nurtured spiritually and to be integrated into the life of the Cause . . . Children find themselves alienated by parents and other adults whether they live in conditions of wealth or poverty. This alienation has its roots in a selfishness that is born of materialism that is at the core of the godlessness seizing the hearts of people everywhere.[8]

The 'rise and consolidation' of materialism is referred to in the Bahá'í writings as a 'disease of the human soul' far more destructive than any of the direct consequences of materialism in the world:

> Its triumph marked a new and ominous stage in the process of social and spiritual degeneration that Shoghi Effendi had identified. Fathered by nineteenth century European thought, acquiring enormous influence through the achievements of American capitalist culture, and endowed by Marxism with the counterfeit credibility peculiar to that system, materialism emerged full-blown in the second half of the twentieth century as a kind of universal religion claiming absolute authority in both the personal and social life of humankind. Its creed was simplicity itself . . . The goal of human life is, or ought to be, the satisfaction of material needs and wants. Society exists to

facilitate this quest, and the collective concern of humankind should be an ongoing refinement of the system, aimed at rendering it ever more efficient in carrying out its assigned task.[9]

With the pervasive spread of materialism, religion has been reduced to a phenomenon marked by prejudices and perceived as a system designed to satisfy individuals' unfulfilled emotional needs or their fanatic spiritual ideology. The influence of a materialistic mindset has engulfed the academic community as well:

> The academic world, once the scene of great exploits of the mind and spirit, settled into the role of a kind of scholastic industry preoccupied with tending its machinery of dissertations, symposia, publication credits and grants.[10]

Addressing the longstanding dogma of materialism, the Universal House of Justice stated in 1985:

> How tragic is the record of the substitute faiths that the worldly-wise of our age have created. In the massive disillusionment of entire populations who have been taught to worship at their altars can be read history's irreversible verdict on their value. The fruits these doctrines have produced, after decades of an increasingly unrestrained exercise of power by those who owe their ascendancy in human affairs to them, are the social and economic ills that blight every region of our world in the closing years of the twentieth century. Underlying all these outward afflictions is the spiritual damage reflected in the apathy that has gripped the mass of the peoples of all nations and by the extinction of hope in the hearts of deprived and anguished millions.
>
> The time has come when those who preach the dogmas of materialism, whether of the east or the west, whether of capitalism or socialism, must give account of the moral stewardship they have presumed to exercise. Where is the 'new

world' promised by these ideologies? Where is the international peace to whose ideals they proclaim their devotion? Where are the breakthroughs into new realms of cultural achievement produced by the aggrandizement of this race, of that nation or of a particular class? Why is the vast majority of the world's peoples sinking ever deeper into hunger and wretchedness when wealth on a scale undreamed of by the Pharaohs, the Caesars, or even the imperialist powers of the nineteenth century is at the disposal of the present arbiters of human affairs?[11]

Two calls to success and prosperity

'Abdu'l-Bahá states that 'two calls to success and prosperity are being raised from the heights of the happiness of mankind'.[12] One is the 'call of civilization, of the progress of the material world'. The other is 'the soul-stirring call of God' for spiritual teachings and the illumination of the world of humanity. However, until material achievements and accomplishments are reinforced by spiritual perfections, no fruit or result can be expected, nor will happiness, which is the ultimate aim of these calls, be attained. Although material and physical achievements bring about prosperity, this progress needs to be sustained through divine education. Otherwise, 'severe calamities and violent afflictions are imminent . . . Therefore, this civilization and material progress should be combined with the Most Great Guidance so that this nether world may become the scene of the appearance of the bestowals of the Kingdom . . .'[13]

'Abdu'l-Bahá further explains that throughout succeeding centuries and ages in history, the call of civilization has been raised and the world of humanity has been progressing day by day until it achieved 'the universal capacity to receive the spiritual teachings and to hearken to the Divine Call'.[14] We in our time are witnessing the quality and intensity of humanity's response to the second call – which will bring either a desirable result or 'violent afflictions'.

Addressing a wayward humanity which has refused to accept the message of Bahá'u'lláh, the Promised One of all ages, the Bahá'í writings disclose the bleak future awaiting humankind as it declines into the abyss of materialism. 'Abdu'l-Bahá warned:

Chaos and confusion are daily increasing in the world. They will attain such intensity as to render the frame of mankind unable to bear them. Then will men be awakened and become aware that religion is the impregnable stronghold and the manifest light of the world, and its laws, exhortations and teaching, the source of life on earth.[15]

The Universal House of Justice, with its profound and divinely inspired vision of the plight of humanity, elaborates further on the culmination of the adolescent age of mankind and the trials and tribulations ahead:

Every discerning eye clearly sees that the early stages of this chaos have daily manifestations affecting the structure of human society; its destructive forces are uprooting time-honoured institutions which were a haven and refuge for the inhabitants of the earth in bygone days and centuries and around which revolved all human affairs. The same destructive forces are also deranging the political, economic, scientific, literary, and moral equilibrium of the world and are destroying the fairest fruits of the present civilization. Political machinations of those in authority have placed the seal of obsolescence upon the root-principles of the world's order. Greed and passion, deceit, hypocrisy, tyranny, and pride are dominating features afflict-ing human relations. Discoveries and inventions, which are the fruit of scientific and technological advancements, have become the means and tools of mass extermination and destruction and are in the hands of the ungodly. Even music, art, and litera-ture, which are to represent and inspire the noblest sentiments and highest aspirations and should be a source of comfort and tranquility for troubled souls, have strayed from the straight path and are now the mirrors of the soiled hearts of this confused, unprincipled and disordered age. Perversions such as these shall result in the ordeals which have been prophesied by the Blessed Beauty in the following words: '. . . the earth will be tormented by a fresh calamity every day and unprecedented commotions will break out.' 'The day is approaching when its [civilization's] flame will devour the cities.'[16]

The Universal House of Justice then comments that in such a difficult period of transition – which it describes as a formative age of the future world civilization – Baha'is should strive 'to build amidst these tumultuous waves an impregnable stronghold which will be the sole remaining refuge for those lost multitudes'.[17]

The cult of individualism

In examining present-day civilization and its crises, one can discern that at the core of it is a 'cult of individualism' which is contributing to the disintegration of contemporary society. It also intensifies the weakening of moral standards and the spread of lawlessness, violence and crime to an extent where no force will be able to provide significant abatement and recovery except through a fundamental change in moral consciousness and human behaviour.[18] Indeed, 'Abdu'l-Bahá explains that

> it is impossible for a human being to turn aside from his own selfish advantages and sacrifice his own good for the good of the community except through true religious faith. For self-love is kneaded into the very clay of man, and it is not possible that, without any hope of a substantial reward, he should neglect his own present material good.[19]

However, if such an individual has faith in God and puts his trust in the Almighty with the hope and expectation of the 'abiding joy and glory of future planes of existence', he will abandon his own profit and will consecrate his heart and soul for the common good.[20]

The cult of individualism, which is the antithesis of a society focused on the good of the community and which is so pervasive in North America and in some other parts of the world, needs to be re-examined. Individualism has given a new meaning to human freedom:

> Concern that each human being should enjoy the freedom of thought and action conducive to his or her personal growth does not justify devotion to the cult of individualism that so deeply corrupts many areas of contemporary life. Nor does concern to ensure the welfare of society as a whole require a deification of the state as the supposed source of humanity's well being . . . Only in a consultative framework made possible by the consciousness of the organic unity of humankind can all aspects of the concern for human rights find legitimate and creative expression.[21]

The process of consultation is central to the task of redefinition and reorganization of the system of human relationships. In this respect, Bahá'u'lláh emphasizes that 'the maturity of the gift of understanding is made manifest through consultation'.[22]

In today's society, seeking truth and coming to an agreement is usually through argument, negotiation and compromise. This long-standing tradition is often handicapped by the culture of protest, propaganda biases and partisan manoeuvring of ideas for personal or collective gain. These are against the spirit of a wise consultative process of problem-solving. In the process of consultation, as understood in the Bahá'í teachings, individuals and groups have to detach themselves from their personal ideas and develop a sense of sharing and cooperation instead of competing through domination. It is an antidote to the current cult of individualism.[23]

In the Bahá'í view, the consciousness of the unity of humankind is to be regarded as the bedrock of any strategy for engaging the inhabitants of the planet to assume responsibility for facing its collective destiny. This consciousness is undoubtedly developing in the world today, but conflict is still too often accepted as the mainstream of human interaction – an attitude that reflects the materialistic view of life which has permeated the social organizations of society during the past two centuries.[24]

The cancer of materialism

Shoghi Effendi uses the metaphor of cancer to underline the insidious nature and pernicious impact of materialism. Depicting the spread of 'cancerous materialism' in the world as '. . . born originally in Europe, carried to excess in the North American continent, contaminating the Asiatic peoples and nations, spreading its ominous tentacles to the borders of Africa and now invading its very heart,'[25] he predicts that the cancer of materialism will have devastating effects on human society.

Cancer develops as a result of cells which begin to multiply and proliferate out of control. Normal cells also grow and multiply, but within the context of biological order. Cancer cells, however, recognize no limits or boundaries; they keep on multiplying and invading neighbouring cells until a malignant tumour is formed. This tumour then spreads to other organs. In brief, cancer develops quietly and then proliferates and destroys. Likewise, materialism has an abnormal pattern of growth, with insidious expansion and destruction. Like a biological cell, every person has the potential to develop this form of pernicious behaviour, just as he or she is also endowed with the capacity to evolve into a virtuous and spiritual individual. Cancer can develop and grow without the conscious awareness of the victim until it reaches to a dangerous state. Materialism also can grow insidiously in individuals without their being aware of the change. Those who become aware of such a cancer may deny its existence – or they may take it as a wake-up call for a new way of life.

Spiritual progress in a material world

According to the Bahá'í teachings, the human soul is a divine mystery far beyond our means of perception. The soul is not governed by the laws of nature; it belongs to the spiritual worlds of God. But the human physical body is subject to the laws of nature because its domain of operation is the material world. As individuals we are therefore endowed with a dual nature, both spiritual and physical.

The philosophers and sages of the past argued about where exactly the soul was in the body. Descartes, for example, believed that the tiny pineal gland in the brain was the seat of the soul. In the Bahá'í view, the soul has no specific place in the body: it is a non-material entity which originates from the worlds of God and, although it is associated with the body, neither enters nor leaves it. The Báb explains that our body, as a physical frame, is the 'throne of the inner temple' (soul).[26]

The relationship of the soul with the body ends with death. The soul returns to its original spiritual world while the body returns to dust, its origin. The soul takes only the good qualities it has developed to the next world; weakness, sin and evil are essentially the expression of an absence of noble virtues. A bad person is a soul poor in divine virtue.[27]

This material world is one of transition in which our soul, through the instrumentality of our physical frame, makes its progress and preparation for the next world. We are like tenants in our dwelling-places on this planet. We are not the owner of the dwelling, nor are we everlasting in our earthly life. Yet sometimes we become so attached to this physical plane that we lose our perspective of the larger universe around us.

'Abdu'l-Bahá, in a telling analogy, compares the life and freedom of a human being in this world with that of a bird:

A bird, on the summit of a mountain, on the high, waving branches, has built for itself a nest more beautiful than the palaces of the kings! The air is in the utmost purity, the water cool and clear as crystal, the panorama charming and enchanting. In such glorious surroundings, he expends his numbered days. All the harvest of the plain are his possessions, having earned all this wealth without the least labour. Hence, no matter how much man may advance in this world, he shall not attain to the station of this bird! Thus it becomes evident that in the matters of this world, however much man may strive and work to the point of death, he will be unable to earn the abundance, the freedom and the independent life of a small bird. This proves and establishes the fact that man is not created for the life of this ephemeral world – nay, rather, is he created for the acquirement of infinite perfections, for the attainment to the sublimity of the world of humanity, to be drawn nigh unto the divine threshold, and to sit on the throne of everlasting sovereignty![28]

Commenting on the meaning 'the world', Bahá'u'lláh states:

Know ye that by 'the world' is meant your unawareness of Him Who is your Maker, and your absorption in aught else but Him. The 'life to come,' on the other hand, signifieth the things that give you a safe approach to God, the All-Glorious, the Incomparable. Whatsoever deterreth you, in this Day, from loving God is nothing but the world . . .[29]

And furthermore:

Know ye that the world and its vanities and its embellishments shall pass away. Nothing will endure except God's Kingdom which pertaineth to none but Him, the Sovereign Lord of all . . . The days of your life shall roll away, and all the things with which ye are occupied and of which ye boast yourselves shall perish . . .[30]

Motion is one of the characteristics of the material as well as of the spiritual world. As 'Abdu'l-Bahá elucidates, in the material world

> absolute repose does not exist . . . Everything moves forward or backward, nothing is without motion. From his birth, man progresses physically until he reaches maturity, then, having arrived at the prime of his life, he begins to decline, the strength and powers of his body decrease, and he gradually arrives at the hour of death.[31]

Likewise, one sees progress and decline in the life of a plant or an animal. But in the life of a human soul there is only progress, there is no decline and no retrogression. A human soul's 'only movement is toward perfection; growth and progress alone constitute the motion of the soul'.[32]

And further,

> 'Progress' is the expression of spirit in the world of matter. The intelligence of man, his reasoning powers, his knowledge, his scientific achievements, all these being manifestations of the spirit, partake of the inevitable law of spiritual progress and are, therefore, of necessity, immortal.[33]

Through the above explanations we can deduce that in the process of material development there is progress and decline, highs and lows. But spiritual progress is continuous, towards perfection. There is no decline. However, the level of progress may vary from person to person.

The mysteries of detachment

Detachment from earthly interests has been defined as a 'state in which a person overcomes his or her attachment to desire for things, people or concepts of the world and thus attains a heightened perspective'.[34] In the western world, detachment is often perceived as a form of deprivation, and is often confused with renunciation of the world, a reclusive life in monasteries or the practice of self-mortification. But its true meaning is much more profound. In the Bahá'í Writings detachment is considered as one of the greatest achievements of human beings, enabling them to scale the loftiest heights of virtue and spirituality.[35]

Bahá'u'lláh states that this world is filled with material bounties and that possessing good things is not attachment. But He warns that the things of this world are transitory and that we should not fix our affections on them, nor should we allow ourselves to be possessed by them. And there is another dimension: detachment can be not only physical but also mental or spiritual – the 'concepts of the world'. For example, too much pride in personal opinions, accomplishments, social status and entitlement are all barriers to spiritual progress. Bahá'u'lláh writes:

> No man shall attain the shores of the ocean of true understanding except he be detached from all that is in heaven and on earth.[36]

We may understand what we are to be detached from on earth, but what do we need to avoid attachment to in heaven? This reflects the fact that detachment has both material and spiritual implications.

Bahá'u'lláh identified three barriers between individuals and God. The first is attachment to the things of this world, the second is attachment to the rewards of the next world and the third is attachment to the 'Kingdom of Names'.[37]

The first barrier represents the challenges to human beings in their evolution from material to spiritual existence. Desire and dependence on the vanities of this world characterize aspects of this barrier. Some people even join a religion with a view to possessing a treasure that will serve their personal interests or their ego. In such circumstances religion becomes an instrument for personal gain or a path to power, and not service to God and humanity.

The second barrier involves the rewards of paradise. Some people (such as suicide bombers) are ready to give their lives for the rewards of the next world, even if that entails endangering the lives of others. This is a reward-oriented attachment to desire of the world to come.

The third barrier is attachment to the 'Kingdom of Names'. Although every created thing manifests the names and attributes of God, becoming attached to any one of these attributes can become a barrier. For example, some may pride themselves on their generosity, others on their kindness or compassion, still others on their sense of justice. While all these qualities are praiseworthy, to pride oneself on having them is attachment to the 'Kingdom of Names'.

So what is detachment? At its most basic level, it is the renunciation of attachment in order to achieve a greater realization of the meaning of creation and of the purpose of life. The strength of one's detachment can be tested in everyday life. 'Abdu'l-Bahá used to tell a story about Ios, the wise and trusted servant of a king.

The King decided to go on a Royal Tour of his kingdom. Preparations started immediately and within a few days the magnificent procession was ready to leave. The ministers of the King's government, ambassadors and diplomats, courtiers and men of importance, soldiers and bandsmen, all splendid in their finery, set out to accompany the King. And, of course, the faithful Ios rode alongside his beloved master at the front of the throng.

Each evening the splendid party made camp and the wonderful imperial tent was erected for the King. This tent was the most beautiful and precious tent you have ever seen – woven from the finest silk, it was decorated with hundreds of jewels and precious stones, which so shone and sparkled . . . one day, as the King and his retinue were making their way through some especially beautiful countryside, the King remembered that he had passed this way before. It had been on this very stretch of road, years ago, that he had first glanced upon the adoring face of his faithful Ios.

In gratitude for that meeting the King, seized of a sudden impulse, took the box of jewels and cast them on the road.

As the procession went on its way the King looked back to see all his followers, all except Ios, forgetful of their duty, scrambling on the ground in great confusion trying to gather up the precious stones.

'Look at Ios,' they muttered to each other, 'see how proud he is, he even despises the King's jewels and makes no effort to pick them up.'

'How is it, Ios,' the King asked him, 'that you do not join the others to gather up my jewels? Are they not precious? Do you despise the very things that were mine?'

'O my King,' replied Ios, 'never in my life have I despised the least thing that is yours. But to be near you and gaze on your face has always been more than sufficient for me. Why should I leave your side to scramble for what you have thrown away?'

And the loyal and steadfast Ios rode on by the side of his grateful master, his gaze never for a moment leaving the face of his beloved King.[38]

Another story illustrates that detachment has nothing to do with the number of possessions one has:

There was once a king who had many spiritual qualities and whose deeds were based on justice and loving-kindness. He often envied the dervish[39] who had renounced the world and appeared to be free from the cares of this material life, for he roamed the country, slept in any place when night fell and chanted the praises of his Lord during the day. He lived in poverty, yet thought he owned the whole world. His only possessions were his clothes and a basket in which he carried the food donated by his well-wishers. The king was attracted to this way of life.

Once he invited a well-known dervish to his palace, sat at his feet and begged him for some lessons about detachment. The dervish was delighted with the invitation. He stayed a few days in the palace and whenever the king was free preached the virtues of a mendicant's life to him. At last the king was converted. One day, dressed in the garb of a poor man, he left his palace in the company of the dervish. They had walked together some distance when the dervish realized that he had left his basket behind in the palace. This disturbed him greatly and, informing the king that he could not go without his basket, he begged permission to return for it. But the king admonished him, saying that he himself had left behind his palaces, his wealth and power, whereas the dervish, who had preached for a lifetime the virtues of detachment, had at last been tested and was found to be attached to this world – his small basket.[40]

Bahá'í history is also replete with examples of detachment. For instance, there was a well-known, wealthy merchant whose father owned one of the best-known turquoise mines of Nishapour, in Iran. He joined Mullá Ḥusayn, the first to embrace the Faith of the Báb, in the heroic attempt to rescue Quddús. On their way to Mazindaran, Mullá Ḥusayn asked his companions to discard their possessions as a symbol of their renunciation of all earthly things and material interests. The merchant was the first to respond; he immediately threw aside his satchel which contained precious turquoise stones brought with him from his father's mine. This was an act of faith and detachment amidst the great adversity of those days.

Bahá'u'lláh writes:

Earthly treasures We have not bequeathed, nor have We added such cares as they entail. By God! In earthly riches fear is hidden and peril is concealed.[41]

Busy not thyself with this world, for with fire We test the gold, and with gold We test Our servants.[42]

In his diary of the days of 'Abdu'l-Bahá's journey in North America, Mírzá Maḥmúd recounts the Master's refusal of all offers of funds and gifts from the friends, a sign of His magnanimity and detachment.

Today some of the friends offered money to the Master but He would not accept it despite their pleading. Instead He told them, 'Distribute it among the poor on my behalf. It will be as though I have given it to them. But the most acceptable gift to me is the unity of the believers, service to the Cause of God, diffusion of the divine fragrances and adherence to the counsels of the Abhá Beauty.'

The believers were saddened because He did not accept their gifts. However, since these were the last days of His visit and He was about to leave, the New York Bahá'ís collected several gifts for the women of the holy household and for the Greatest Holy Leaf . . .

Some of the believers agreed among themselves to go to 'Abdu'l-Bahá and cling to His robe until He accepted their gifts. They came and begged He accept their offerings. The Master called them, saying:

'I am most grateful for your services; in truth you have served me. You have extended hospitality. Night and day you have been ready to serve and to diffuse the divine fragrances. I shall never forget your services, for you have no purpose but the will of God and you desire no station but entry into the Kingdom of God. Now you have brought presents for the members of my family. They are most acceptable and excellent but better than all these are the gifts of the love of God which remain preserved in the treasuries of the heart. These gifts are evanescent but those are eternal; these jewels must be kept in boxes and vaults and they will eventually perish but those jewels remain in the treasuries of the heart and will remain throughout the world of God for eternity. Thus I will take to them your love, which is the greatest of all gifts. In our house they do not wear diamond rings nor do they keep rubies. That house is sanctified above such adornments.

'I, however, have accepted your gifts; but I entrust them to you for you to sell and send the proceeds to the fund for the Mashriqu'l-Adhkár [House of Worship] in Chicago.'

When the friends continued to plead with Him, He said: 'I want to take from you a present which will endure in the eternal world and a jewel which belongs to the treasures of the heart. This is better.[43]

Detachment also has implications for our expectations while engaged in prayer and meditation. Even worship, an act of such spiritual significance, cannot escape the scrutiny of detachment. The Báb advises,

Worship thou God in such wise that if thy worship lead thee to the fire, no alteration in thine adoration would be produced, and so likewise if thy recompense should be paradise. Thus and thus alone should be the worship which befitteth the one True God. Shouldst thou worship Him because of fear, this would be unseemly in the sanctified Court of His presence, and could not be regarded as an act by thee dedicated to the Oneness of His Being. Or if thy gaze should be on paradise, and thou shouldst worship Him while cherishing such a hope, thou wouldst make God's creation a partner with Him, notwithstanding the fact that paradise is desired by men.[44]

In a letter to a believer, Shoghi Effendi comments on the expectation of a worshipper:

> The true worshipper, while praying, should endeavour not so much to ask God to fulfil his wishes and desires, but rather to adjust these and make them to conform to the Divine Will. Only through such an attitude can one derive that feeling of inner peace and contentment which the power of prayer alone can confer.[45]

In one of His prayers, the Báb reveals how God in His divine wisdom will test individuals:

> Indeed shouldst Thou desire to confer blessing upon a servant Thou wouldst blot out from the realm of his heart every mention or disposition except Thine Own mention; and shouldst Thou ordain evil for a servant by reason of that which his hands have unjustly wrought before Thy face, Thou wouldst test him with the benefits of this world and of the next that he might become preoccupied therewith and forget Thy remembrance.[46]

In the mystic stages of the Seven Valleys we learn that the traveller passing through the Valley of Contentment 'burneth the veils of want'.[47] This consumption of the veils of desire is an expression of the conquest of the lower nature by the power of the higher or spiritual nature. In this stage, the traveller may be outwardly poor but is inwardly rich and endowed with spiritual strength. The final station of this journey, the Valley of True Poverty and Absolute Nothingness, is the culmination of detachment and the dawn of a new emancipation. Detachment is a state of freedom from the captivity of the perishable dominion, whether it be 'outer wealth or personal opinions', and is 'dying from self and living in God'.[48]

During my career as a physician I have often wondered about

the wisdom of the physical and emotional pain and suffering endured by patients in their terminal stages, and how God in His benevolent wisdom prepares them to detach and separate themselves from the world to which they will soon no longer belong. But this should not be perceived as an encouragement to avoid alleviation of pain and discomfort. Indeed, with modern medicine, and all the forms of tranquillizers and analgesics now available, it is now possible to make passing to the next world less disturbing. There is more and more debate about how to die happily; some overzealous companies even present their insurance products with such magnanimity as though they are divinely ordained gatekeepers of heaven! It is interesting how the consumer mindset and the pursuit of happiness can haunt us to the very end. Hard and arduous is the plight of those who don't want to give up their earthly abode.

Since the purpose of religion is to guide humanity to true happiness, is detachment a bridge to our ultimate destiny?

Meanings of self and transformation

In the Bahá'í view, self has two meanings, as Shoghi Effendi explains. One relates to the individual identity created by God: passages such as 'he hath known God who hath known himself' are a reference to this kind of self.[49] The other meaning is 'self' as the ego, 'the dark, animalistic heritage each one of us has, the lower nature that can develop into a monster of selfishness, brutality, lust and so on'. It is the latter sense of self that we must struggle against and overcome in order to be liberated from its influence. Self-sacrifice means to subordinate this lower nature to a higher and nobler side of ourselves.[50]

Self can be a 'veil' which deprives individuals of truth. 'Suffer not yourselves to be wrapt in the dense veils of your selfish desires,' writes Bahá'u'lláh.[51] The term 'self-love' has been referred to in the Bahá'í Writings as 'a strange trait and the means of the destruction of many important souls in the world. If man be imbued with all good qualities but be selfish, all the other virtues will fade or pass away and eventually he will grow worse.'[52]

In present-day psychology and the general perceptions of people, self-love is the ultimate state of selfhood, a cherished goal, especially among youth. From popular music to a range of psychoactive and stimulating illicit drugs, all are tools for the perfecting of self-love and the gratification of natural impulses. Self-love can also grow without the assistance of these extrinsic elements: it can be due to self-centredness and narcissism to the exclusion of others, including loved ones. Excessive greed, selfish pride and self-glorification are just a few symptoms of this form of self.

The human ability to change and to convert lower or animal attributes into higher spiritual qualities is referred to as spiritual transformation and development. This is 'spiritual progress'. But such a vital change is not easy; it becomes possible through the 'breaths of the Holy Spirit and is the awakening of the conscious soul of man . . .'[53]

'Abdu'l-Bahá elaborates on spiritual transformation through the acquisition of heavenly qualities and attributes. He uses the expression 'sacrifice' to mean bringing about such a transformation. In discussing how to distinguish the qualities and attributes of the world of nature from those of the world of God, He gives the example of a material substance such as iron and how its qualities can be changed:

> Observe its qualities; it is solid, black, cold. These are the characteristics of iron. When the same iron absorbs heat from the fire, it sacrifices its attribute of solidity for the attributes of fluidity. It sacrifices its attribute of darkness for the attribute of light, which is a quality of the fire. It sacrifices its attribute of coldness to the quality of heat which the fire possesses so that in the iron there remains no solidity, darkness or cold. It becomes illumined and transformed, having sacrificed its qualities to the qualities and attributes of the fire.[54]

Following this metaphor, 'Abdu'l-Bahá tells us that human beings, by severing themselves from the attributes of this material world, sacrifice its qualities and exigencies in order to manifest 'the perfections of the Kingdom'.[55] We also perceive from the metaphor that transformation to the state of possessing a higher quality or attribute is not free from pain and hardship

'Abdu'l-Bahá emphasizes that a heavenly and illumined individual stands 'in the station of sacrifice' and expresses the hope that Bahá'ís, through divine providence and bounties, may be 'entirely severed from the imperfections of the world of nature, purified from selfish, human desires, receiving life from the Kingdom of Abhá and attaining heavenly graces'.[56]

This process of transformation is unique; the force behind such an empowerment to change from one state or quality to another is potent and profound. Bahá'u'lláh elucidates the dynamics of the phenomenon of change in the following words:

> Is it within human power, O Ḥakím, to effect in the constituent elements of any of the minute and indivisible particles of matter so complete a transformation as to transmute it into purest gold? Perplexing and difficult as this may appear, the still greater task of converting satanic strength into heavenly power is one that We have been empowered to accomplish. The Force capable of such a transformation transcendeth the potency of the Elixir itself. The Word of God, alone, can claim the distinction of being endowed with the capacity required for so great and far-reaching a change.[57]

In the future, the behavioural sciences will be enlightened with new insights to facilitate the transformation of human character. In the next chapter we will explore some of the implications of such a change, and how it can be brought about.

CHAPTER 11

SPIRITUAL DIMENSIONS OF HUMAN PROSPERITY

Material progress ensures the happiness of the human world.
Spiritual progress ensures the happiness and eternal continuance
of the soul.
'Abdu'l-Bahá[1]

Spirituality and personal transformation

Personal transformation is a popular topic today, much debated
and written about. But it is not possible without self-evaluation,
reflection and objectivity. Personal transformation is a process
which takes place when the soul is empowered to express its
full potential. Each individual is endowed with the capacity to
realize this potential. But as no one can fully comprehend the
nature and significance of the soul, defining spirituality is a difficult task, particularly today when spirituality is either denied or
misinterpreted. And we are living in a time when everyone wants
to change everybody but himself. No one seems to want to take
responsibility for his or her own spiritual well-being.

Observing the situation in the world today, we are reminded
that

> while new levels of consensus have been reached in global
> programmes to promote health, sustainable development
> and human rights, the situation on the ground in many areas

has deteriorated. The alarming spread of militant racialism and religious fanaticism, the cancerous growth of materialism, the epidemic rise of crime and organized criminality, the widespread increase in mindless violence, the ever-deepening disparity between rich and poor, the continuing inequities faced by women, the intergenerational damage caused by the pervasive break-down of family life, the immoral excesses of unbridled capitalism and the growth of political corruption – all speak to this point.[2]

To bring about a moral and spiritual transformation to such a troubled global community is a formidable task. Perhaps one of the first important challenges with respect to the application of moral principles is the current lack or loss of a clear vision about the true purpose of life and the meaning of civilization. For the majority of people, their view of the purpose of life is influenced by materialistic thinking without spiritual mindfulness. Others base their views on a fanatic and distorted religious ideology which no longer conforms to the original essence of divine education which they have espoused. Yet another group, indifferent to either of the above notions, feels lost and hopeless about the plight of humanity.

In such a mosaic of human ideologies, promoting human virtues and intrinsic spiritual values may be perceived as a utopian notion. Yet the well-being and prosperity of any civilized society depends on a system of values and teachings which are not man-made, racially biased or politically motivated, but inspired by divine revelation which can respond to the needs and challenges of that society – today, a global society.

For Bahá'ís, the purpose of life is explained by Bahá'u'lláh and 'Abdu'l-Bahá in many different contexts. On an individual level, it is expressed in a prayer used daily by Bahá'ís: 'I bear witness, O my God, that Thou hast created me to know Thee and to worship Thee . . .'[3] In a wider context, 'All men have been created to carry forward an ever-advancing civilization'.[4] The founders of the world religions, 'divine educators', have been sent by God throughout history to enable humanity to acquire these capacities. This 'progressive revelation' is a unique characteristic of Bahá'í teaching.

It is beyond the scope of this book to discuss in detail how human beings have come to their present stage of development. The following statement by 'Abdu'l-Bahá elucidates a Bahá'í understanding of evolution and the future destiny of humanity.

In the world of existence man has traversed successive degrees until he has attained the human kingdom. In each degree of his progression he has developed capacity for advancement to the next station and condition. While in the kingdom of the mineral he was attaining the capacity for promotion into the degree of the vegetable. In the kingdom of the vegetable he underwent preparation for the world of the animal and from thence he has come onward to the human degree or kingdom. Throughout this journey of progression he has ever and always been potentially man.

In the beginning of his human life man was embryonic in the world of the matrix. There he received capacity and endowment for the reality of human existence. The forces and powers necessary for this world were bestowed upon him in that limited condition. In this world he needed eyes; he received them potentially in the other. He needed ears; he obtained them there in readiness and preparation for his new existence. The powers requisite in this world were conferred upon him in the world of the matrix so that when he entered this realm of real existence he not only possessed all necessary functions and powers but found provision for his material sustenance awaiting him.

Therefore, in this world he must prepare himself for the life beyond. That which he needs in the world of the Kingdom must be obtained here. Just as he prepared himself in the world of the matrix by acquiring forces necessary in this sphere of existence, so likewise the indispensable forces of the divine existence must be potentially attained in this world.

What is he in need of in the Kingdom which transcends the life and limitation of this mortal sphere? That world beyond is a world of sanctity and radiance; therefore it is necessary that in this world he should acquire these divine attributes. In that world there is need of spirituality, faith, assurance, the knowledge and love of God. These he must attain in this world so that after his ascension from the earthly to the heavenly Kingdom he shall find all that is needful in that life eternal ready for him.[5]

Bahá'u'lláh compares the world to the human body: individuals are like cells, which are interrelated in their functions with respect to the organic growth of the body. The cells are different from each other in the various organs but are united in their biological goal of maintaining the vitality of the entire body. There is a unity in diversity in the microcosm of the work of cells and organs of the body, as there should be in the human community at large. This is a reciprocal relationship. Human consciousness in an individual, undistracted by the diversity of cells and their functions, continues to rule, preserving the integrity and well-being of the person as a whole.[6]

Spiritual progress in the material world requires the development of capacity to acquire virtues to fulfil the true purpose of life. 'To act like the beasts of the field is unworthy of man,' writes Bahá'u'lláh. 'Those virtues that befit his dignity are forbearance, mercy, compassion and loving-kindness towards all the peoples and kindreds of the earth.'[7]

The Bahá'í concept of spirituality is based on the concept that there is an everlasting relationship between the soul and its Creator. This is a dynamic and evolutionary process whose primary purpose is to draw the soul nearer to God. By turning to God the soul will be empowered to bring about that personal transformation which manifests itself in relation to others. The creative words of Bahá'u'lláh are endowed with the power to transform hearts. References are made in all sacred scriptures to the meaning of the metaphor 'heart', which in physical terms is the lifeline of human existence. 'Heart' is also a symbolic expression of human conscience.

In the Bahá'í Writings there are references to suggest that the heart is the seat of revelation, a home, a city upon which God's grace will descend. For example, Bahá'u'lláh writes, 'O Son of Being! Thy heart is My home; sanctify it for My descent.'[8] And also:

> O Son of Dust! All that is in heaven and earth I have ordained for thee, except the human heart, which I have made the habitation of My beauty and glory; yet thou didst give My home and dwelling to another than Me and whenever the manifestation of My holiness sought His own abode, a stranger found He there and, homeless, hastened to the sanctuary of the Beloved.[9]

In this passage, Bahá'u'lláh speaks of 'home', 'friend', and 'stranger'. The stranger which occupies the heart could be material attachment or an egoistic self-centredness. Personal transformation will be very difficult if not impossible so long as this stranger is present in the home.

The human heart needs to be illumined with the spirit of faith. To do so, it must detach itself from love of the material world, otherwise it will become a host to the 'stranger' and be filled with 'self-love'. Bahá'u'lláh writes:

> O My Friend in Word! Ponder awhile. Hast thou ever heard that friend and foe should abide in one heart? Cast out then the stranger, that the Friend may enter His home.[10]

The human heart is like a mirror. A mirror covered by dust can't reflect light until it is cleaned and cleared of dust. In the words of Bahá'u'lláh:

> . . . the heart is the dwelling of eternal mysteries, make it not the home of fleeting fancies; waste not the treasure of thy precious life in employment with this swiftly passing world. Thou comest from the world of holiness – bind not thine heart to the earth . . .[11]

The development of spirituality is a gradual and life-long process for each person. Spirituality is an expression of one's attraction to God and the progress of the soul toward its Creator. This progress is like the journey of a traveller who longs for the end of the journey, traversing valleys, mountains and plains and meeting all conditions, both opportunities and obstacles. In this analogy, the soul (the traveller) looks forward to the end of its journey in this world, longing for reunion with its Beloved in the realm of eternity. It encounters opportunities and barriers, which it must overcome in order to grow and develop. If it weren't for the reunion with the Beloved after all these trials and tribulations, the journey would have no end or meaning.

This concept of the journey of the soul has parallels in all sacred scripture and religious literature, notably, for the West, in Bunyan's *Pilgrim's Progress*. In *The Seven Valleys* Bahá'u'lláh illustrates the stages, cities and valleys that a soul will have to traverse in order to reach the abode of the Beloved. The journey begins with the Valley of Search, where the traveller must 'cleanse the heart – which is the wellspring of divine treasures – from every marking' and from imitation of others.[12] This is a search whose quality is that of the search of a lover for the beloved; to be successful it must be free from all forms of prejudice. Then comes the Valley of Love, where the traveller must give up his or her self-interest and personal desires in order to find the Beloved. Once through this stage, the traveller will enter the Valley of Knowledge and subsequently pass through other Valleys – Unity, Contentment,

Wonderment –to reach the Valley of Poverty and Absolute Nothingness. In this Valley the traveller becomes poor, utterly nothing in himself, but rich in drawing near to the Creator. During the journey the soul encounters signs and guiding lights to ensure its progress in the path of love and knowledge for God.

We have said earlier that to acquire spirituality one has to acquire faith. And to acquire faith one needs to open one's heart to the Manifestation of God. Today, Bahá'ís believe, this is Bahá'u'lláh, the latest of the divine educators sent by God to humanity. Opening one's heart means to detach oneself from all defilement and earthly attachments, in other words, to detach oneself from that 'stranger' and to develop the love and knowledge of God. The Bahá'í Writings not only give us a new vision of life, but a road map for personal development.

Spirituality is a phenomenon which knows no boundaries. It seeks no status, no nationality, no language barrier or gender differences. It knows no limit of knowledge, nor does it discriminate as to colour or race: a healthy soul is entirely free from prejudice. Progress is the essential characteristic of the soul. Spirituality makes no distinction between the poor and the rich, although the rich may find it harder to attain and sustain this experience. You don't have to have a university degree in order to be spiritual!

'Abdu'l-Bahá identified seven 'means' which are necessary to spiritual transformation.[13] These are:

1. The knowledge of God
2. The love of God
3. Faith
4. Philanthropic deeds
5. Self-sacrifice
6. Severance from this world
7. Sanctity and holiness

Among the obstacles along the path to spirituality are materialism, egotism and loss of contact with the divine reality. Materialism

and attachment to worldly vanities are among the most challenging obstacles to overcome. The individual development of
spirituality requires not only knowledge of sacred teachings but
also the will to translate this knowledge into action and service
to humanity, in order to contribute to the advancement of an
everlasting civilization, to pray and meditate about the purpose of
life and its spiritual destiny and to live one's life according to the
divine teachings for the age one lives in. Active teaching of these
things is itself considered essential to spiritual growth.

'Abdu'l-Bahá states that the way to acquire a thirst for spirituality is to 'meditate on the future life'.[14] This kind of meditation
and reflection awakens the soul from the slumber of self-centredness and egotism. Shoghi Effendi states that the universal crisis
affecting mankind is 'essentially spiritual in its causes',[15] drawing
attention to the spiritual bankruptcy of present-day society.
The current disintegration and decline of civilization, of which
many are all too aware, is a reflection of the spiritual crisis within
individuals.

In such a climate, spiritual transformation becomes exceed-
ingly important. For Bahá'ís, it is an 'essential purpose' of their
Faith which demands action on the part of each individual:

Transformation is the essential purpose of the Cause of
Bahá'u'lláh, but it lies in the will and effort of the individual
to achieve it in obedience to the Covenant. Necessary to the
progress of this life-fulfilling transformation is knowledge
of the will and purpose of God through regular reading and
study of the Holy Word.[16]

Bahá'u'lláh has stated clearly in His Writings the essential requisites for our spiritual growth and these are stressed again
and again by 'Abdu'l-Bahá in His talks and Tablets. One can
summarize them briefly in this way:

1. The recital each day of one of the Obligatory Prayers
with pure-hearted devotion.

2. The regular reading of the Sacred Scriptures, specifically at least each morning and evening, with reverence, attention and thought.

3. Prayerful meditation on the Teachings, so that we may understand them more deeply, fulfil them more faithfully, and convey them more accurately to others.

4. Striving every day to bring our behaviour more into accordance with the high standards that are set forth in the Teachings.

5. Teaching the Cause of God.

6. Selfless service in the work of the Cause and in the carrying on of our trade or profession.[17]

These 'essential requisites' for spiritual growth are a daily prescription which enable believers not only to nurture and sustain their spiritual empowerment but also to find the practical implications of the teachings of Bahá'u'lláh in service to mankind.

Spiritual susceptibility

Capability for spiritual susceptibility is one of the bounties that a person can attain in this earthly life. 'Abdu'l-Bahá explains that this capability seems to vanish under the influence of materialism and 'divine civilization become(s) decadent'; in such a society 'people are submerged in the sea of materialism'.[18] He used the concept of submersion to describe the forces of materialism. When under this influence, people's sensibilities are attuned to these material forces; their perceptions become purely physical. Even those who attend churches or temples may not be free from such influences. For some, worship and devotion is simply a means of keeping up the traditions of their ancestors: 'the darkness of imitations encompasses the world'.[19]

In His talks in the West, especially during His visit to North America, 'Abdu'l-Bahá frequently raised people's awareness of the spiritual dimensions of human life and society as opposed to the materialistic attachments of the world. He often drew a contrast between the material and spiritual aspects of life and civilization.

In His opening remarks to a talk given at Green Acre in 1912, while praising the physical beauty of the venue 'Abdu'l-Bahá also expressed the hope that a spiritual charm might surround the place so that its beauty would be perfect. He noted that people are devoted to 'the attractions of this world, without aspiration beyond the life that is vanishing and mortal'. He observed that in schools and temples of learning, 'knowledge of the sciences acquired is based on material observations only; there is no realization of Divinity in their methods and conclusions . . . They are not interested in attaining knowledge of the mysteries of God or understanding the secrets of the heavenly Kingdom'; tangible evidence becomes the only basis of their learning.'[20] His critical analysis of the materialistic society underlines the dichotomy between intrinsic and extrinsic values and the need for a harmony between the two. For materialists, intrinsic values that stem from spiritual and divine teachings don't exist.

'Abdu'l-Bahá compares humanity as a whole to the individual human body. No matter how much the body is trained and developed in strength and beauty, the person will be unable to make real progress unless the mind is correspondingly advanced. Spiritual and transcendental advancement are unique to human beings, for God has created man in His own image and empowered him with the potential to achieve that likeness. The material world and its creatures are not endowed with this special capacity. Earthly phenomena are subject to natural law; they are captives of nature and the 'sense world'. But human beings are created with a power through which they can perceive 'intellectual or spiritual realities'.[21] 'Abdu'l-Bahá explains that a human being has 'the power to attain those ideals and thereby differentiate and consciously distinguish himself an infinite degree above the kingdoms of existence below him.[22]

Human beings are likened to a lamp, or a glass, where the light within the glass is their spiritual reality. No matter how perfectly translucent the glass may be, it stays dark if there is no light within it. So is our physical reality imperfect, unless we are enlightened with spiritual virtues and understand the purpose of creation. Otherwise, we are like a body which, although beautiful, is without the gift of life.

A story from the Middle East tells of a caliph who was deeply in love with his wife. One day she became afflicted by a disease for which there was no cure; this caused the caliph much distress and he sought the help of the best physicians, but all in vain. When she died, his grief was so extreme that he refused to bury her. Her beauty had so profoundly captivated his mind that separation from her seemed impossible to him. He ordered a crystal casket, into which her body was placed. Each day he would sit at the foot of the casket of his beloved and immerse himself in all his delightful memories. But the body began to decay and disintegrate. He lamented over the disappearance of her charm and beauty, but it reached a point where the body had become so ugly and malodorous that he couldn't stand it and asked that she be buried.

The point of this story is that a body, even one of utmost beauty, cannot exist for long without a soul. Many today are worshippers of the seductively glamorous but soulless bodies of material fancy, unable to recognize that there is no light or life in them. This failure to distinguish the deeper meaning of life from deceptive material attachments can lead to much disillusionment and cause many misconceptions.

> Unless society learns to attribute more importance to spiritual matters, it would never be fit to enter the golden era foretold by Bahá'u'lláh. The present calamities are parts of this process of purgation, through them alone will man learn his lesson. They are to teach the nations that they have to view things internationally, they are to make the individual attribute more importance to his moral, than his material welfare.[23]

'Abdu'l-Bahá urged the Bahá'ís to give precedence to moral distinction rather than more worldly honours:

> I desire distinction for you. The Bahá'ís must be distinguished from others of humanity. But this distinction must not depend upon wealth – that they should become more affluent than other people. I do not desire for you financial distinction. It is not an ordinary distinction I desire, not scientific, commercial, industrial distinction. For you I desire spiritual distinction – that is, you must become eminent and distinguished in morals.[24]

Bahá'u'lláh uses the metaphor of a tree to elucidate the importance of acquiring praiseworthy attributes and virtues. While a fruit-bearing tree that is fruitless is no use at all, a tree that bears fruit fulfils its purpose. This is equally true of human beings:

> The fruits of the human tree are exquisite, highly desired and dearly cherished. Among them are upright character, virtuous deeds and a goodly utterance. The springtime for earthly trees occurreth once every year, while the one for human trees appeareth in the Days of God – exalted be His glory. Were the trees of men's lives to be adorned in this divine Springtime with the fruits that have been mentioned, the effulgence of the light of Justice would, of a certainty, illumine all the dwellers of the earth and everyone would abide in tranquillity and contentment beneath the sheltering shadow of Him Who is the Object of all mankind.[25]

So although the popular view has it that personal wealth is the source of joy and peace in this world, what really counts is noble character and praiseworthy virtues – these are the most precious fruits of this life.

. . . the happiness and greatness, the rank and station, the pleasure and peace, of an individual have never consisted in his personal wealth, but rather in his excellent character, his high resolve, the breadth of his learning, and his ability to solve difficult problems.[26]

This statement by 'Abdu'l-Bahá challenges the traditional view, prevalent in many cultures, that individuals should be judged by what they *have* rather than by who they *are* with regard to their moral integrity, noble deeds and servitude to humanity. The latter way of valuing human beings will probably be an important feature of the future civilization, in which the acquiring of human virtues will be celebrated as among the most praiseworthy accomplishments.

In his brilliant and divinely inspired analysis of the United States, Shoghi Effendi characterizes the magnitude of that country's spiritual, moral, social and political crisis as extremely serious:

> The steady and alarming deterioration in the standard of morality as exemplified by the appalling increase of crime, by political corruption in ever widening and ever higher circles, by the loosening of the sacred ties of marriage, by the inordinate craving for pleasure and diversion, and by the marked and progressive slackening of parental control, is no doubt the most arresting and distressing aspect of the decline that has set in, and can be clearly perceived, in the fortunes of the entire nation.
>
> Parallel with this, and pervading all departments of life . . . is the crass materialism, which lays excessive and ever-increasing emphasis on material well-being, forgetful of those things of the spirit on which alone a sure and stable foundation can be laid for human society.[27]

Shoghi Effendi nevertheless reminds the American Bahá'ís that in spite of the evils of the 'excessive and binding materialism' which surrounds them, their country is nevertheless destined to become the 'standard-bearer of the New World Order'. He tells them:

> It is by such means as this that Bahá'u'lláh can best demonstrate to a heedless generation His almighty power to raise up from the very midst of a people, immersed in a sea of materialism, a prey to one of the most virulent and long-standing forms of racial prejudice, and notorious for its political corruption, lawlessness and laxity in moral standards, men and women who, as time goes by, will increasingly exemplify those essential virtues of self-renunciation, of moral rectitude, of chastity, of indiscriminating fellowship, of holy discipline, and of spiritual insight that will fit them for the preponderating share they will have in calling into being that World Order and that World Civilization of which their country, no less than the entire human race, stands in desperate need.[28]

CHAPTER 12

RETHINKING THE CONCEPTS OF WEALTH AND WELL-BEING

. . . although material civilization is one of the means for the
progress of the world of mankind, yet until it becomes combined
with Divine civilization, the desired result, which is the felicity
of mankind, will not be attained.
'Abdu'l-Bahá[1]

The Bahá'í Faith defines economy in a broad context, relating it to the spiritual reality of human beings. The present world economy, based on growth and profit-making policies, works mainly in the interests of the rich; on the other hand, money is blamed as being 'the root of all evil'. But it is not the fault of money as such: it is human greed for money which is the problem.

When we look at human society as a collection of souls in a global community, with equal rights to betterment and progress, we become more conscious of the needs of others. Through this perception we realize that the interests of society must transcend the pursuit of individual self-interest. This is not possible, however, unless individuals truly believe in the unity of the human race as one family and are willing to be altruistic and equitable – to sacrifice personal interest in order to promote the prosperity and the welfare of others. The prerequisite for accomplishing this noble task is love of people, regardless of their colour, education or nationality. Without a spiritual understanding of the purpose of life, true love will not be sustainable, for the persuasive force of selfish desire is universal and too tempting to ignore.

In a spiritualized economy, material gain through work and service to humanity has a special significance and meaning: work, the source of income, is also to be regarded as an act of worship if it is conducted in the spirit of service. This relationship connecting material gain with a spiritual experience can have a transformative effect on our perception of the economy and our attitude toward money. It can expand our vision and awareness of the necessity of a spiritual solution to economic problems, as enunciated in the teachings of Bahá'u'lláh. Therefore, it should come as no surprise that the Bahá'í teachings see the future world economy as a spiritual economy.

One Bahá'í economist puts it in a way with which many others would agree:

> The economic problem is fundamentally not one of scarcity of goods and services but rather their inequitable distribution amongst the peoples of the world. To achieve a better distribution requires a reduction in personal and national self-interest and a lessening of the greed that characterizes our culture today.[2]

'Abdu'l-Bahá's evaluation of our self-centred society is also enlightening:

> Today, all the peoples of the world are indulging in self-interest and exert the utmost effort and endeavour to promote their own material interests. They are worshipping themselves and not the divine reality, nor the world of mankind. They seek diligently their own benefit and not the common weal. This is because they are captives of the world of nature and unaware of the divine teachings, of the bounty of the Kingdom and of the Sun of Truth. But ye, praise be to God, are at present especially favoured with this bounty.[3]

Bahá'u'lláh exhorts us to 'Be anxiously concerned with the needs of the age ye live in, and centre your deliberations on its exigencies and requirements . . .'[4] One of the needs of humanity today is to be released from the captivity of the prison which they have built around themselves, the prison of self-indulgence and greed. This imprisonment is reinforced by the power of the wealthy and enterprises focused only on profit.

In the Bahá'í system, part of what we earn does not belong to us; it belongs to God. An individual, after deducting debts and essential expenses, should pay a certain amount of his or her wealth into a special fund known as 'the Right of God' (Ḥuqúqu'lláh) which will be disbursed for the good of mankind. This law is a cornerstone of the future 'divine economy'; it will become 'a source of prosperity and blessing'.[5] As a result of it there will be a change of attitude toward material possessions and wealth, a spiritual and more equitable attitude toward the management of the economy.

> . . . the acquisition of wealth is not in itself a fearsome objective, it is a practical necessity. The problem with wealth arises from inappropriate attitudes toward possessing and using it . . .
> As in so many other aspects of personal life, Bahá'u'lláh's teachings provide a means for safeguarding us from the test of wealth by ordaining the law of Ḥuqúqu'lláh, providing the opportunity to contribute to the Bahá'í Funds, and encouraging philanthropic endeavours for the well-being of all.[6]

This expression of true love and ability to consciously and willingly detach oneself from one's own self-interest for a higher spiritual ideal is a sign of human maturity: it is self-regulation in the context of obedience. It protects individuals from narcissistic self-indulgence while at the same time encouraging the spirit of generosity, sacrifice and world-mindedness for the benefit of society. As the Universal House of Justice comments:

This law enables the friends to recognize the elevation of their economic activity to the level of divine acceptability, it is a means for the purification of their wealth and a magnet attracting divine blessings.[7]

The Right of God is a law which will enhance the spiritual solution to economic problems and greatly contribute to the spiritualization of the financial affairs of humanity. Consequently, it will

contribute to the spiritualization of humanity through the promotion of a new attitude toward the acquisition and use of material resources. It will provide the material resources necessary for great collective enterprises designed to improve all aspects of life and will be a powerful element in the growth of a world civilization.[8]

Furthermore, it will permeate our consciousness with the capacity of knowing how to be generous and content; it will enable us to be connected with the suffering of humanity through our love for the Creator and our commitment to social justice.

Although it appears to be simply a material offering, it has a profound spiritual significance; 'it is the source of grace, abundance, and of all good,' writes Bahá'u'lláh.[9] It will also help in the elimination of extremes of wealth and poverty, and in increasing mindfulness of the need for a more equitable distribution of resources.

In a world where at one extreme material riches are used to stockpile military armaments while at the other extreme, millions of people are dying of hunger, starvation and disease, the Right of God not only raises human consciousness of the necessity for an equitable sharing of wealth and for social justice; it also promotes the use of riches for spiritual transformation and the advancement of civilization. This is a form of giving which, although it is a sacred obligation, is left entirely to the judgement of the individual (who is responsible to God) and not to any worldly pressure or force. This reflects the evolution of the human mind and soul in this era, now capable of discharging a responsibility with joy and willingness without the slightest outside pressure or intervention. The Right of God brings a new and revolutionary transformation in human attitude toward wealth, combined with a sense of self-discipline, not from fear of punishment or the hope of reward. It is from pure love of the Creator. What a great difference it will make when this obligation becomes known by the world of humanity.

> The significance of the Right of God has yet to permeate the consciousness of the mass of the followers of Bahá'u'lláh. Many believers remain oblivious of a mighty law, the observance of which has been characterized by Bahá'u'lláh Himself as 'conducive to prosperity, to blessing, and to honour and divine protection' and as 'the source of grace, abundance, and of all good'.[10]

How different is this principle from present-day corrupt and bankrupt economic systems, where governments must crack down on tax evasion, money laundering and many other forms of corruption to bring about order, and where people neither trust the system nor are willing to pay their share of taxation.

Given the fact that human beings are deeply inclined to be selfish and to strive to satisfy their own needs and desires above those of others, the development of a natural altruistic motivation is a remarkable advance in human evolution and ethics. William Hatcher once made an insightful analysis of the role of motivation in response to law, indicating that at any particular time, one of the following motivations might be predominant in our relationship to a law such as Ḥuqúqu'lláh: (1) fear of the consequences of failure; (2) the promise of reward; (3) a sense of duty – an expression of faithfulness; (4) the pure love of God, without any hope of reward or fear of the consequences of failure.

'The Writings of our Faith appeal to each of these motivations,' said Hatcher. However, '. . . the highest all motivations is that of the intrinsic love of God, without regard to duties, obligations or consequences . . .'[11] The fulfilment of this motivation requires the development of spiritual discipline and autonomy, which are some of the ingredients of personal growth and transformation.

Our world is passing through an historic transition. All its turmoil is paving the way for the ushering in of a new civilization with a new world order. There are unprecedented changes on every level of human society. The old world order and outworn traditional beliefs and habits are changing; we are moving toward a more equitable civilization which will be based on both a material and spiritual foundation. Not only will the landscape of politics and governance of countries change, but religious, economic and educational systems will also undergo transformation. 'Abdu'l-Bahá said,

> It is evident, therefore. that counterfeit and spurious religious teaching, antiquated forms of belief and ancestral imitations which are at variance with the foundations of divine reality must also pass away and be reformed. They must be abandoned and new conditions be recognized. The morals of humanity must undergo change. New remedies and solutions for human problems must be adopted. Human intellects themselves must change and be subject to the universal reformation.[12]

These changes will bring new opportunities to reflect and act on the creative words of the Revelation of Bahá'u'lláh, destined to regenerate the world of humanity.

> In the midst of a civilization torn by strifes and enfeebled by materialism, the people of Bahá are building a new world. We face at this time opportunities and responsibilities of vast magnitude and great urgency. Let each believer in his inmost heart resolve not to be seduced by the ephemeral allurements of the society around him, nor to be drawn into its feuds

and short-lived enthusiasms, but instead to transfer all he can from the old world to that new one which is the vision of his longing and will be the fruit of his labours.[13]

There is always resistance to change, including changing the old concept of a materialistic economy. In 2006 the Universal House of Justice asked:

Have not the unquenchable thirst for, and the feverish pursuit after, earthly vanities, riches and pleasures so consolidated their power and influence as to assume authority over such human values as happiness, fidelity and love?[14]

Swiftly-moving events since then have challenged the materialistic economy: the rapid and dramatic deterioration in the financial fortunes of humanity has raised serious questions about the integrity and sustainability of the current economic system and has called for a rethinking of the fundamental principles that govern our present materialistic society. The economic crisis of 2008–09 awakened the masses of humanity to the bitter realization that wealth by itself cannot guarantee either security or happiness.

The collapse of longstanding financial corporations and time-honoured establishments is part of the disintegration process foreseen in the Bahá'í Writings and underlines the crucial need to establish spiritual foundations for a just and equitable system of economic planning and management . . . Parallel with the accelerated disintegration of the material and moral fabric of the present day society, the regenerative forces of the Revelation of Bahá'u'lláh have given rise to an ever increasing discernment of the immense wisdom in the application of the mighty law of Ḥuqúqu'lláh which is 'a source of inestimable blessings for all humanity'.[15]

In a world 'preoccupied with self-indulgence'[16] this law will contribute to the revival of society and to the establishment of a civilization based on spiritual values for all humankind.

Toward a spiritual civilization

At this turbulent time in the development of our civilization, when the proliferation of nuclear weapons continues to threaten the very existence of the global community, one may wonder what the chances of the human race surviving are. But this depends not so much on technology as on human values and a consciousness of man's ultimate destiny – a truth which was increasingly recognized as the 20th century drew to its close. One American scholar said that man's existential crisis was due to man himself – technologically 'a giant, morally a dwarf'.[17] And decades before that, Albert Einstein warned,

> Our world is threatened by a crisis of such dimensions that it seems to have outstripped those who have the most important decisions for good or ill within their power. The unleashed might of the atom has changed everything, except our thinking. We are consequently moving towards an unparalleled catastrophe. We shall need a substantially new way of thinking if mankind is to survive.[18]

The 'new way of thinking' that Einstein referred to is not possible through either science or technology. Indeed, 'science can neither bring about a change of consciousness nor discern new standards of value, let alone set absolute standards . . .'[19]

But it is characteristic of divine revelation to bring about change and transformation in human consciousness through a system of education and knowledge which has been the wellspring of new civilization throughout history. According to the Bahá'í teachings, 'The Word of God, alone, can claim the distinction of being endowed with the capacity required for so great and far-reaching a change.'[20]

Humanity as a whole has been going through a devastating period of collective adolescence, whose catastrophic effects have included

> the deliberate extermination of millions of helpless human beings, the invention and use of new weapons of destruction capable of annihilating whole populations, the rise of ideologies that suffocated the spiritual and intellectual life of entire nations, damage to the physical environment of the planet on a scale so massive that it may take centuries to heal, and the incalculably greater damage done to generations of children taught to believe that violence, indecency, and selfishness are triumphs of personal liberty. Such are only the more obvious of a catalogue of evils, unmatched in history, whose lessons our era will leave for the education of the chastened generations who will follow us.[21]

All of these have fed the sense of helplessness many people feel. Characteristic too has been the worldwide loss of trust, both in the institutions of society and between people. No wonder, then, that the idea that human beings are intrinsically aggressive and therefore forever condemned to aggressive conduct has gained such currency. The Bahá'í teachings, however, challenge this theory; aggressive conduct is viewed rather as 'a distortion of the human spirit' influenced by flaws in education, cultural habits and attitudes as well as environment.

> Most particularly, it is in the glorification of material pursuits, at once the progenitor and common feature of all such ideologies, that we find the roots which nourish the falsehood that human beings are incorrigibly selfish and aggressive. It is here that the ground must be cleared for the building of a new world fit for our descendants.
>
> That materialistic ideals have, in the light of experience, failed to satisfy the needs of mankind calls for an honest

acknowledgement that a fresh effort must now be made to find the solutions to the agonizing problems of the planet. The intolerable conditions pervading society bespeak a common failure of all, a circumstance which tends to incite rather than relieve the entrenchment on every side. Clearly, a common remedial effort is urgently required. It is primarily a matter of attitude. Will humanity continue in its waywardness, holding to outworn concepts and unworkable assumptions? Or will its leaders, regardless of ideology, step forth and, with a resolute will, consult together in a united search for appropriate solutions?[22]

In an insightful document *Who is Writing the Future?*, the inseparability of the spiritual aspects of society from the development of civilization is underlined: 'the entire enterprise that we call civilization is itself a spiritual process.'[23] This concept challenges the current popularity of atheistic and materialistic theories:

> If social and intellectual evolution is in fact responding to a moral intelligence inherent in existence, a great deal of the theory determining contemporary approaches to decision-making is fatally flawed. If human consciousness is essentially spiritual in nature – as the vast majority of ordinary people have always been intuitively aware – its developmental needs cannot be understood or served through an interpretation of reality that dogmatically insists otherwise.[24]

Referring to the significance of the new era of human society, Bahá'u'lláh made the following prophetic statement in the 19th century, 'A new life is, in this age, stirring within all the peoples of the earth; and yet none hath discovered its cause or perceived its motive.'[25] Commenting on the suffering of humanity, he wrote, 'Regard the world as the human body which, though at its creation whole and perfect, hath been afflicted, through various causes, with grave disorders and maladies.'[26]

The vision and teachings of Bahá'u'lláh are, Bahá'ís believe, the remedy. His counsels have far-reaching implications for the well-being, happiness and prosperity of the entire world – and not only for Bahá'ís. He challenges us all to broaden our vision, to and go beyond preoccupation with ourselves:

> Do not busy yourselves in your own concerns; let your thoughts be fixed upon that which will rehabilitate the fortunes of mankind and sanctify the hearts and souls of men. This can best be achieved through pure and holy deeds, through a virtuous life and a goodly behaviour.[27]

We can be under no illusions that changes from the present state of affairs of humanity to the future civilization based on social justice, peace and the unity of humankind will be easy. A host of individual and social habits and behavioural attitudes, rooted in the cultural characteristics of people for thousands of years, will not be abandoned simply through education or legislative action. The severe suffering and calamities experienced by people worldwide may well be the ultimate way, through divine wisdom, that humanity will be transformed and a new and equitable future civilization established.[28]

Changing the present forces of war and exploitation and the pernicious influence of a materialistic way of life into a more equitable and harmonious spirit of altruism and cooperation will require a profound shift in consciousness and a re-examination of the true purpose of life. But this change of paradigm will greatly transform the landscape of human prosperity and enhance the betterment of humankind. Shoghi Effendi outlines this Bahá'í vision of the future:

> Destitution on the one hand, and gross accumulation of ownership on the other, will disappear. The enormous energy dissipated and wasted on war, whether economic or political, will be consecrated to such ends as will extend the range of

human inventions and technical development, to the increase of the productivity of mankind, to the extermination of disease, to the extension of scientific research, to the raising of the standard of physical health, to the sharpening and refinement of the human brain, to the exploitation of the unused and unsuspected resources of the planet, to the prolongation of human life, and to the furtherance of any other agency that can stimulate the intellectual, the moral, and spiritual life of the entire human race . . .

. . . such a consummation – the coming of age of the human race – must signalize, in its turn, the inauguration of a world civilization . . . Who is it that can imagine the lofty standard which such a civilization, as it unfolds itself, is destined to attain?[29]

CONCLUSION

This book has explored materialism with a specific focus on the moral and social consequences of a materialistic mindset and lifestyle. It has examined psychological, sociological and spiritual perspectives on the theme, substantiated by extensive scientific research reported in the literature. It challenges the materialistic view that matter is the centrepiece of life, that whatever is not matter does not exist –a view that denies spirituality, conscience and feeling. Issues of wealth and poverty, as well as moral degradation and the decline of social order, have been discussed. The role of greed and excessive attachment to material things has been analysed. The book has also addressed non-material challenges such as the roles of egotism, arrogance and indifference to the plight of millions who die each year from starvation and disease. This indifference, as well as the deterioration of human behaviour, are rooted in the loss of values and spiritual perspectives on life.

In challenging the unbridled accumulation of wealth, or the economic injustices and corruption of our modern world it has not been my intention to endorse poverty or an ascetic lifestyle. Rather, my purpose is to promote moderation, modesty and contentment in a world heavily engaged in hedonism and self-indulgence – to advocate for a sensible balance between the spiritual and material aspects of life as two pillars of an equitable civilization.

The problem of wealth and poverty is not only an economic

and material issue; it is also a moral dilemma. The solution to such a dilemma, therefore, cannot be only scientific; there must also be a spiritual principle involved. The moral principles of human affairs have their roots in world religions, and have done so throughout history. It has been through religious teachings that 'masses of people in all ages and lands have developed the capacity to love. They have learned to discipline the animal side of their natures, to make great sacrifices for the common good, to practise forgiveness, generosity and trust, to use wealth and other resources in ways that serve the advancement of civilization.'[1] Conversely, materialism and hedonism are not purely psychological or instinctual: they are expressions of a lack of depth in one's spiritual perspective of the purpose and meaning of life in this world.

The following words of Shoghi Effendi call us to an increased awareness as we ponder the challenges before us in moving toward the establishment of the World Order of Bahá'u'lláh:

> . . . today's intensely materialistic civilization, alas, most perfectly exemplified by the United States, has far exceeded the bounds of moderation, and, as Bahá'u'lláh has pointed out in His Writings, civilization itself, when carried to extremes, leads to destruction. The . . . friends should be on their guard against this deadly influence to which they are so constantly exposed, and which we can see is undermining the moral strength of not only America, but indeed of Europe and other parts of the world to which it is rapidly spreading.[2]

Materialism in moral terms, as discussed in this book, can have destructive consequences and may permeate society as a form of social dysfunction. It is an acquired condition and state of mind which develops as a result of a number of factors, including materialistic education, parental attitudes and socio-cultural influences. To remedy this condition, a reconstruction of society's mindset and attitude toward the accumulation of wealth and greedy attachment to it is needed, through a consciousness of and belief in intrinsic moral values and the spiritual reality of existence which transcend dependence on material wealth as a lifestyle. Such a conviction will encourage a sense of world-embracing love for humanity, empathy and altruism, especially toward those who are deprived and underprivileged. As a result, individuals will be able to move away from a self-oriented frame of mind to an other-oriented and God-conscious vision of life. They will also become more sensitive to the needs and interests of others as a source of self-actualization.

In such a society, human values will be judged differently from today. People will be valued not because of their wealth, fame or status, but rather for their generosity of spirit and their service to the world community. Selfless contribution to the well-being of others will be considered praiseworthy, as will the willingness to forgo or sacrifice one's own interests for the interests and needs of those who are less fortunate. This may sound an ambitious, if not utopian, concept – and it is true that the achievement of a goal so intimately related to social justice and true fellowship can only be possible through the development of a genuine love for people regardless of their race, colour, wealth, educational or ideological background. But such a sincere love, I believe, will become possible through a system of education which is divine in origin and responds to the spiritual and material needs and requirements of our time. Expounding the importance of cooperation and reciprocity in society, 'Abdu'l-Bahá said:

> The supreme need of humanity is cooperation and reciprocity. The stronger the ties of fellowship and solidarity amongst men, the greater will be the power of constructiveness and accomplishment in all the planes of human activity. Without cooperation and reciprocal attitude the individual member of human society remains self-centered, uninspired by altruistic purposes, limited and solitary in development . . . [3]

The teachings of Bahá'u'lláh contain perspectives and 'gems of inestimable value' for such a profound transformation:

> Be generous in prosperity, and thankful in adversity. Be worthy of the trust of thy neighbour, and look upon him with a bright and friendly face. Be a treasure to the poor, an admonisher to the rich, an answerer of the cry of the needy, a preserver of the sanctity of thy pledge. Be fair in thy judgement, and guarded in thy speech. Be unjust to no man, and show all meekness to all men. Be as a lamp unto them that walk in darkness, a joy to the sorrowful, a sea for the thirsty, a haven for the distressed, an upholder and defender of the victim of oppression. Let integrity and uprightness distinguish all thine acts. Be a home for the stranger, a balm to the suffering, a tower of strength for the fugitive. Be eyes to the blind, and a guiding light unto the feet of the erring. Be an ornament to the countenance of truth, a crown to the brow of fidelity, a pillar of the temple of righteousness, a breath of life to the body of mankind, an ensign of the hosts of justice, a luminary above the horizon of virtue, a dew to the soil of the human heart, an ark on the ocean of knowledge, a sun in the heaven of bounty, a gem on the diadem of wisdom, a shining light in the firmament of thy generation, a fruit upon the tree of humility.[4]

EXCERPTS FROM THE BAHÁ'Í WRITINGS

All the Prophets have come to promote divine bestowals, to found the spiritual civilization and teach the principles of morality. Therefore, we must strive with all our powers so that spiritual influences may gain the victory. For material forces have attacked mankind. The world of humanity is submerged in a sea of materialism. The rays of the Sun of Reality are seen but dimly and darkly through opaque glasses. The penetrative power of the divine bounty is not fully manifest.[1]

Fear the sighs of the poor and of the upright in heart who, at every break of day, bewail their plight, and be unto them a benignant sovereign. They, verily, are thy treasures on earth. It behoveth thee, therefore, to safeguard thy treasures from the assaults of them who wish to rob thee. Inquire into their affairs, and ascertain, every year, nay every month, their condition, and be not of them that are careless of their duty.[2]

The days of your life are far spent, O people, and your end is fast approaching. Put away, therefore, the things ye have devised and to which ye cleave, and take firm hold on the precepts of God, that haply ye may attain that which He hath purposed for you, and be of them that pursue a right course. Delight not yourselves in the things of the world and its vain ornaments, neither set your hopes on them. Let your reliance be on the remembrance of God, the Most Exalted, the Most Great. He will, erelong, bring to naught all the things ye possess. Let Him be your fear, and forget not His covenant with you, and be not of them that are shut out as by a veil from Him.[3]

Wealth is praiseworthy in the highest degree, if it is acquired by an individual's own efforts and the grace of God, in commerce, agriculture, art and industry, and if it be expended for philanthropic purposes. Above all, if a judicious and resourceful individual should initiate measures which would universally enrich the masses of the people, there could be no undertaking greater than this, and it would rank in the sight of God as the supreme achievement . . .[4]

But if conditions are such that some are happy and comfortable and some in misery; some are accumulating exorbitant wealth and others are in dire want – under such a system it is impossible for man to be happy and impossible for him to win the good pleasure of God. God is kind to all. The good pleasure of God consists in the welfare of all the individual members of mankind.[5]

Be not troubled in poverty nor confident in riches, for poverty is followed by riches, and riches are followed by poverty. Yet to be poor in all save God is a wondrous gift, belittle not the value thereof, for in the end it will make thee rich in God, and thus thou shalt know the meaning of the utterance, 'In truth ye are the poor,' and the holy words, 'God is the all-possessing,' shall even as the true morn break forth gloriously resplendent upon the horizon of the lover's heart, and abide secure on the throne of wealth.[6]

O ye loved ones of God! Know ye that the world is even as a mirage rising over the sands, that the thirsty mistaketh for water. The wine of this world is but a vapour in the desert, its pity and compassion but toil and trouble, the repose it proffereth only weariness and sorrow. Abandon it to those who belong to it, and turn your faces unto the Kingdom of your Lord the All-Merciful, that His grace and bounty may cast their dawning splendours over you, and a heavenly table may be sent down for you, and your Lord may bless you, and shower His riches upon you to gladden your bosoms and fill your hearts with bliss, to attract your minds, and cleanse your souls, and console your eyes.[7]

Detachment is as the sun; in whatsoever heart it doth shine it quencheth the fire of covetousness and self. He whose sight is illumined with the light of understanding will assuredly detach himself from the world and the vanities thereof . . . Let not the world and its vileness grieve you. Happy is he whom riches fill not with vain-glory, nor poverty with sorrow.[8]

With reference to what is meant by an individual becoming entirely forgetful of self: the intent is that he should rise up and sacrifice himself in the true sense, that is, he should obliterate the promptings of the human condition, and rid himself of such characteristics as are worthy of blame and constitute the gloomy darkness of this life on earth – not that he should allow his physical health to deteriorate and his body to become infirm.[9]

Man must sever himself from the influences of the world of matter, from the world of nature and its laws; for the material world is the world of corruption and death. It is the world of evil and darkness, of animalism and ferocity, bloodthirstiness, ambition and avarice, of self-worship, egotism and passion; it is the world of nature. Man must strip himself of all these imperfections, must sacrifice these tendencies which are peculiar to the outer and material world of existence.

On the other hand, man must acquire heavenly qualities and attain divine attributes. He must become the image and likeness of God. He must seek the bounty of the eternal, become the manifestor of the love of God, the light of guidance, the tree of life and the depository of the bounties of God. That is to say, man must sacrifice the qualities and attributes of the world of nature for the qualities and attributes of the world of God.[10]

Nothing that existeth in the world of being hath ever been or will ever be worthy of mention. However, if a person be graciously favoured to offer a pennyworth – nay, even less – in the path of God, this would in His sight be preferable and superior to all the treasures of the earth.[11]

Ye are the trees of My garden; ye must give forth goodly and wondrous fruits, that ye yourselves and others may profit there-from. Thus it is incumbent on every one to engage in crafts and professions, for therein lies the secret of wealth, O men of under-standing! For results depend upon means, and the grace of God shall be all-sufficient unto you. Trees that yield no fruit have been and will ever be for the fire.[12]

This station [the Valley of True Poverty and Absolute Nothing-ness] is the dying from self and the living in God, the being poor in self and rich in the Desired One. Poverty as here referred to sig-nifieth being poor in the things of the created world, rich in the things of God's world. For when the true lover and devoted friend reacheth to the presence of the Beloved, the sparkling beauty of the Loved One and the fire of the lover's heart will kindle a blaze and burn away all veils and wrappings.[13]

The primary purpose, the basic objective, in laying down power-ful laws and setting up great principles and institutions dealing with every aspect of civilization, is human happiness; and human happiness consists only in drawing closer to the Threshold of Almighty God, and in securing the peace and well-being of every individual member, high and low alike, of the human race; and the supreme agencies for accomplishing these two objectives are the excellent qualities with which humanity has been endowed.[14]

BIBLIOGRAPHY

'Abdu'l-Bahá. *'Abdu'l-Bahá in London: Addresses and Notes of Conversations.* London: Bahá'í Publishing Trust, 1982.

— *Paris Talks: Addresses Given by 'Abdu'l-Bahá in 1911.* London: Bahá'í Publishing Trust, 12th ed. 1986.

— *The Promulgation of Universal Peace: Talks Delivered by 'Abdu'l-Bahá during His Visit to the United States and Canada in 1912.* Comp. Howard MacNutt. Wilmette, IL: Bahá'í Publishing Trust, 2nd ed. 1982.

— *The Secret of Divine Civilization.* Wilmette, IL: Bahá'í Publishing Trust, 1957.

— *Selections from the Writings of 'Abdu'l-Bahá.* Haifa: Bahá'í World Centre, 1978.

— *Some Answered Questions.* Haifa: Bahá'í World Centre, 2014.

— *Tablets of Abdul-Baha Abbas.* New York: Bahá'í Publishing Committee. Vol. 1, 1930; vol. 2, 1940; vol. 3, 1930. Reprinted from the original edition 1909–1916.

— *Tablets of the Divine Plan.* Wilmette, IL: Bahá'í Publishing Trust, 1993.

— Tablet to Auguste Forel, in *Auguste Forel and the Bahá'í Faith.* Oxford: George Ronald, 1978. Also in *The Bahá'í World,* vol. 15, p. 38.

Action Aid, United Kingdom. *Fact File.* Available at http://www.actionaid.org.uk.

Adams, M. *Better Happy than Rich? Canadians, Money, and the Meaning of Life.* Toronto: Viking, 2000.

Ahuvia, A. C. 'Individualism/Collectivism and Cultures of Happiness: A Theoretical Conjuncture on the Relationship between Consumption, Culture and Subjective Well-Being at the National Level', in *Journal of Happiness Studies,* vol. 31 (2002), no. 1, pp. 23–36.

— and N. Wong. 'Materialism: Origins and Implications for Personal Well-Being', in Flemming Hansen (ed.): *European Advances in Consumer*

Research, vol. 2. Provo, UT: Association for Consumer Research, 1995, pp. 172–178.

Allport, G. W. and J. M. Ross. 'Personal Religious Orientation and Prejudice', in *Journal of Personality and Social Psychology*, vol. 5 (1967), pp. 432–443.

Alper, M. *The God Part of the Brain: A Scientific Interpretation of Human Spirituality and God.* New York: Rogue, 2001.

— 'Obesity in Children and Teens', in *American Academy of Child and Adolescent Psychiatry*, no. 79 (May 2008), p. 1. Available at http://www. aacap.org/cs/root/facts_for_families/.

Amiel, B. 'I am Hearing a Lot about Loneliness', in *Maclean's* magazine (Canada), 7 December 2009.

Andrees, Beate and Patrick Belser. *Forced Labour: Coercion and Exploitation in the Private Economy.* Geneva: ILO; Boulder, CO: Lynne Rienner, 2009.

Arbab, Farzam. 'Knowledge and Civilization: Implications for the Community and the Individual', in *The Bahá'í World 1997–1998*, pp. 157–178. Haifa: Bahá'í World Centre, 1999.

Arehart-Treichel, J. 'Research Shines Spotlight on Narcissistic Personality Disorder', in *Psychiatric News* (US), 1 August 2008, p. 38. Available at http://pn.psychiatryonline.org/.

The Báb. *Selections from the Writings of the Báb.* Haifa: Bahá'í World Centre, 1976.

Badiei, A. *Stories Told by 'Abdu'l-Bahá.* Oxford: George Ronald, 2003.

Bahá'í Canada. Periodical. Toronto: National Spiritual Assembly of the Bahá'ís of Canada.

Bahá'í International Community. *Eradicating Poverty: Moving Forward as One.* New York: Bahá'í International Community United Nations Office, 2008.

— *One Common Faith.* Haifa: Bahá'í World Centre, 2005.

— *The Prosperity of Humankind.* Haifa: Bahá'í International Community Office of Public Information, 1995.

— *Rethinking Prosperity: Forging Alternatives to a Culture of Consumerism.* Contribution to the 18th Session of the United Nations Commission on Sustainable Development, New York, 3 May 2010. Available at http://bic.org/statements-and-reports/bic-statements/10-0503.htm.

— *Turning Point for All Nations.* New York: Bahá'í International Community United Nations Office, 1995.

— *Who is Writing the Future? Reflections on the Twentieth Century.* Haifa: Bahá'í International Community Office of Public Information, 1999.

Bahá'í Prayers. Wilmette, IL: Bahá'í Publishing Trust, 1991.

The Bahá'í World 1968–1973. Vol. 15. Haifa: Bahá'í World Centre, 1976. New series: *The Baha'i World 1997–1998.* Haifa: Bahá'í World Centre, 1999.

Bahá'u'lláh. *Epistle to the Son of the Wolf* (1891). Trans. Shoghi Effendi. Wilmette, IL: Bahá'í Publishing Trust, 1976.

— *Gleanings from the Writings of Bahá'u'lláh.* Wilmette, IL: Bahá'í Publishing Trust, 2nd ed. 1976.

— *The Hidden Words of Bahá'u'lláh.* Wilmette, IL: Bahá'í Publishing Trust, 1985.

— *The Kitáb-i-Aqdas: The Most Holy Book* Haifa: Bahá'í World Centre, 1992.

— *Kitáb-i-Íqán: The Book of Certitude.* Wilmette, IL: Bahá'í Publishing Trust, 1950.

— *Prayers and Meditations by Bahá'u'lláh* (1938). Trans. Shoghi Effendi. Wilmette, IL: Bahá'í Publishing Trust, 1987.

— *The Seven Valleys and the Four Valleys.* Wilmette, IL: Bahá'í Publishing Trust, 1991.

— *The Summons of the Lord of Hosts: Tablets of Bahá'u'lláh.* Haifa: Bahá'í World Centre, 2002.

— *Tablets of Bahá'u'lláh Revealed After the Kitáb-i-Aqdas.* Haifa: Bahá'í World Centre, 1978.

Barrie, V. 'Happiest Places Have Highest Suicide Rates'. Online article, 21 April 2011, available at http://www.hamilton.edu/news/story/wus-study-shows-happiest-places-have-highest-suicide-rates.

Beauregard, M. and O'Leary, D. (eds). *The Spiritual Brain: A Neuroscientist's Case for the Existence of the Soul.* New York: Harper One, 2007.

Becker, A. E. and R. A. Burwell. 'Acculturation and Disordered Eating in Fiji', presented at the annual meeting of the American Psychiatry Association, Washington DC, May 1999.

Belk, R. W. 'Materialism: Trait Aspects of Living in the Material World', in *Journal of Consumer Research*, vol. 12 (1985), pp. 265–279.

— 'Worldly Possessions: Issues and Criticisms', in *Advances in Consumer Research*, vol. 10 (1983), pp. 514–519.

Bezruchka, Stephen. 'The Effect of Economic Recession on Population Health', in *Canadian Medical Association Journal*, vol. 181 (2009), no. 5 (September), pp. 281–285.

—, R. Namekata and M. C. Sistrom. 'Improving Economic Equality and Health: The Case of Postwar Japan', in *American Journal of Public Health*, vol. 98 (2008), pp. 589–94.

The Bhagavad Gita. Trans. Juan Mascaró. London: Penguin, 1962, 2003.

British Broadcasting Association (BBC). 'UK Children Damaged by Materialism', in *BBC News*, 26 February 2008. Available at www.bbc.co.uk/2/hi/uk_news/7262936.stm.

Bouckaert, Luk and Laszlo Zsolnai (eds). *Handbook of Spirituality and Business*. London: Palgrave, 2011.

Brown, Lloyd and Lisa Brown. *The Embodiment of My Name*, paper presented at the International Environment Forum 4th Annual Conference, 12–14 December 2000, Orlando, Florida. Available at http://www.bcca.org/ief/dbrowooc.htm.

Burroughs, J. E. and A. Rindfleisch, 'Materialism and Well-being: A Conflicting Values Perspective', in *Journal of Consumer Research*, vol. 29 (2002), pp. 348–370.

Campbell, A. *The Sense of Well-being in America*. New York: McGraw-Hill, 1981.

Carlin, Flora. 'The Pursuit of Happiness', in *Psychology Today*, January/February 2009.

Castello, M. 'Will Ethan Couch, the 'Affluenza' Teen, Get Off Lightly Again?', reported by CNN, 29 December 2015. Available at http://www.cnn.com/2015/12/29/us/affluenza-teen-ethan-couch-detained-in-mexico/index.html.

Centers for Disease Control and Prevention. *Leading Causes of Mortality and Morbidity and Contributing Behaviors in the United States*. New York: CDC, 1997. Online article available at http://www.cdc.gov/nccdphp/dash/ahsumm/ussumm.htm.

— *Economic Facts About US Tobacco Use and Tobacco Production*. Fact sheet. Atlanta, Georgia: CDC/Office on Smoking and Health, 2005. Available at http://www.cdc.gov/tobacco/data_statistics/fact_sheets/economics/econ_facts/index.htm.

Chavez Rojas, J. A. *The Impact of Capitalism and Materialism on Generosity: A Cross-national Examination*. University of Iowa: Iowa Research Online, 2014. Available at http://ir.uiowa.edu/cgi/viewcontent.cgi?article=5344&context=etd.

Chew, Phyllis. *The Chinese Religion and the Bahá'í Faith*. Oxford: George Ronald, 1993.

Clark, N. 'Volatile Worlds, Vulnerable Bodies: Confronting Abrupt Climate Change', in *Theory, Culture and Society*, vol. 27 (2010), no. 2–3, pp. 31–53.

Clay, R. A. 'Advertising to Children: Is it Ethical?', in *Monitor on Psychology*, vol. 31 (2000), no. 8. Available at http://www.apa.org/monitor/sepoo/advertising.html.

The Compilation of Compilations: Prepared by the Universal House of Justice 1963–1990. 2 vols. Maryborough, Victoria: Bahá'í Publications Australia, 1991.

Compston, A. 'Decade of the Brain', in *Brain*, no. 128 (2005), pp. 1741–1742.

Corrigan, P. *The Sociology of Consumption*. London: Sage, 1997.

Crick, F. *The Astonishing Hypothesis: The Scientific Search for the Soul*. New York: Charles Scribner's Sons, 1994.

Crow, S. and Prendergast, J. 'Stop Your Gadget Greed from Fueling Tragedy in Congo', in *The Christian Science Monitor*, 30 April 2009. Available at www.csmonitor.com/Commentary/Opinion/2009/0430/po9so2-coop.html.

Csikszentmihalyi, M. 'If We Are So Rich, Why Aren't We Happy?', in *American Psychologist*, vol. 54 (1999), no. 10, pp. 821–827.

— 'Materialism and the Evolution of Consciousness' in T. Kasser and A. D. Kanner (eds): *Psychology and Consumer Culture*.

Cushman, P. 'Why the Self is Empty: Toward a Historically Situated Psychology', in *American Psychologist*, vol. 45 (1990), pp. 599–611.

Dalai Lama XIV (Tenzin Gyatso). *The Universe in a Single Atom*. New York: Morgan Road Books, 2005.

Davis, Melinda. *The New Culture of Desire: 5 Radical New Strategies that will Change your Business and Your Life*. New York: Free Press, 2002.

De la Fuente, A. 'Race and Inequality in Cuba, 1899–1981', in *Journal of Contemporary History*, vol. 30 (1995), pp. 131–168.

Dean, L. R., J. S. Caroll and C. Yang. 'Materialism, Perceived Financial Problems and Marital Satisfaction' in *Family and Consumer Sciences Research Journal*, vol. 35 (2007), no. 3, pp. 260–281.

Deci, E. L. and R. M. Ryman. 'The "What" and the "Why" of Goal Pursuits: Human Needs and the Self-determination of Behaviour', in *Psychological Inquiry*, vol. 11 (2000), pp. 227–268.

Diener, E., J. Horwitz and R. A Emmons. 'Happiness of the Very Wealthy', in *Social Indicators,* vol. 16 (1985), pp. 263–274.

The Divine Art of Living: Selections from the Writings of Bahá'u'lláh and 'Abdu'l-Bahá. Comp. Mabel Hyde Paine, rev. Anne Marie Scheffer. Wilmette, IL: Bahá'í Publishing Trust, 1986.

Dominguez, Joe and Vicki Robin. *Your Money or Your Life.* New York: Viking Penguin, 1992.

Easterbrook, G. *The Progress Paradox: How Life Gets Better While People Feel Worse.* New York: Random House, 2003.

— 'The Real Truth About Money', in *Time* magazine, 17 January 2005.

Edwards, Paul (ed.). *Encyclopedia of Philosophy.* Vol. 5. New York: Macmillan/Free Press, 1967.

Egeland, J. A. and A. M. Hostetter. 'Amish Study, I: Affective Disorders among the Amish, 1976–1980', in *The American Journal of Psychiatry,* vol. 140 (1983), pp. 56–61.

Eliade, Mircea (ed.). *Encyclopedia of Religion.* New York: MacMillan, 1987.

Ellis, A. W., S. J. Holmes and R. L. Wright. 'Age of Acquisition and the Recognition of Brand Names: On the Importance of Being Early', in *Journal of Consumer Psychology,* vol. 20 (2010), no. 1, pp. 43–52.

Environmental Defense Fud. 'Climate Change's Effects Plunder the Planet'. Online article, 2017, at http://www.edf.org/climate/climate-change-impacts.

Frankl, Viktor. *Man's Search for Meaning.* Boston: Pocket Books, 1975.

Freud, Sigmund. *Civilization and its Discontents.* New York: W.W. Norton, 1961.

Fromm, Erich. *Escape from Freedom.* New York: Rinehart, 1941.

— *To Have or To Be?* New York: Harper and Row, 1976.

Ghadirian, A-M. *Ageing: Challenges and Opportunities.* Oxford: George Ronald, 1991.

— *Alcohol and Drug Abuse: A Psychosocial and Spiritual Approach to Prevention.* Oxford: George Ronald, 2007.

— *Alzheimer's Disease: An Eclipse before Sunset.* Charleston, SC: Create Space, 2016.

— *Creative Dimensions of Suffering.* Wilmette, IL: Bahá'í Publishing Trust, 2009.

— 'Depression: Biological, Psychosocial, and Spiritual Dimensions and

Treatment', in *The Journal of Bahá'í Studies*, vol. 25 (2015), no. 3, pp. 25–60.

— *Doukhobors and the Bahá'í Faith: Tolstoy and His Appreciation of the Bahá'í Faith.* Thornhill, Ont: Baha'i Canada Publications, 1989.

— *In Search of Nirvana: A New Perspective on Alcohol and Drug Dependency.* Oxford: George Ronald, 1985, 1989.

— 'Intergenerational Responses to Persecution', in Y. Danieli (ed): *International Handbook on Multigenerational Legacies of Trauma.* New York: Plenum Press, 1998, pp. 513–532.

— 'Psychological and Spiritual Dimensions of Persecution and Suffering', in *Journal of Baha'i Studies*, vol. 6 (1994), no. 3, pp. 1–26.

— *Steadfastness in the Covenant: Responding to Tests and Tribulations.* Oxford: George Ronald, 2014.

— *Substance Abuse: A Baha'i Perspective.* Riviera, FL: Palabra Publications, 2000.

— WHO Course on Psychiatric Hospital Organization and Management. World Health Organization, Montreal Collaborating Centre for Research and Training in Mental Health, Douglas Hospital Centre, Montreal (Verdun): WHO, 1983.

— and H. E. Lehmann (eds). *Environment and Psychopathology.* New York: Springer, 1993.

Gilbert, David, Tom Walley and Bill New. 'Lifestyle Medicines', in *British Medical Journal*, vol. 321, 25 November 2000, pp. 1341–1344.

Ghaemi, N. *The Concepts of Psychiatry.* Baltimore, MD: Johns Hopkins University Press, 2003.

Giubilini, A. and F. Minerva, F. 'After-birth Abortion: Why Should the Baby Live?'. Online article in *Journal of Medical Ethics*, 23 February and 13 April 2012, available at http//dx.doi.org/10.1136/medethics-2011-100411.

Global Footprint Network. 'World Footprint: Do We Fit on the Planet?' Online article, 11 November 2015, available at http://www.footprintnetwork.org/en/index.php/GFN/page/world_footprint/.

Gold, I. 'Reduction in Psychiatry', in *The Canadian Journal of Psychiatry*, vol. 54 (2009), no. 8.

Goldbart, S., D. T. Joffe and J. Difuria. 'Money, Meaning and Identity: Coming to Terms with Being Wealthy', in T. Kasser and A. D. Kanner (eds): *Psychology and Consumer Culture*, pp. 189–210.

Graham, B. 'The Bahá'í Faith and Economics: A Review and Synthesis' in *Bahá'í Studies Review*, vol. 7 (1997).

Gray, M. 'The Affluenza Defense: Judge Rules Rich Kid's Rich Kid-ness Makes Him Not Liable for Deadly Drunk Driving Accident', reported by CNN, 12 December 2013. Available at http://newsfeed.time.com/2013/12/12/the-affluenza-defense-judge-rules-rich-kids-rich-kid-ness-makes-him-not-liable-for-deadly-drunk-driving-accident/.

Grof, P. 'Psychiatry and Neuroscience: Reduction or Pluralism', in *The Canadian Journal of Psychiatry*, vol. 54 (2009), no. 8.

Hanley, Paul. *Eleven*. Victoria, BC: Friesen Press, 2014.

Harris, Misty. 'Targeting Could Build Lifelong Brand Recognition: Study.' Canwest News Service, 23 October 2009.

Hatcher, William. Talk given at the Ḥuqúqu'lláh Conference, New York, November 1992, in *Institution of Ḥuqúqu'lláh Newsletter*, no. 9 (May 1993).

Hellevik, O. 'Economy, Values and Happiness in Norway', in *Journal of Happiness Studies,* vol. 4 (2003), no. 3, pp. 243–283.

Hesketh, T. , L. Lu and Z.W. Xing. 'The Consequences of Son Preference and Sex-selective Abortion in China and Other Asian Countries', in *Canadian Medical Association Journal* (CMAJ), vol. 183 (2011), no. 12, pp. 1374–1377.

Hidaka, B. 'Depression as a Disease of Modernity: Explanations for Increasing Prevalence', in *Journal of Affective Disorders*, vol. 140 (2012), pp. 205–214.

Hogenson, Kathryn Jewett. *Lighting the Western Sky: The Hearst Pilgrimage and the Establishment of the Bahá'í Faith in the West*. Oxford: George Ronald, 2010.

Ḥuqúqu'lláh: The Right of God. Comp. Research Department, Bahá'í World Centre. Wilmette, IL: Bahá'í Publishing Trust, 2007.

Inglehart, Ronald. *The Silent Revolution: Changing Values and Political Styles among Western Publics*. Princeton, NJ: Princeton University, 1977.

Insel, T. R. and R. Quirion. 'Psychiatry as a Clinical Neuroscience Discipline', in *Journal of the American Medical Association*, vol. 294 (2005), no. 17, pp. 2221–2224.

International Environment Forum. *Education for Sustainability*. Bahá'í Conference on Social and Economic Development in the Americas, December 2004. Available at www.bcca.org/ief/sedwksh2.htm.

International Institute for Strategic Studies (IISS). *The Military Balance 2010*. London: IISS, 2010.

International Labour Organization (ILO). *The Cost of Coercion: 2009 Global Report on Forced Labour*. Geneva: ILO, 2009.

International Religious Foundation. *World Scripture: A Comparative Anthology of Sacred Texts*. Paragon House, 1995. Available online.

Johnson, Thomas L. 'What is the Relationship between Consumerism and Materialism?' Online article, 20 March 2014, available at https://www.quora.com/What-is-the-relationship-between-consumerism-and-materialism.

Kashdan, T. B. and W. E. Breen. 'Materialism and Diminished Well-being: Experiential Avoidance as a Mediating Mechanism', in *Journal of Social and Clinical Psychology*, vol. 26 (2007), no. 5, pp. 521–539.

Kasser, T. *The High Price of Materialism*. Cambridge, MA: MIT Press, 2002.

— and A. Ahuvia. 'Materialistic Values and Well-being in Business Students', in *European Journal of Social Psychology*, vol. 32 (2002), pp. 137–146.

— and A. D. Kanner (eds). *Psychology and Consumer Culture*. Washington DC: American Psychological Association, 2004.

— and R. M. Ryan. 'A Dark Side of the American Dream: Correlates of Financial Success as a Central Life Aspiration', in *Journal of Personality and Social Psychology*, vol. 65 (1993), pp. 410–422.

—; — . 'Further Examining the American Dream: Differential Correlates of Intrinsic and Extrinsic Goals', in *Personality and Social Psychology Bulletin,* vol. 22 (1996), no. 3, pp. 280–287.

— and K. M. Sheldon. 'What Makes for a Merry Christmas?', in *Journal of Happiness Studies,* vol. 3 (2002), pp. 313–329.

— ; —; C. E. Couchman and K. M. Sheldon. 'Materialistic Values: Their Causes and Consequences', in T. Kasser and A. D. Kanner (eds): *Psychology and Consumer Culture.*

Keller, Helen. Cited in 'Odes to Joy', in *Time* magazine, 17 January 2005, p. 68.

— *Helen Keller's Journal: 1936–1937*. Garden City, NY: Doubleday, Doran & Co., 1938.

Khadem, Ramin. 'Ḥuqúqu'lláh and Prosperity: The Institution of Huququ'llah'. Online article, available at www.huquq.org.

Khursheed, Anjam. *The Universe Within: An Exploration of the Human Spirit.* Oxford: Oneworld, 1995.

Kilbourne, J. 'The More You Subtract, the More You Add: Cutting Girls Down to Size', in T. Kasser and A. D. Kanner (eds): *Psychology and Consumer Culture.*

Koplewicz, H. S., A. Gurian and K. Williams. 'The Era of Affluence and its Discontents', in *Journal of the American Academy of Child and Adolescent Psychiatry*, vol. 48 (2009), no. 11, p. 1053.

Kurzius, Brian. *Fire and Gold: Benefiting From Life's Tests.* Oxford: George Ronald, 1995.

Lane, R. E. 'The Road Not Taken: Friendship, Consumerism and Happiness', in *Critical Review*, vol. 8 (1994), no. 4, pp. 521–554.

Lemonick, Michael D. 'The Biology of Joy', in *Time* magazine, 17 January 2005.

Leschoier, I. and S. S. Gallagher. 'Unintentional Injury', in R. J. Diclemente. B. H. Williams and L. E. Ponton (eds): *Handbook of Adolescent Health Risk Behavior.* New York: Plenum Press, 1996, pp. 225–258.

Levin, J. S. 'Religion and Health: Is There an Association, Is it Valid, and Is it Causal?', in *Social Science and Medicine*, vol. 38 (1994), no. 11, pp. 1475–1482.

Levin, D. E. and S. Linn. 'The Commercialization of Childhood: Understanding the Problem and Finding Solutions', in T. Kasser and A. D. Kanner: *Psychology and Consumer Culture.*

Lights of Guidance: A Bahá'í Reference File. Comp. Helen Hornby. New Delhi: Bahá'í Publishing Trust, 5th ed. 1997.

Lo, Andrew W. 'Fear, Greed and Crisis Management: A Neuroscientific Perspective', cited by Stephen J. Dubner in *The New York Times* blog *Freakonomics: The Hidden Side of Everything.* Available at http://freakonomics.blogs.nytimes.com/2009/01/09/.

Luthar, S. 'The Culture of Affluence: Psychological Costs of Material wealth', in *Child Development*, vol. 74 (2003), pp. 1581–1591.

— and E. Becker. 'Privileged but Pressured? A Study of Affluent Youth', in *Child Development*, vol. 73 (2002), pp. 1593–1610.

MacLeish, A. 'The Poet and the Press', in *Atlantic Monthly*, March 1959, pp. 44–46.

Macnair, T. 'Obesity in Children'. BBC report, 17 December 2009. Available at http://www.bbc.co.uk/health/conditions/obesity2.shtml.

MacQueen, K. 'A Conversation with Ken MacQueen', in *Maclean's* magazine, 29 March 2010, pp. 19–21.

Martz, Erin. 'Principles of Eastern Philosophies Viewed from the Framework of Yalom's Four Existential Concerns', in *International Journal for the Advancement of Counselling*, vol. 24 (2002), no. 1, pp. 31–42.

Maslow, A. H. *Motivation and Personality*. New York, Harper and Row, 2nd ed. 1970.

McGinnis, J. M. and W. H. Foege. 'Actual Causes of Death in the United States', in *Journal of the American Medical Association*, no. 270 (1993), pp. 55–60.

Medina, J. F. *Faith, Physics and Psychology*. Wilmette, IL: Bahá'í Publishing Trust, 2006.

Merriam-Webster's Deluxe Dictionary. Pleasantville, NY: Reader's Digest Association, 1998.

Montagu, A. *The Nature of Human Aggression*. New York: Oxford University Press, 1976.

Moore, Charles. 'Moral Materialism'. Online article, 2010, available at www.plough.com/eng/topics/justice/social-justice/moral-materialism.

Morss, Elliott R. 'The Economics of the Global Entertainment Industry'. Online article, 26 June 2009, available at http://www.morssglobalfinance.com/the-economics-of-the-global-entertainment-industry/.

Moynihan, R, I. Heath, and D. Henry. 'Selling Sickness: The Pharmaceutical Industry and Disease', in *British Medical Journal*, vol. 324 (2002), pp. 886–891.

Nabíl-i- A'zam (Muhammad-i-Zarandí). *The Dawn-Breakers: Nabíl's Narrative of the Early Days of the Bahá'í Revelation*. Trans. Shoghi Effendi. Wilmette, IL: Bahá'í Publishing Trust, 1932.

Myers, D. G. 'The Funds, Friends and Faith of Happy People', in *The American Psychologist*, vol. 55 (2000), pp. 56–67.

— *The Pursuit of Happiness*. New York: Avon, 1993.

The New Encyclopaedia Britannica, Micropaedia. Chicago: Encyclopaedia Britannica, 1988, vol. 2.

Paris, J. 'Psychiatry and Neuroscience', in *The Canadian Journal of Psychiatry*, vol. 54 (2009), no. 8.

Park, Madison. 'Despondent Dads Driven to Kill Loved Ones', on CNN, 19 May 2009. Available at www.cnn.com/2009/CRIME/05/19/murder.suicide.families/.

Parwini, Zora. 'Poverty Forces Bangladeshi Women to Turn to Organ Trade'. Online article, 18 May 2005, available at www.wsws.org/articles/2005/may2005/bang-m18.shtml.

Peen, J., R. Schoevers, A. Beekers and J. Dekker. 'The Current Status of Urban–Rural Differences in Psychiatric Disorders', in *Acta Psychiatrica Scandinavica*, vol. 121 (2010), pp. 84–93.

Piachaud, David. 'Freedom To Be a Child: Commercial Pressures on Children', in *Social Policy and Society*, vol. 7 (2008), no. 4, pp. 445–456.

Pieters, R. 'Bidirectional Dynamics of Materialism and Loneliness: Not Just a Vicious Cycle', in *Journal of Consumer Research*, vol. 40 (2013).

Pittman, F. S. 'Children of the Rich', in *Family Process*, vol. 24 (1985), pp. 461–472 [PubMed: 4085614].

van Praag, H. M. 'Does Psychiatry Really Know "Solid Disease Diagnosis"?', in *The Canadian Journal of Psychiatry*, vol. 55 (2010), no. 2.

Pruett, Dave. 'Toward a Post-materialistic Science', in *The Huffington Post*, 1 October 2014. Available at http://www.huffingtonpost.com/dave-pruett/toward-a-postmaterialistic-science_b_5842730.html.

Psychology and Knowledge of Self. Comp. Research Department of the Universal House of Justice. Available at http://bahairesearch.com.

Pyarelal. *Mahatma Gandhi: The Last Phase.* Vol. X, part II. Ahmedabad: Navaijan, 1958. Available at http://www.mkgandhi.org/ebks/mahatma-gandhi-volume-ten.pdf.

Qur'án. *The Koran.* Trans. J. M. Rodwell. London: Dent, 1953.

Richins, M. L. 'Media, Materialism, and Human Happiness', in *Advances in Consumer Research*, vol. 14 (1987), pp. 352–356.

— and S. Dawson. 'A Consumer Values Orientation for Materialism and its Measurement: Scale Development and Validation', in *Journal of Consumer Research*, vol. 19 (1992), pp. 303–316.

Robbins, Richard. *Global Problems and the Culture of Capitalism.* Boston: Allyn and Bacon, 1999.

Rosenberg, E. L. 'Mindfulness and Consumerism', in T. Kasser and A. D. Kanner (eds): *Psychology and Consumer Culture.*

Sachs, Jeffrey D. 'Common Wealth', in *Time* magazine in partnership with CNN, 13 March 2008. Available at www.time.com/time/specials2007/article.

Schaefer, Udo. *The Imperishable Dominion.* Oxford: George Ronald, 1983.

Shah, Anup. 'Climate Change and Global Warming'. Online article, 2

February 2015, available at http://www.globalissues.org/issue/178/ climate-change-and-global-warming.

— 'Climate Justice and Equity'. Online article, 8 January 2012, available at http://www.globalissues.org/article/231/climate-justice-and-equity.

Sheldon, S., J. L. Greenberg and T. A. Pyszazynski. 'Death-denying Materialism', in T. Kasser and A. D. Kanner, (eds): *Psychology and Consumer Culture.*

Shoghi Effendi. *The Advent of Divine Justice.* Wilmette, IL: Bahá'í Publishing Trust, 1963.

— *Citadel of Faith.* Wilmette, IL: Bahá'í Publishing Trust, 1965.

— *God Passes By* (1944). Wilmette, IL: Bahá'í Publishing Trust, 1965.

— *Letters from the Guardian to Australia and New Zealand 1923–1957.* Sydney: National Spiritual Assembly of the Bahá'ís of Australia, 1970.

— *Messages to Canada.* National Spiritual Assembly of the Baha'is of Canada, 1965.

— *The Promised Day is Come* (1941). Wilmette, IL: Bahá'í Publishing Trust, 1985.

— *The World Order of Bahá'u'lláh* (1938). Wilmette, IL: Bahá'í Publishing Trust, 1991.

Shoumatoff, A. 'Agony and Ivory', in *Vanity Fair*, August 2011. Available at http://www.vanityfair.com/news/2011/08/elephants-201108.

Singer, P. and A. Sagan. 'Are We Ready for a "Morality Pill"?', in *The New York Times*, 28 January 2012.

Somerville, M. *Birds on an Ethics Wire: Battles about Values in the Culture Wars.* Montreal: McGill University Press, 2015.

— *Death Talk: The Case Against Euthanasia and Physician-Assisted Suicide.* Montreal: McGill University Press, 2001.

Sperling, Gene B. 'The Case for Universal Basic Education for the World's Poorest Boys and Girls'. New York: Council on Foreign Relations, 2005. Online article, available at www.cfr.org.

Spiegel, J. M. 'Commentary: Daring to Learn from a Good Example and Break the "Cuba Taboo"', in *International Journal of Epidemiology*, vol. 35 (2006), pp. 825–826.

Star of the West. Periodical, 25 vols. 1910–1935. Rpt. Oxford: George Ronald, 1978. Available on CD-ROM, Talisman Educational Software, 2001.

Storm, S. 'Capitalism and Climate Change: Can the Invisible Hand Adjust the Natural Thermostat?', in *Development and Change*, vol. 40 (2009), no. 6, pp. 1011–1038. Available at http://onlinelibrary.wiley.com/doi/10.1111/j.1467-7660.2009.01610.x/abstract.

Swinyard, William R., Kau Ah-Keng and Phua Hui-Yin. 'Happiness, Materialism and Religious Experience in the US and Singapore', in *Journal of Happiness Studies*, vol. 2 (2001), pp. 13–32.

Tapia Granados, José A. and Ana V. Diez Roux. 'Life and Death During the Great Depression', in *Proceedings of the National Academy of Sciences of the United States of America* (2009).

Taherzadeh, A. *The Child of the Covenant*. Oxford: George Ronald, 2000.

— *The Revelation of Baha'u'llah*. 4 vols. Oxford: George Ronald, 1974–86.

Tang, Thomas Li-Ping. 'Money. The Meaning of Money, Management, Spirituality, and Religion', in *Journal of Management, Spirituality and Religion*, vol. 7 (2010), no. 2.

Tone, A. *The Age of Anxiety: A History of America's Turbulent Affair with Tranquilizers*. New York: Basic Books, 2009.

'Underage, Overweight', in *Scientific American*, May 2010, p. 30.

Union of Concerned Scientists. 'Is Global Warming Linked to Severe Weather?' Online article, 17 June 2011, available at http://www.ucsusa.org/global_warming/science_and_impacts/impacts/global-warming-rain-snow-tornadoes.html#.VpRp4PkrK71.

United Nations. 'Secretary-General Calls for $30 Billion to Restructure World Agriculture, Create Long-Term Food Security'. Press release, 30 November 2008. Available at http://www.un.org/esa/ffd/doha/press/foodsideevent.pdf.

United Nations Children's Fund (UNICEF). *The State of the World's Children 2008: Child Survival*. New York: UNICEF, 2008.

United Nations Department of Public Information. 'Secretary-General, Addressing Side Event, Spells Out Areas "Crying Out for Action" to Advance Implementation of Water and Sanitation Agenda'. Press release, 25 September 2008. Available at http://www.un.org/News/Press/docs/2008/sgsm11813.doc.htm.

United Nations Development Programme (UNDP). *Human Development Report 2007/2008: Fighting Climate Change: Human Solidarity in a Divided World*. New York: UNDP, 2008.

— *Tackling Corruption, Transforming Lives*. Asia–Pacific Human Development Report. New Delhi: Macmillan India, 2008.

BIBLIOGRAPHY

United Nations Office of Drugs and Crime (UNODC). *World Drug Report 2006*. Vienna: UNODC, 2006. Available at www.unodc.org.

— *World Drug Report 2008*. Vienna: UNODC, 2008. Available at www.unodc.org.

The Universal House of Justice. *Century of Light*. Haifa: Bahá'í World Centre, 2001.

— Letter to the Believers in Iran, 2 March 2013.

— Letter to the Deputies and Representatives of the Institution of Ḥuqúqu'lláh, 14 February 1997.

— *Messages from the Universal House of Justice 1963–1986: The Third Epoch of the Formative Age*. Comp. Geoffry W. Marks. Wilmette, IL: Bahá'í Publishing Trust, 1996.

— Message to the Bahá'ís of the World, 1 March 2017.

— Message to the Bahá'ís of the World, Riḍván 2008.

— Message to the Conference of the Continental Boards of Counsellors, 28 December 2010.

— Message to the Conference of the Continental Boards of Counsellors, 29 December 2015.

— *The Promise of World Peace*. Haifa: Bahá'í World Centre, 1985.

— *Turning Point: Selected Messages of the Universal House of Justice and Supplementary Material 1996–2006*. Riviera Beach, FL: Palabra Publications, 2006.

— *A Wider Horizon: Selected Messages of the Universal House of Justice 1983–1992*. Riviera Beach, FL: Palabra, 1992.

Van Boven, L. and T. Gilovich. 'To Do or to Have? That is the Question', in *Journal of Personality and Social Psychology*, vol. 85 (2003), no. 6, pp. 1198–1202.

Wallace, Alan B. *The Taboo of Subjectivity: Toward a New Science of Consciousness*. Oxford: Oxford University Press, 2000.

Wallace, J. M. and T. A. Forman. 'Religion's Role in Promoting Health and Reducing Risk among American Youth', in *Health Education and Behavior*, vol. 25 (1998), no. 6, pp. 721–741.

Warner, E. 'The Role of Belief in Healing', in *Canadian Medical Association Journal*, vol. 128 (1983).

Wilson, Andrew (ed.). *World Scripture: A Comparative Anthology of Sacred Texts*. New York: International Religious Foundation, 1991. Available at http://www.unification.net/ws/.

Wilson, Edward O. *On Human Nature*. Cambridge, MA: Harvard University Press, 1978.

Wilkinson, R. and K. E. Pickett. *The Spirit Level: Why More Equal Societies Almost Always Do Better*. London: Penguin, 2009.

Zarqání, Mírzá Maḥmúd. *Maḥmúd's Diary: The Diary of Mírzá Maḥmúd-i-Zar'qání Chronicling 'Abdu'l-Bahá's Journey to America*. Trans. M. Sobhani with S. Macias. Oxford: George Ronald, 1998.

REFERENCES

Introduction

1   See www.allaboutphilosophy.org/Materialism.htm.
2   ibid.
3   ibid.
4   Moore, 'Moral Materialism'.
5   ibid.
6   Eliade (ed.), Encyclopedia of Religion, p. 282.
7   Pruett, 'Toward a Post-Materialistic Science'.
8   ibid.
9   See wordnetweb.princeton.edu/perl/webwn.
10 Ahuvia and Wong, 'Materialism: Origins and Implications for Personal Well-being', pp. 172–8.
11 See www. en.wiktionary.org/wiki/materialism.
12 Csikszentmihalyi, 'Materialism and the Evolution of Consciousness', p. 92.
13 ibid.
14 ibid.
15 Letter from the Universal House of Justice to the Bahá'ís of the World, 1 March 2017.
16 Belk, 'Materialism: Trait Aspects of Living in the Material World'.
17 Brezinka, cited in Schaefer, Imperishable Dominion, p. 85.
18 'Abdu'l-Bahá, Promulgation of Universal Peace, p. 177.
19 Dalai Lama, talk on 'Cultural Compassion' in Riga, Latvia, 9 September 2013. Available at www.dalailama.com/news/2013.

1. Perspectives on Materialism

1   The Universal House of Justice, Message to the Bahá'ís of the World, Riḍván 2008.
2   See http://en.wikipedia.org/wiki/Materialism.
3   Swinyard et al., 'Happiness, Materialism and Religious experience in the US and Singapore', p. 15.

4   Richins and Dawson, 'A Consumer Values Orientation for Material-
    ism and its Measurement', cited in Swinyard et al., op. cit. p. 15.
5   Belk, 1985; Richins, 1987; Richins and Dawson, 1992.
6   Swinyard et al., op. cit. p. 18.
7   Allport and Ross, 'Personal Religious Orientation and Prejudice'.
8   Swinyard et al., op. cit. p. 17.
9   Kashdan and Breen, 'Materialism and Diminished Well-being', p.
    522.
10 Compare the statement of Bahá'u'lláh that true liberty is to be found
    in obedience to divine law: 'Consider the pettiness of men's minds.
    They ask for that which injureth them, and cast away the thing that
    profiteth them. They are, indeed, of those that are far astray. We find
    some men desiring liberty, and priding themselves therein. Such men
    are in the depths of ignorance' (Kitáb-i-Aqdas, para. 122).
11 See Csikszentmihalyi, 'If We Are So Rich, Why Aren't We Happy?'
12 Matson, cited in Khursheed, The Universe Within, p. 41.
13 Csikszentmihalyi, 'If We Are So Rich, Why Aren't We Happy?', p.
    821.
14 Cited in S. Sheldon, J. L. Greenberg and T. A. Pyszazynski. 'Death-
    denying Materialism', in Kasser and Kanner (eds): Psychology and
    Consumer Culture, pp. 138–9.
15 The following statement by Baha'u'llah reflects the fact that the spiri-
    tual strength latent within an individual is everlasting: 'O Son of Man!
    Thou art My dominion and My dominion perisheth not; wherefore
    fearest thou thy perishing? Thou art My light and My light shall never
    be extinguished; why dost thou dread extinction? Thou art My glory
    and My glory fadeth not; thou art My robe and My robe shall never
    be outworn. Abide then in thy love for Me, that thou mayest find Me
    in the realm of glory' (Bahá'u'lláh, Hidden Words, Arabic no. 14).
16 'Capitalism', in The New Encyclopaedia Britannica, Micropaedia, vol.
    2, p. 831.
17 Chavez Rojas, The Impact of Capitalism and Materialism on Generosity:
    A Cross-national Examination.
18 Johnson, 'What is the Relationship between Consumerism and
    Materialism?'
19 See for example Inglehart, The Silent Revolution: Changing Values and
    Political Styles among Western Publics.
20 Chavez Rojas, op. cit., p. 3.
21 ibid. p. 33.
22 Bahá'í International Community, Rethinking Prosperity: Forging
    Alternatives to a Culture of Consumerism.
23 ibid.
24 Kasser et al., 'Materialistic Values: Their Causes and Consequences',

in Kasser and Kanner (eds): *Psychology and Consumer Culture*, pp. 14–22.

25   ibid.
26   Bahá'u'lláh, Kitáb-i-'Ahd, para. 1, in *Tablets*, p. 219.
27   Kasser et al., op.cit.
28   ibid.
29   ibid. p. 16.
30   Kasser, *The High Price of Materialism*, p. 3.
31   Fromm, *Escape from Freedom*, pp. 109–10.
32   Kasser, *The High Price of Materialism*, p. 78.
33   Freud, *Civilization and its Discontents*, p. 24.
34   ibid. p. 10.
35   ibid. p. 45.
36   ibid. p. 25.
37   ibid.
38   ibid.
39   ibid. pp. 26–8.
40   ibid. pp. 28–9.
41   ibid. pp. 68–70.
42   ibid. p. 81.

2 Exploiting Desire: The Rise of Consumerism

1   Gandhi, as quoted in Pyarelal, *Mahatma Gandhi: The Last Phase*, p. 668.
2   See www.globalissues.org/article/236/creating-the-consumer.
3   Robbins, *Global Problems*, pp. 14–24.
4   ibid. pp. 15–16.
5   Fromm, *To Have or To Be?*, pp. 24–42.
6   Kasser and Kanner (eds), *Psychology and Consumer Culture*, pp. 3–4.
7   Khursheed, *The Universe Within*, p. 41.
8   Ahuvia, 'Individualism/Collectivism and Cultures of Happiness', p. 23.
9   Rosenberg, 'Mindfulness and Consumerism', pp. 110–11.
10   Levin and Linn, 'The Commercialization of Childhood', pp. 213, 218.
11   ibid. p. 214.
12   ibid.
13   ibid. p. 223.
14   'Underage, Overweight', in *Scientific American*, May 2010, p. 30.
15   ibid.
16   Ellis, Holmes and Wright, 'Age of Acquisition and the Recognition of Brand Names: The Importance of Being Early'.
17   ibid. See also Misty Harris's syndicated article 'Targeting Could Build Lifelong Brand Recognition'.

18 Levin and Linn, 'The Commercialization of Childhood', p. 225.
19 The Universal House of Justice, *Turning Point*, p. 136.
20 Kilbourne, J. "The More You Subtract, the More You Add: Cutting Girls Down to Size", p. 252.
21 ibid.
22 Becker and Burwell, 'Acculturation and Disordered Eating in Fiji'.
23 Kasser, cited in Clay, 'Advertising to Children: Is it Ethical?', p. 52.
24 BBC News, 'UK Children Damaged by Materialism'.
25 The Universal House of Justice, Message to the Conference of Continental Counsellors, 28 December 2010.

3 Materialism and Discontent

1   Socrates, quoted in Tang, 'Momey. The Meaning of Money, Management, Spirituality, and Religion', p. 180.
2   See Goldbart et al., 'Money, Meaning and Identity'.
3   Myers, 'The Funds, Friends and Faith of Happy People', pp. 56–67.
4   ibid. See also Easterbrook, 'The Real Truth About Money'; and www.wikihow.com/Escape-Materialism-and-Find-Happiness.
5   Easterbrook, op. cit. p. 64.
6   Hellevik, 'Economy, Values and Happiness in Norway'.
7   Campbell, *The Sense of Well-being in America.*
8   Diener et al., 'Happiness of the Very Wealthy'.
9   Csikszentmihalyi, 'If We Are So Rich, Why Aren't We Happy?'
10 ibid.
11 Myers, *The Pursuit of Happiness*, p. 57, cited by Csikszentmihalyi.
12 Kasser et al., 'Materialistic Values: Their Causes and Consequences', pp. 14–22.
13 Easterbrook, 'The Real Truth About Money', p. 64.
14 ibid.
15 MacLeish, 'The Poet and the Press'.
16 Attributed to 'Abdu'l-Bahá in the diary of Ahmad Sohrab, *Star of the West*, vol. 8, no. 2, p. 17. Also available in Kurzius, *Fire and Gold*, p. 171.
17 'Abdu'l-Bahá, *Paris Talks*, no. 35, p. 110.
18 Warner, 'The Role of Belief in Healing', p. 1108.
19 Bahá'u'lláh, 'Words of Wisdom', in *Tablets*, pp. 155–6.
20 'Abdu'l-Bahá, *Tablets*, vol. 3, p. 557.
21 'Abdu'l-Bahá, *Selections*, no. 188, pp. 220–21.
22 Ghadirian, *Alcohol and Drug Abuse*, pp. 85–6.
23 'Abdu'l-Bahá, *Promulgation of Universal Peace*, p. 335.
24 'Abdu'l-Bahá, *Secret of Divine Civilization*, p. 99.
25 Carlin, 'The Pursuit of Happiness', p. 62.
26 Cited by Lemonick, 'The Biology of Joy', p. 50.

27 Keller, cited in 'Odes to Joy', p. 68.

28 'Abdu'l-Bahá, in *The Divine Art of Living*, p. 29.

4 Materialism and Mental Health

1 The Universal House of Justice, Message to the Conference of Continental Counsellors, 28 December 2010.

2 Hidaka, 'Depression as a Disease of Modernity: Explanations for Increasing Prevalence', p. 208.

3 ibid.

4 Peen et al., 'The Current Status of Urban–Rural Differences in Psychiatric Disorders'.

5 Egeland and Hostetter, 'Amish Study, I: Affective Disorders among the Amish, 1976–1980'.

6 Barrie, 'Happiest Places have Highest Suicide Rates'.

7 ibid.

8 For further details on depression, modernity and affluence in relation to spirituality, see my 2015 article: 'Depression: Biological, Psychosocial and Spiritual Dimenstions and Treatment.'

9 Lane, 'The Road Not Taken: Friendship, Consumerism and Happiness'.

10 ibid. p. 526.

11 ibid. p. 528.

12 ibid. p. 544.

13 ibid. pp. 529–30.

14 Kasser et al., 'Materialistic Values: Their Causes and Consequences', pp. 14–22.

15 The term 'narcissism' comes from Greek mythology. Narcissus was a handsome youth who repulsed the love of the nymph Echo. Aphrodite, goddess of love, punished him for his cruelty by making him fall in love with his own image reflected in a fountain. His hopeless attempts to approach the object of his love led to despair; he died of thirst. In our materialistic world there are many Narcissuses who have a deep thirst for true love but are so fascinated by and preoccupied with their own self-love that they remain imprisoned in their worship of themselves. This phenomenon calls to mind the following words of Bahá'u'lláh: 'O Son of Spirit! I created thee rich, why dost thou bring thyself down to poverty? Noble I made thee, wherewith dost thou abase thyself?' (*Hidden Words*, Arabic no. 13.)

16 Grant study cited in Arehart-Treichel, 'Research Shines Spotlight on Narcissistic Personality Disorder'.

17 Martz, 'Principles of Eastern Philosophies'.

18 Somerville, *Death Talk*, p. 113.

19 Ghadirian, *Alcohol and Drug Abuse*, pp. 135–9.

20 MacQueen, 'A Conversation with Ken MacQueen', p. 19.
21 Tone, *The Age of Anxiety*, p. xii.
22 ibid. p. xvi.
23 ibid. p. xviii.
24 Park, 'Despondent Dads Driven to Kill Loved Ones'.
25 ibid.
26 Bahá'u'lláh, *Hidden Words*, Arabic no. 14.
27 Shoghi Effendi, *Citadel of Faith*, pp. 124–5.
28 http://en.wikipedia.org/wiki/Materialism.
29 Montagu, *The Nature of Human Aggression*, p. 57.
30 Fromm, cited in Khursheed, *The Universe Within*, pp. 79–80.
31 'Abdu'l-Bahá, *The Secret of Divine Civilization*, pp. 97–8.
32 ibid. p. 98.
33 Bahá'u'lláh, *Gleanings from the Writings of Bahá'u'lláh*, CLXIV, p. 342.
34 Koplewicz, Gurian and Williams, 'The Era of Affluence and its Discontents', p. 1053.
35 See https://en.wikipedia.org/wiki/Affluenza.
36 Koplewicz et al., op cit.
37 Luthar and Becker, 'Privileged but Pressured? A Study of Affluent Youth'.
38 Pittman, 'Children of the Rich', p. 470.
39 Luthar, 'The Culture of Affluence: Psychological Costs of Material Wealth'.
40 Singer and Sagan, 'Are We Ready for a "Morality Pill"'?
41 Gray, 'The Affluenza Defense'.
42 Castello, 'Will Ethan Couch, the 'Affluenza' Teen, Get Off Lightly Again?'
43 Keller, *Helen Keller's Journal: 1936–1937*, p. 60.
44 Luthar, 'The Culture of Affluence: Psychological Costs of Material Wealth'.
45 Bezruchka, 'The Effect of Economic Recession on Population Health'.
46 Wilkinson and Pickett, *The Spirit Level: Why More Equal Societies Almost Always Do Better* (2009).
47 Tapia Granados and Diez Roux, 'Life and Death During the Great Depression'. Also cited in Arehart-Treichel, 'Research Shines Spotlight on Narcissistic Personality Disorder', p. 24.
48 Bezruchka et al., 'Improving Economic Equality and Health: The Case of Postwar Japan'.
49 De la Fuente, 'Race and Inequality in Cuba, 1899–1981'.
50 Spiegel, 'Commentary: Daring to Learn from a Good Example and Break the "Cuba Taboo"'.
51 Wilkinson and Pickett, op. cit.
52 Bezruchka, 'The Effect of Economic Recession on Population Health'.

53 Wilkinson and Pickett, op. cit.
54 See http://www.healthyminds.org/Home-Page-Feature/Mental-Health-and-Economy.aspx.
55 Bezruchka, 'The Effect of Economic Recession on Population Health'.
56 Kasser, *The High Price of Materialism*, p. 64.
57 Pieters, 'Bidirectional Dynamics of Materialism and Loneliness: Not Just a Vicious Cycle'.
58 Amiel, 'I am Hearing a Lot about Loneliness', in *Maclean's* magazine (Canada), 7 December 2009, p. 12.
59 Bahá'u'lláh, *Hidden Words*, Arabic no. 12.
60 Wallace and Forman, 'Religion's Role in Promoting Health and Reducing Risk among American Youth'.
61 'Obesity in children and teens', in *American Academy of Child and Adolescent Psychiatry*, no. 79, May 2008, p. 1.
62 'Underage, Overweight', in *Scientific American*, May 2010, p. 30.
63 MacNair, 'Obesity in children'.
64 McGinnis and Foege, 'Actual Causes of Death in the United States'.
65 Levin, 'Religion and Health: Is There an Association, Is it Valid, and Is it Causal?'
66 Wallace and Forman, 'Religion's Role in Promoting Health and Reducing Risk among American Youth'.
67 ibid.
68 ibid.
69 ibid.
70 Leschoier and Gallagher, 'Unintentional Injury'.
71 Centers for Disease Control and Prevention, 'Leading Causes of Mortality and Morbidity and Contributing Behaviors in the United States, pp. 1–2.
72 Morss, 'The Economics of the Global Entertainment Industry'.
73 'Abdu'l-Bahá, *Tablets*, vol. 3, pp. 673–4.

5 Materialistic Science and Bioethics

1 'Abdu'l-Bahá, *Some Answered Questions*, no. 64, p. 272.
2 Beauregard and O'Leary, *The Spiritual Brain*, pp. 42–3.
3 See for example Ghaemi, *The Concepts of Psychiatry* (2003); Insel and Quirion, 'Psychiatry as a Clinical Neuroscience Discipline' (2005); Grof, 'Psychiatry and Neuroscience' (2009); Gold, 'Reduction in Psychiatry' (2009); Paris, 'Psychiatry and Neuroscience' (2009).
4 Crick, *The Astonishing Hypothesis: The Scientific Search for the Soul*, p. 3.
5 Gold, 'Reduction in Psychiatry', p. 507.
6 ibid. p. 508.
7 Paris, 'Psychiatry and Neuroscience', p. 513.

8   For example, Compston, 'Decade of the Brain'.

9   Wilson, *On Human Nature*, p. 42.

10 Alper, *The God Part of the Brain*, p. 56.

11 Beauregard and O'Leary, *The Spiritual Brain*, p. 45.

12 ibid. p. 292.

13 Dalai Lama, *The Universe in a Single Atom*, p. 207.

14 van Praag, 'Does Psychiatry Really Know "Solid Disease Diagnosis"?', p. 64.

15 Wallace, *The Taboo of Subjectivity*, p. 136.

16 'Abdu'l-Bahá, Tablet to Auguste Forel, p. 8; also in *Bahá'í World*, vol. 15, p. 38.

17 Arbab, 'Knowledge and Civilization', p. 159.

18 'Abdu'l-Bahá, *Promulgation of Universal Peace*, p. 140.

19 ibid. p. 49.

20 Arbab, 'Knowledge and Civilization', p. 160.

21 Somerville, *Birds on an Ethics Wire: Battles about Values in the Culture Wars*.

22 ibid. p. 173.

23 'Abdu'l-Bahá, *Paris Talks*, no. 2, p. 4.

24 'Abdu'l-Bahá, *Promulgation of Universal Peace*, p. 49.

25 Giubilini and Minerva, 'After-birth abortion: Why should the baby live?' (Abstract to the article).

26 ibid.

27 ibid.

28 ibid.

29 Hesketh, Lu and Xing, 'The Consequences of Son Preference and Sex-selective Abortion in China and Other Asian Countries'.

30 ibid. p. 1374.

31 ibid.

32 Somerville, op. cit, p. 177.

33 ibid. p. 180.

6 Finding the Balance: Materialism and Intrinsic Values

1   'Abdu'l-Bahá, *The Secret of Divine Civilization*, p. 2.

2   Kasser and Ryan, 'Further Examining the American Dream'.

3   Kasser and Ahuvia, 'Materialistic Values and Well-being in Business Students'.

4   Goldbart et al., 'Money, Meaning and Identity'.

5   ibid.

6   Needleman, *Money and the Meaning of Life*.

7   Goldbart et al., 'Money, Meaning and Identity'.

8   ibid.

9   Bahá'u'lláh, in *Ḥuqúqu'lláh: The Right of God*, no. 10, p. 13.

10   Cushman, 'Why the Self is Empty'.
11   ibid.
12   Dominguez and Robin, *Your Money or Your Life*, pp. 22–3.
13   United Nations, *World Drug Report 2006*.
14   Maslow, *Motivation and Personality*, pp. 59–61.
15   ibid. pp. 59–60.
16   ibid. See also http://pandc.ca/?page=maslow.
17   Einstein, cited in Mitchell, *The Enlightened Mind*, pp. 191–2.
18   'Abdu'l-Bahá, *The Secret of Divine Civilization*, pp. 2–3.
19   From a letter written on behalf of Shoghi Effendi, 18 February 1954, in *Lights of Guidance*, no. 391, p. 114.
20   Shoghi Effendi, *The Promised Day Is Come*, p. 41.
21   'Abdu'l-Bahá, *Selections*, no. 68, pp. 103–4.
22   From a letter written on behalf of Shoghi Effendi, 8 January 1949, in Kurzius (ed.) *Fire and Gold*, p. 78.
23   Bahá'u'lláh, in *Bahá'í Prayers*, p. 28.
24   From a letter written on behalf of Shoghi Effendi, 8 December 1935, in *Lights of Guidance*, no. 449, p. 135.
25   'Abdu'l-Bahá, *Promulgation of Universal Peace*, p. 195.
26   ibid. p. 184.
27   Bahá'u'lláh, Súriy-i-Ra'ís, para. 34, in *Summons of the Lord of Hosts*, p. 154.
28   Bahá'u'lláh, *Gleanings*, no. CLIII, para. 6, p. 327.
29   Eliade, *Encyclopedia of Religion*, p. 307.
30   ibid. p. 308.
31   ibid.
32   ibid. pp. 309–10.
33   ibid. 310.
34   Bhagavad Gita 3: 40–41.
35   ibid. 2 : 62–6.
36   Eliade, *Encyclopedia of Religion*, p. 313.
37   ibid. pp. 308–13, passim.
38   Matt. 16: 26.
39   Cited in Chew, *The Chinese Religion*, p. 104.
40   Allama Prabhu, Vacama 91, cited in Wilson (ed), *World Scriptures*, Ch.7, 'The Human Condition: Selfish Desire, Lust and Greed'.
41   Qur'án 45: 23, cited ibid.
42   Eliade, *Encyclopedia of Religion*, p. 314.
43   'Abdu'l-Bahá, *The Secret of Divine Civilization*, pp. 59–60.
44   'Abdu'l-Bahá, *Selections*, no. 176, p. 204.
45   'Abdu'l-Bahá, *Paris Talks*, no. 18: 'The Two Natures in Man', pp. 55–7.
46   For further discussion of this subject see Taherzadeh, *The Revelation of Bahá'u'lláh*, vol. 3, pp. 78–9.

47 'Abdu'l-Bahá, *Some Answered Questions*, no. 64, p. 236.
48 Shoghi Effendi, *Letters from the Guardian to Australia and New Zealand*, p. 1.
49 'Abdu'l-Bahá, *Some Answered Questions*, no. 64, pp. 272–3.
50 Bahá'u'lláh, *Gleanings*, no. CLIII, para. 8, p. 328.
51 'Abdu'l-Bahá, *Selections*, no. 157, p. 186.
52 Bahá'u'lláh, *Epistle to the Son of the Wolf*, p. 56.
53 Matt. 6: 19–21.
54 According to Belk, 'Worldly Possessions'.
55 Kasser and Sheldon, 'What Makes for a Merry Christmas?'.
56 Kasser, 'Materialistic Value Orientation', in Bouckaert and Zsolnai, *Handbook of Spirituality and Business*.
57 Burroughs and Rindfleisch, 'Materialism and Well-being'.
58 Kasser, 'Materialistic Value Orientation', in Bouckaert and Zsolnai, *Handbook of Spirituality and Business*.
59 ibid.
60 Medina, *Faith, Physics and Psychology*, p. 459.
61 Van Boven and Gilovich, 'To Do or to Have? That is the Question'.
62 Kashdan and Breen, 'Materialism and Diminished Well-Being', p. 522.
63 ibid., citing Fromm, 1976; Kasser, 2002; Deci and Ryan, 2000; and Maslow, 1970.
64 Kasser, *The High Price of Materialism*.
65 Davis, *The New Culture of Desire*, pp. 138–9.
66 ibid. pp. 139–41.
67 ibid. p. 141.
68 Quoted in Adams, *Better Happy than Rich?*.
69 Corrigan, *The Sociology of Consumption*, pp. 68–9.
70 Lo, 'Fear, Greed and Crisis Management: A Neuroscientific Perspective'.
71 Bickel, cited in 'Self-destructive Acts', p. 19.
72 ibid.
73 Carlin, 'The Pursuit of Happiness'.
74 'Abdu'l-Bahá, *'Abdu'l-Bahá in London*, p. 87.
75 Bahá'u'lláh, *Gleanings*, CXXIII, p. 261.

7 Wealth, Poverty and Moral Values

1 The Universal House of Justice, Message to the Bahá'ís of the World, 1 March 2017.
2 Goldbart et al., 'Money, Meaning and Identity'.
3 Matt. 19:24.
4 Bahá'u'lláh, Bishárát, in *Tablets*, p. 24.
5 Bahá'u'lláh, *Gleanings*, CXXVIII, para. 4, p. 276.

6   Bahá'u'lláh, *Hidden Words*, Persian no. 53.
7   Bahá'u'lláh, cited in *Ḥuqúqu'lláh: The Right of God*, no. 10. Also available in *The Compilation of Compilations*, vol. 1, p. 496.
8   Bahá'u'lláh, *Gleanings*, CLIII, para. 8, p. 328.
9   Bahá'u'lláh, cited in Shoghi Effendi, *The Advent of Divine Justice*, pp. 30–31.
10 'Abdu'l-Bahá, *Tablets*, vol. 2, p. 292. See also Hogenson, *Lighting the Western Sky*, Appendix 3 and note.
11 'Abdu'l-Bahá, *Some Answered Questions*, no. 64, p. 271.
12 'Abdu'l-Bahá, *Promulgation of Universal Peace*, p. 302.
13 ibid.
14 'Abdu'l-Bahá, Tablet to the Hague, in *Selections*, no. 227, p. 302.
15 Bahá'u'lláh, *Kitáb-i-Íqán*, para. 142, pp. 131–2.
16 'Abdu'l-Bahá, in *Bahá'í Prayers*, p. 58.
17 Bahá'u'lláh, *Gleanings*, XLIII, para. 3, p. 93.
18 ibid.
19 Bahá'u'lláh, *Hidden Words*, Arabic no. 56.
20 Bahá'u'lláh, *Gleanings*, CXV, para. 13, pp. 245–6.
21 Letter from the Universal House of Justice to Deputies and Representatives of the Institution of Ḥuqúqu'lláh, 14 February 1997.
22 'Abdu'l-Bahá, *Promulgation of Universal Peace*, p. 221.
23 Bahá'u'lláh, cited in the compilation *Psychology and Knowledge of Self*.
24 Bahá'u'lláh, *Gleanings*, LXXV, para. 1, p. 143.
25 'Abdu'l-Bahá, cited in the compilation *Psychology and Knowledge of Self*.
26 Shoghi Effendi, letter to an individual, 14 December 1941, cited in 'Living the Life', *The Compilation of Compilations*, vol. 2, no. 1295, p. 11; also in the compilation *Psychology and Knowledge of Self*.
27 Shoghi Effendi, letter to an individual, 8 January 1949, cited in the compilation *Psychology and Knowledge of Self*.
28 'Abdu'l-Bahá, *Selections*, no. 35, pp. 71–2.
29 'Abdu'l-Bahá, *Tablets*, vol. 1, p. 214.
30 Bahá'u'lláh, *Hidden Words*, Arabic no. 42.
31 Bahá'u'lláh, *Gleanings*, V, para. 2, pp. 7–8.
32 Bahá'u'lláh, cited by Shoghi Effendi, *The Advent of Divine Justice*, p. 31.
33 Shoghi Effendi, ibid. p. 30.
34 Bahá'u'lláh, cited by Shoghi Effendi, ibid. p. 32.
35 Shoghi Effendi, ibid. p. 33.
36 See http://www.nytimes.com/2005/01/05/opinions/05kris.html?ex=1262.
37 See Anup Shah's website which brings together many of these recent statistics, available at www.globalissues.org.

38 UNICEF, *The State of the World's Children 2008*, p. 1.
39 The following statistics were collected from various UN reports by Shah, www.globalissues.org.
40 Action Aid (United Kingdom). *Fact File*; see also Sperling, *The Case for Universal Basic Education.*
41 Centers for Disease Control and Prevention. *Economic Facts About US Tobacco Use and Tobacco Production* (2005 data).
42 United Nations press release, 30 November 2008.
43 'The estimated cost of closing the gap between current trends and what is needed to meet the target ranges from $10 billion to $18 billion per year'. United Nations Department of Public Information. Press release, 25 September 2008.
44 International Institute for Strategic Studies, *The Military Balance 2010.*
45 Bahá'í International Community, *Rethinking Prosperity*, p. 3.
46 See UNDP, *Tackling Corruption, Transforming Lives.*
47 Bahá'í International Community, *The Prosperity of Humankind*, p. 2.
48 Murray, 'Finding Healing Hands', p. 1.
49 ibid.
50 ibid.
51 Bahá'í International Community, *The Prosperity of Humankind*, pp. 9–10.

8 Global Warming, Climate Change and Environmental Degradation

1 Letter from the Universal House of Justice to the Believers in Iran, 2 March 2013.
2 Shah, 'Climate Change and Global Warming'.
3 Storm, 'Capitalism and Climate Change: Can the Invisible Hand Adjust the Natural Thermostat?'
4 Shah, 'Climate Justice and Equity'.
5 Global Footprint Network. 'World Footprint: Do We Fit on the Planet?'
6 ibid.
7 Hanley, *Eleven*, p. 51.
8 Union of Concerned Scientists, 'Is Global Warming Linked to Severe Weather?'
9 ibid.
10 Clark, 'Volatile Worlds, Vulnerable Bodies: Confronting Abrupt Climate Change', p. 32.
11 Union of Concerned Scientists, op. cit.
12 UNDP, *Human Development Report 2007/2008*. See also https://en.wikipedia.org/wiki/Climate_change_and_poverty.
13 Letter from Shoghi Effendi to an individual, 17 February 1933, in

The *Compilation of Compilations*, vol. 1, p. 84.

14 Environmental Defense Fund, 'Climate Change's Effects Plunder the Planet'.
15 ibid.
16 ibid.
17 ibid.
18 International Environment Forum, Conference on Education for Sustainability.
19 Brown and Brown, *The Embodiment of My Name*.

9 Consequences of Materialism

1 'Abdu'l-Bahá, *Promulgation of Universal Peace*, p. 335.
2 Bahá'í International Community, *Eradicating Poverty*, paras. 3, 17.
3 ibid. para. 9.
4 Piachaud, 'Freedom To Be a Child'.
5 ibid.
6 Information in this section is taken from a number of sources. See ILO, *The Cost of Coercion: 2009 Global Report on Forced Labour*; Andrees and Belser: *Forced Labour: Coercion and Exploitation in the Private Economy* (2009); websites such as www.endhumantrafficking-now; www.globalissues.net; www.ilo.org.
7 See the website of Human Rights Education Associates at www.hrea.org.
8 ibid., where definitions of these eight forms of forced labour are given, together with lists of the countries where they take place.
9 See *UNA–USA's Global Classrooms: World Health Organization*, available at www.unausa.org.
10 ibid.
11 Parwini, 'Poverty Forces Bangladeshi Women to Turn to Organ Trade'.
12 For sources of information in this section see www.un.org/peace/africa/Diamond.html; http://princessjewelry.com/Conflict-Diamonds.asp; and http://brilliantearth.com/conflict-diamond-trade/.
13 www.un.org/peace/africa/Diamond.html.
14 Jer. 17:1.
15 On CNN, the BBC, and in newspaper articles such as Crow and Prendergast, 'Stop Your Gadget Greed from Fueling Tragedy in Congo'.
16 Crow and Prendergast, ibid.
17 Shoumatoff, 'Agony and Ivory'.
18 Gilbert et al., 'Lifestyle Drugs', p. 1341.
19 Cited by Moynihan et al., 'Selling Sickness', p. 888.
20 ibid.
21 'Abdu'l-Bahá, *Promulgation of Universal Peace*, p. 4.
22 Bahá'u'lláh, *Hidden Words*, Persian no. 6.

23 Bahá'u'lláh, *Kitáb-i-Íqán*, para. 214, p. 193.
24 Sachs, 'Common Wealth'.
25 ibid.
26 ibid.
27 Letter written on behalf of the Universal House of Justice to an individual, 7 October 2005, in *Ḥuqúqu'lláh*, no. 32, p. 11.
28 Shoghi Effendi, cited in Bahá'u'lláh, *The Kitáb-i-Aqdas*, note 38, p. 182.
29 Bahá'í International Community, *Turning Point for All Nations*, Part IV (A), note 31.
30 Shoghi Effendi, *The World Order of Bahá'u'lláh*, pp. 19, 24.
31 Graham, 'The Bahá'í Faith and Economics'.
32 Shoghi Effendi, *God Passes By*, p. 315.
33 Bahá'u'lláh, *Gleanings*, LXXXII, para. 5, p. 160.
34 Bahá'u'lláh, *Prayers and Meditations*, CLXXVI, para. 14, p. 272.

10 Bahá'í Perspectives on Materialism

1 The Universal House of Justice, Message to the Conference of the Continental Boards of Counsellors, 29 December 2015, para. 46.
2 'Abdu'l-Bahá, *Paris Talks*, no. 39, p. 124.
3 Shoghi Effendi, *The Advent of Divine Justice*, p. 47.
4 Shoghi Effendi, *Letters from Guardian to Australia and New Zealand*, p. 3.
5 Shoghi Effendi, *Citadel of Faith*, p. 149.
6 ibid. p. 125.
7 Bahá'í International Community, *One Common Faith*, pp. 3–4.
8 The Universal House of Justice, Message to the Bahá'ís of the World, Riḍván 2000, in *Turning Point*, p. 136.
9 The Universal House of Justice, *Century of Light*, p. 89.
10 ibid.
11 The Universal House of Justice, *The Promise of World Peace*, p. 7.
12 'Abdu'l-Bahá, *Selections*, no. 225, p. 283.
13 ibid. pp. 283–5 passim.
14 ibid. p. 285.
15 'Abdu'l-Bahá, quoted by the Universal House of Justice in 'Message to Iranian Bahá'ís throughout the World', 10 February 1980, in *Messages from the Universal House of Justice 1983–1986*, no. 246, p. 434.
16 The Universal House of Justice, ibid. pp. 434–5.
17 ibid. p. 435.
18 The Universal House of Justice, *Century of Light*, p. 90.
19 'Abdu'l-Bahá, *The Secret of Divine Civilization*, pp. 96–7.
20 ibid. p. 97.
21 Bahá'í International Community, *The Prosperity of Humankind*, p. 5.
22 ibid. p. 6.

23 ibid. p. 7.

24 ibid. p. 3.

25 Shoghi Effendi, *Citadel of Faith*, p. 125.

26 The Báb, *Selections*, p. 95.

27 Taherzadeh, *The Revelation of Bahá'u'lláh*, vol. 1, p. 73.

28 'Abdu'l-Bahá, *Tablets of the Divine Plan*, pp. 45–6.

29 Bahá'u'lláh, *Gleanings*, CXXVIII, para. 4, p. 276.

30 ibid. LXV, para. 8, p. 125.

31 'Abdu'l-Bahá, *Paris Talks*, no. 29, pp. 86–7.

32 ibid. p. 87.

33 ibid. p. 88.

34 See Wikipedia, http://en.wikipedia,org/wiki/Detachment.

35 See Taherzadeh, *The Revelation of Bahá'u'lláh*, vol. 2, pp. 34–9.

36 Bahá'u'lláh, *Kitáb-i-Íqán*, para. 1, p. 3.

37 For a discussion of detachment from the 'Kingdom of Names', see Taherzadeh, *The Revelation of Bahá'u'lláh*, vol. 2, pp. 34–9.

38 Badiei, *Stories Told by 'Abdu'l-Bahá*, pp. 26–7.

39 According to the *Encyclopedia of Religion* (Eliade, 1987, p. 240), 'the Persian word "derwish" is most likely derived from the term "darwiz" which means "poverty", "neediness" and "begging". It also implies simplicity, limitation of material needs and reliance on God for sustenance. However, it also carries negative connotations such as neglect of self and society and indifference toward cleanliness.

'By the term "spiritual poverty" Islam and Sufism refer to a condition where possessions are nothing but "poverty". The term Darwish appeared in the Persian literature and Sufi texts in the early 10th century and included broader variations in meaning such as humility, charity, self-discipline, asceticism, "hermit" and "wandering Sufi". Later on it also denoted an honorific bestowed upon certain important Sufis: the title of darwish or darwishi is a sign of great honour and respect in Sufism. The famous Persian poet Hafiz writes:
    Rawdiy-i khuld-i barin khalwat-i darwishanast
    Mayiy-i muhtashimin khidmat-i darwishanast
    The sublime eternal Paradise is the spiritual retreat of the dervishes;
    The essence of grandeur is the service of the dervishes.'

40 Taherzadeh, *The Revelation of Bahá'u'lláh*, vol. 1, pp. 76–7.

41 Bahá'u'lláh, *Tablets*, p. 217.

42 Bahá'u'lláh, *Hidden Words*, Arabic no. 55.

43 Zarqání, *Maḥmúd's Diary*, pp. 415–16.

44 The Báb, *Selections*, pp. 77–8.

45 Letter on behalf of Shoghi Effendi to an individual believer, 26 October 1938, in 'The Importance of Prayer, Meditation and the Devotional Attitude', *Compilation of Compilations*, vol. 2, no. 1768, p. 240.

46 The Báb, in *Bahá'í Prayers*, p. 151.
47 Bahá'u'lláh, *The Seven Valleys*, p. 29.
48 ibid. p. 36.
49 Quoted by Bahá'u'lláh, *Kitáb-i-Íqán*, para. 107, p. 102.
50 Letter on behalf of Shoghi Effendi to an individual believer, 10 December 1947, in 'Living the Life', *Compilation of Compilations*, vol. 2, no. 1318, p. 18.
51 Bahá'u'lláh, *Gleanings*, LXXV, para. 1, p. 143.
52 'Abdu'l-Bahá, *Tablets*, vol. 1, p. 136.
53 'Abdu'l-Bahá, *Promulgation of Universal Peace*, p. 142.
54 ibid. p. 452.
55 ibid.
56 ibid.
57 Bahá'u'lláh, *Gleanings*, XCIX, p. 200.

11 Spiritual Dimensions of Human Prosperity

1 'Abdu'l-Bahá, *Promulgation of Universal Peace*, p. 335.
2 Bahá'í International Community, *Turning Point for All Nations*.
3 *Bahá'í Prayers*, p. 4.
4 Bahá'u'lláh, *Gleanings*, CIX, para. 2, p. 215.
5 'Abdu'l-Bahá, *Promulgation of Universal Peace*, pp. 225–6.
6 See Bahá'í International Community, *The Prosperity of Humankind*, p. 3.
7 Bahá'u'lláh, *Gleanings*, CIX, para. 2, p. 215.
8 Bahá'u'lláh, *Hidden Words*, Arabic no. 59.
9 ibid. Persian no. 27.
10 ibid. Persian no. 26.
11 Bahá'u'lláh, *Seven Valleys*, p. 35.
12 ibid. p. 5.
13 'Abdu'l-Bahá, *Promulgation of Universal Peace*, p. 226.
14 'Abdu'l-Bahá, quoted in 'The Importance of Deepening our Knowledge and Understanding of the Faith', in *Compilation of Compilations*, vol. 1, no. 427, p. 204.
15 Shoghi Effendi, letter to an individual believer, 8 December 1935, in 'The Importance of Prayer, Meditation and the Devotional Attitude', *Compilation of Compilations*, vol. 2, no. 1762, p. 238.
16 The Universal House of Justice, Message to the Bahá'ís of the World, Riḍván 1989, in *A Wider Horizon*, p. 64.
17 Letter from the Universal House of Justice to the National Spiritual Assembly of the Bahá'ís of Norway, 1 September 1983, in *Messages from the Universal House of Justice 1979–1986*, no. 375, p. 589.
18 'Abdu'l-Bahá, *Promulgation of Universal Peace*, pp. 221, 261.
19 ibid. p. 221.

20   ibid. pp. 261–2.
21   ibid. p. 302.
22   ibid. p. 262.
23   Letter on behalf of Shoghi Effendi to an individual, 14 October 1931, in *Lights of Guidance*, no. 447, p. 133.
24   'Abdu'l-Bahá, *Promulgation of Universal Peace*, p. 190.
25   Bahá'u'lláh, *Tablets*, p. 257.
26   'Abdu'l-Bahá, *The Secret of Divine Civilization*, pp. 23–4.
27   Shoghi Effendi, *Citadel of Faith*, pp. 124–5.
28   Shoghi Effendi, *The Advent of Divine Justice*, pp. 19–20.

12 Rethinking the Concepts of Wealth and Well-being

1   'Abdu'l-Bahá, *Selections*, no. 227, p. 303.
2   Khadem, 'Ḥuqúqu'lláh and Prosperity', p. 4.
3   'Abdu'l-Bahá, *Selections*, no. 68, pp. 103–4.
4   Bahá'u'lláh, *Gleanings*, CVI, para. 1, p. 213.
5   Bahá'u'lláh, in *Ḥuqúqu'lláh: The Right of God*, no. 16.
6   Letter from the Universal House of Justice to an individual, 7 October 2005, ibid. no. 32.
7   The Universal House of Justice, *A Wider Horizon*, p. 173.
8   Letter from the Universal House of Justice to the Deputies and Representatives of the Institution of Ḥuqúqu'lláh, 12 January 2003, in *Ḥuqúqu'lláh: The Right of God*, no. 31.
9   Bahá'u'lláh, ibid. no. 13.
10   Letter from the Universal House of Justice to the Deputies and Representatives of the Institution of Ḥuqúqu'lláh, 14 February 1997.
11   William Hatcher, talk given at the Ḥuqúqu'lláh Conference, New York, November 1992.
12   'Abdu'l-Bahá, *Promulgation of Universal Peace*, p. 144.
13   Letter from the Universal House of Justice to the Bahá'ís of East and West, 18 December 1963, in *Messages from the Universal House of Justice 1963–1986*, no. 13, p. 27.
14   The Universal House of Justice, Message to the Bahá'ís of the World, Riḍván 2006, in *Turning Point*, p. 216.
15   Letter from the Board of Trustees of Ḥuqúqu'lláh in Canada, to delegates at the 2009 Canadian Bahá'í National Convention, in *Bahá'í Canada* (July/August 2009), p. 12.
16   Letter from the Universal House of Justice to the Deputies and Representatives of the Institution of Ḥuqúqu'lláh, 14 February 1997.
17   Grover Foley, quoted by Schaefer, *The Imperishable Dominion*, p. 207.
18   Einstein, quoted ibid. p. 206.
19   Schaefer, ibid. p. 208.
20   Bahá'u'lláh, *Gleanings*, XCIX, p. 200.

21 Bahá'í International Community, *Who is Writing the Future?*, part 3, p. 15.
22 The Universal House of Justice, *The Promise of World Peace*, pp. 1–2.
23 Bahá'í International Community, *Who is Writing the Future?*, part 1, p. 1.
24 ibid. p. 17.
25 Bahá'u'lláh, *Gleanings*, XCVI, para. 2, p. 196.
26 ibid. CXX, para. 1, pp. 254–5.
27 Bahá'u'lláh, *Tablets*, p. 86.
28 Bahá'í International Community, *Who is Writing the Future?*, part 5, p. 22.
29 Shoghi Effendi, 'The Unfoldment of World Civilization', in *The World Order of Bahá'u'lláh*, p. 204.

Conclusion
1 Bahá'í International Community, *The Prosperity of Humankind*, p. 8.
2 Shoghi Effendi, *Messages to Canada*, p. 67.
3 'Abdu'l-Bahá, *Promulgation of Universal Peace*, p. 338.
4 Bahá'u'lláh, *Gleanings*, CXXX, p. 285.

Excerpts from the Bahá'í Writings
1 'Abdu'l-Bahá, *Promulgation of Universal Peace*, p. 12.
2 Bahá'u'lláh, *Gleanings*, CXIV, p. 236.
3 ibid. LXVI, pp. 127–8.
4 'Abdu'l-Bahá, *The Secret of Divine Civilization*, p. 24.
5 'Abdu'l-Bahá, in *Star of the West*, vol. 13, no. 9 (December 1922), p. 229.
6 Bahá'u'lláh, *Hidden Words*, Persian no. 51.
7 'Abdu'l-Bahá, *Selections*, no. 157, p. 186.
8 Bahá'u'lláh, in *The Divine Art of Living*, p. 66.
9 'Abdu'l-Bahá, *Selections*, no. 153, p. 180.
10 'Abdu'l-Bahá, *Promulgation of Universal Peace*, pp. 451–2.
11 Bahá'u'lláh, in *Ḥuqúqu'lláh : The Right of God*, no. 4.
12 Bahá'u'lláh, *Hidden Words*, Persian no. 80.
13 Bahá'u'lláh, *The Seven Valleys*, p. 36.
14 'Abdu'l-Bahá, *The Secret of Divine Civilization*, p. 60.

INDEX

hair loss 149
Haiti 120
Hanley, Paul 131
happiness 3-4, 8-10, 17-18, 21,
    22-3, 31-5, 37-42, 45-9, 59, 70,
    79, 88, 101, 102-3, 105, 144,
    157, 162, 177, 180, 191-2, 200,
    204, 211, 212, 213
harmony 41, 61, 77, 93-4, 189
Hatcher, William 198-9
Harvard University 36, 39
health 9, 13, 16, 28, 31, 34, 39,
    43-71, 73-4, 79-80, 87, 104,
    117, 121-3, 125, 134-5, 143,
    148-9, 151, 180, 186, 205, 212
healthcare, medical care 46, 61, 63,
    64-5, 69, 122, 125-7, 143, 149
Hearst, Phoebe 112
heart, human (met.) 27, 29, 37, 39,
    71, 86, 93, 94, 95, 97, 100, 119,
    133, 152, 156, 157, 159-61,
    164, 165, 175, 176, 184-6, 187,
    199, 204, 209, 210, 211, 212
hedonism 10, 103, 104, 206, 207
Hellevik, Ottar 32
Hesketh, T. 80
Hidaka, Brandon 43-4
Hinduism 92-3, 95
HIV/AIDS 67, 69, 117, 121,
    125-6, 145
homicide see murder
honesty 98, 110, 156, 202-3
honour 38, 42, 57, 83, 112, 115,
    117, 191, 198, 245
humanity, destiny of 41, 159, 166,
    177, 182, 187, 201
Human Development Report (HDR)
    124
human nature 10, 55, 57, 73, 77,
    125, 159
    dual (lower, higher) 3, 167
    spiritual 13, 55
human qualities 97

    see also specific entries
human papilloma virus (HPV) 69
human rights 4, 78, 139, 140, 142,
    145-6, 165, 180, 194
humility 115-17, 209, 245
hunger 31, 42, 67, 120, 124, 139,
    143, 162, 197
    spiritual 57, 90, 91, 135
Ḥuqúqu'lláh (Right of God) 114,
    196-200

Iceland 45
ideology 10, 12-13, 18, 87, 161,
    181, 203
Imam Ṣádiq 113
income 11, 14-15, 21, 23, 31-3,
    336, 47, 64, 70, 102-3, 121-2,
    127, 131, 140, 141, 144, 156-7,
    195
India 80, 81, 146, 154
indifference 4, 59, 91, 138, 152,
    206, 245
individualism 20, 29, 46, 50, 160,
    164-5
Industrial Revolution 20, 139-40
infanticide 81
Inglehart, Ronald 12
insecurity 14-15, 43, 50, 55
integrity 110, 183, 192, 200, 209
International Environment Forum
    (IEF) 135
International Labour Organization
    (ILO) 141
International Monetary Fund
    (IMF) 70
Internet 24
intrinsic goals, values 2, 5, 9, 12,
    14, 16, 34, 44, 83-6, 103-4,
    138, 181, 189, 199, 202, 208
Ios, story of, 171-2
Iran 143, 173, 245
Ireland 45
iron 178

ABOUT THE AUTHOR

Dr Abdu'l-Missagh Ghadirian is a Professor Emeritus of McGill University, Faculty of Medicine, and a Distinguished Life Fellow of the American Psychiatric Association. As author, educator and researcher, he has published extensively on psychosocial and spiritual issues and spoken at many universities and public events around the world.

He is the author of several books, including the first edition of this book on materialism which received the Distinguished Scholarship award of the Association for Bahá'í Studies in 2011. Among his other recent publications are *Creative Dimensions of Suffering* (2009) and *Steadfastness in the Covenant: Responding to Tests and Tribulations* (2014). His current interest is the exploration of the interrelationship between religion and science in the advancement of civilization.